AMERICA
FROM THE AIR

MetroBooks

Texts
Robert J.Moore, Jr.

Editorial coordination
Laura Accomazzo

Graphic design
Luana Gobbo

North American edition
Managing editor JoAnn Padgett
Project editor Elizabeth McNulty

Contents

© 1999 White Star S.r.l.
Via C. Sassone, 24 - 13100 Vercelli, Italy.

This edition published by MetroBooks, an imprint of Friedman/Fairfax Publishers, by arrangement with White Star S.r.l.

Library of Congress Cataloging-in-Publication Data available

First reprint in 2000

ISBN 1-58663-116-0
M1098765432

Printed by Grafedit, Italy

1 Low clouds lend an air of mystery and excitement to New York Harbor, the gateway to the most populous city in the United States. The Statue of Liberty, in the foreground, has welcomed citizens, visitors and immigrants hoping to make a better life since 1886.

2-3 The snow-covered, fantastic landscape of southwestern Utah is on display at Bryce Canyon National Park. The bright red sandstone has eroded into fantastic shapes in the "hoodoo" formations at bottom left.

4-5 The snowy summit of Alaska's magnificent Mount McKinley, the highest point in the Western Hemisphere, seems almost luminescent when set off by a crystal clear sky.

6-7 The Pacific Coast Highway winds through the Big Sur Country of California, crossing Bixby Creek Canyon on the graceful bridge at the center. Backed by the Coastal Range and caressed by the waves of the Pacific Ocean, the highway is one of the most scenic routes in the United States.

8 top One of the Art Deco towers of San Francisco's Golden Gate Bridge welcomes visitors and residents to northern California and the West Coast of the U.S.

8 bottom The United States' most precious monuments and public buildings are clustered along the National Mall, the heart of the nation's capital in Washington, D.C.

9 As seen from space, the North American continent's distinguishing features are laid out before us like a map. To the north, Hudson's Bay forms an indentation into Canada, with the five Great Lakes delineating the border with the United States. The craggy Atlantic coastline includes the mouth of the St. Lawrence River on the east, running down to the tip of Florida and the islands of the Caribbean Sea. The mighty mass of the Rocky Mountains and the Sierras dominates the Pacific Coast, running from Alaska in the northwest down through Mexico to the south. The flat central portion of the continent is drained by the mighty Mississippi River system.

10-11 In this satellite view of the entire U.S., one can see the nine "regions" selected for this book. Although the nation could be divided in many different ways, in this case topography and history have caused the selection of zones: the North Atlantic States, the Middle Atlantic States, the Sunbelt, the Midwest, the Continental Divide and Rocky Mountains, the Desert Region, the Pacific Coast, Alaska and Hawaii.

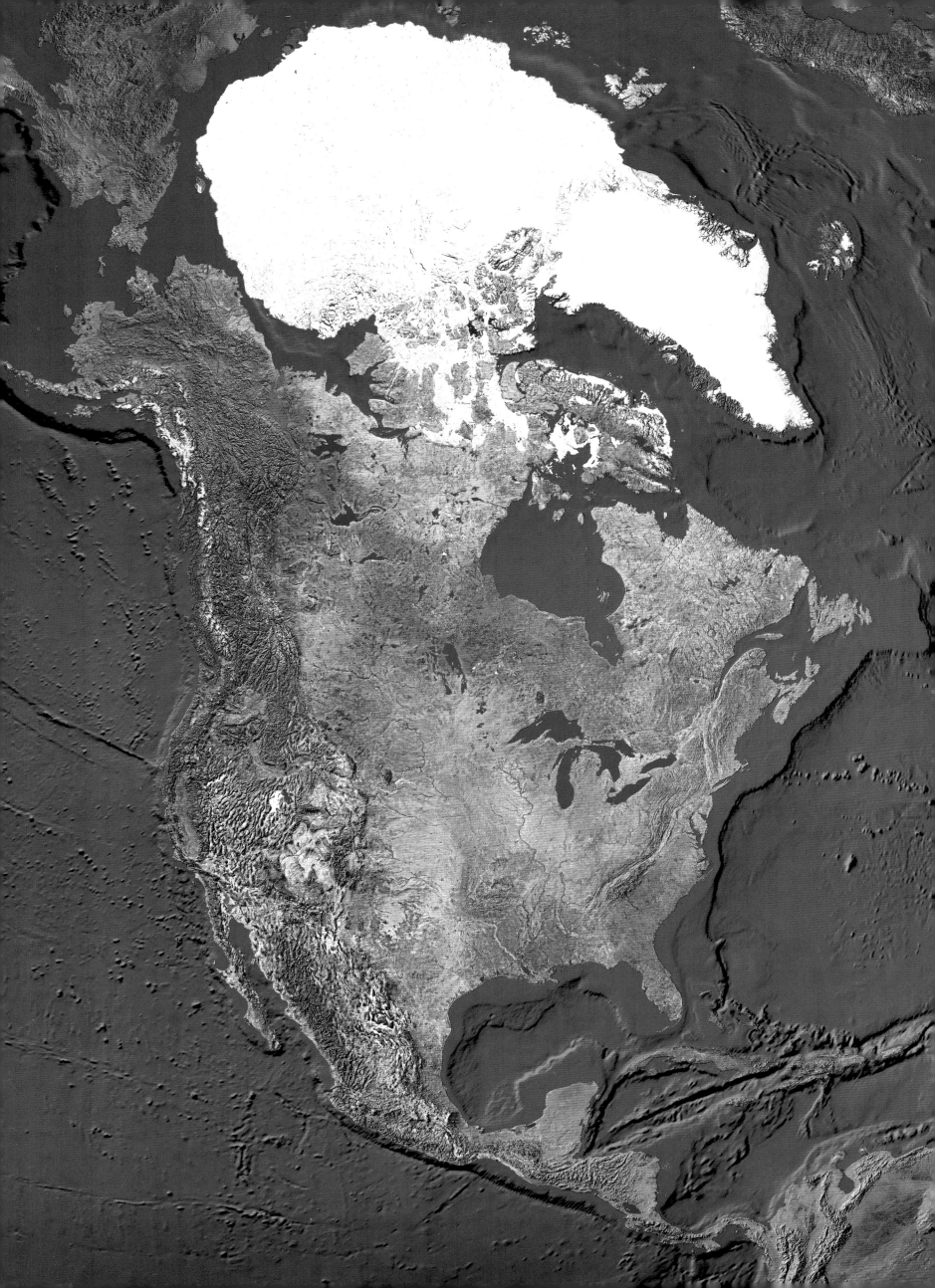

PACIFIC
OCEAN

**The Pacific
Coast**

**The Rocky
Mountain Region**

•Seattle

San Francisco •

**The Desert
Southwest**

Denver •

•Las Vegas

Los Angeles •

San Diego • Phoenix • Albuquerque •

•Honolulu

Alaska

•Anchorage

Hawaii

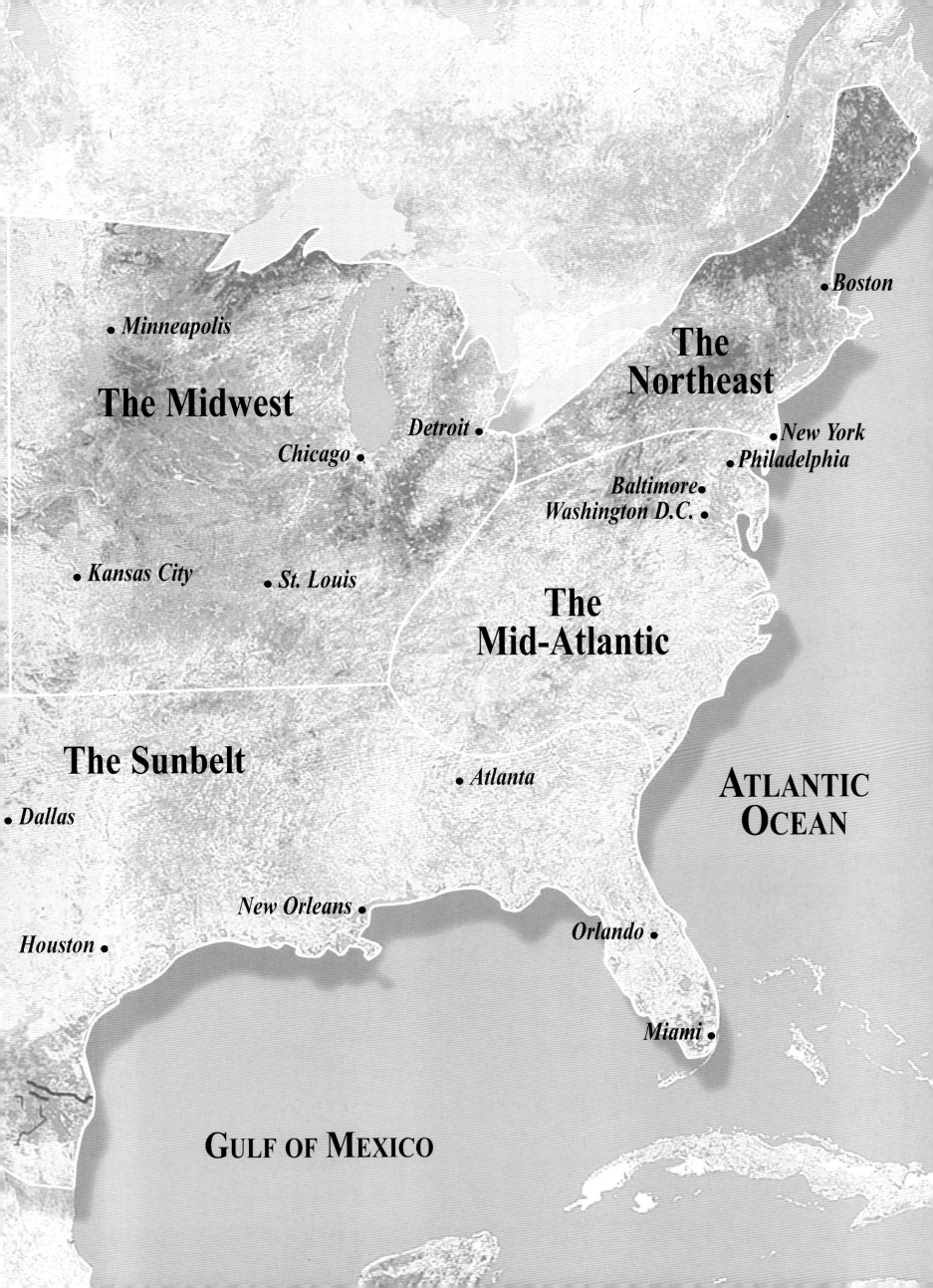

Introduction

The United States of America is a vast country, composed of fifty states, each with its own unique geography, history and cultural makeup. Its landscape encompasses a mosaic of people, places and things. This prosperous, colorful and beautiful land of many surprises continues to reach out to settlers and travelers, challenging those who would try to conquer its mountains, rivers and canyons as well as those who would get to know its mosaic of people, regional and cultural variations. In just over 200 years this patchwork quilt of a nation forged a unique history, traditions, and an attitude toward government, justice and religion different from anyplace else on earth.

Because there has been a constant stream of immigration to America since colonial days, the character of the people of the United States is more difficult to describe than that of other nations. The U.S. has been called a "melting pot," meaning that its large number of cultures, religions and ethnic groups have melded into a cohesive, single people. In addition to its unique mixture of people, what makes the United States special is the variety and grandeur of its geography. It was the land, after all, in its abundance and variety,

Climactic conditions range from semi-tropical to temperate, from desert to Mediterranean to rainforest.

This mere recital of topographical features and statistics, however, does not begin to tell the story of how this vast geographical area was conquered and placed under one flag. The first human settlers were peoples of various tribal groups, each developing unique lifestyles suited to the area in which they lived. Many anthropologists suggest that these Native Americans or American Indians reached America via the Bering Strait from Asia, once high enough above the water to

allow passage over a "land bridge." Indian people themselves reject this claim, and describe various points of origin on the North American continent itself. Many Indians believe that they and the American continent are inseparable, one and the same from the dawn of time. Most Indian people and tribal groups tried to live in harmony with their environment rather than striving to triumph over it. The geography, the land itself, was sacred to them. In much of the U.S., the

12 left Pueblo Bonito at Chaco Culture National Historical Park in northwestern New Mexico is one of the finest ancient structures in North America. Occupied from about A.D. 50 to A.D. 1150, Chaco Culture has thirteen major ruins and at least 300 smaller structures. Pueblo Bonito was a 5 story building with 800 rooms and 30 circular kivas built in the 10th century A.D.

12-13 Islands near Maine's Acadia National Park on the Atlantic coast display their lush beauty on a bright summer day. The Atlantic coastline's wave-eroded granite cliffs and glacially-carved hills and valleys were preserved in this park area in 1919.

12 bottom The U.S.S. Constitution, oldest commissioned warship still afloat, resides at anchor in Charlestown Navy Yard, Boston, Massachusetts. "Old Ironsides" as she was nicknamed by her crew, was launched in Boston in 1797. She achieved her greatest fame in the War of 1812 when she sank the British frigates Guerrière and Java and in a single battle captured the enemy sloops Cyane and Levant. Outdated but saved from destruction by an inspirational poem in 1830, the 200 year old warship has survived to be restored and serves as a tourist attraction.

that drew settlers to its shores from the very beginning. Although there are deeper canyons, taller waterfalls, longer rivers, vaster deserts and higher mountains elsewhere on earth, few countries can claim such a rich, beautiful and varied topography as can the United States. There are 3,675,911 square miles within its borders; it is 2,807 miles from the Atlantic coast to the Pacific, and 1,598 miles from the Canadian border to the southern extremity of the U.S. Its coastline runs for 12,383 miles when Alaska and Hawaii are included, for 4,993 miles without. The United States borders on just two nations, the Dominion of Canada on the north and the Republic of Mexico on the south. The highest point in the United States is Mount McKinley [Denali] in Alaska, 20,320 feet above sea level; the lowest is in Death Valley, California, 282 feet below sea level. The Mississippi-Missouri river system is the fourth longest in the world, and dominates the central portion of the United States. Three major mountain ranges, the Appalachians, the Rockies and the Sierras each have their own character and distinctive topography. All run roughly north and south, providing an abundance of water and a variety of weather conditions for the nation.

same land the Indians knew can be seen from the air.

Europeans began to explore the present-day U.S. in the 1500s, led by the Spanish, French and English. Many European nations colonized America, and fought wars between themselves for supremacy.
In the late 18th century thirteen colonies along the Atlantic coast, claimed by Great Britain, began to turn away from their "mother country." These colonies were led by groups of men who felt that rules, regulations and laws were being forced upon them by Britain. As a result, a rebellion began in 1775 which soon grew into a full-blown armed insurrection. On July 4, 1776, the ringing words of Thomas Jefferson's Declaration of Independence were adopted by the Continental Congress in Philadelphia, and 13 disparate colonies became the United States of America. After a hard-fought war for independence, which ended in 1783, the United States drifted into a period of uncertainty. Then in the summer of 1787 delegates from each state arrived in Philadelphia to write a constitution for the new nation. The extraordinary document they drafted was the foundation for a government that has endured ever since.

13 top A historic port, New York served as a gateway to America for millions of immigrants. In the distance are the skyscrapers of lower Manhattan.

13 center The granite walls of Fort Adams protected Narrangansett Bay and the harbor of Newport, Rhode Island for over 100 years. The site was used as a fortification from the time of the American Revolution.

13 bottom Cahokia Mounds State Park is located in Illinois, across the Mississippi River from St. Louis. The middle Mississippi region was once home to a flourishing culture of Native American who built earthen mounds, like the one in the photo.

Autumn in the Northeast is accented by a warm spell called "Indian Summer."

If we boarded an airplane to view the northeastern part of the United States, part of the vast territory wrested in warfare from Great Britain 200 years ago, we would observe a fascinating variety of topographical features which change from season to season. Passing over the rocky seashores of the Maine, New Hampshire and Massachusetts coastlines, for example, one can watch the continual pounding they take from the angry Atlantic Ocean. The rocky shoreline tapers to the incredible sandy fishhook of Cape Cod, which juts outward from the coast for 35 miles, then northward 30 miles further. From the air we can see cranberry bogs red with berries, and gorgeous beaches loaded with people on holiday each summer. The shoreline is dotted with little fishing villages, with picturesque docks jutting out into the

water, and motorized fishing boats regularly departing each morning for the open sea. Pictures of the dockside fishing shacks, hung with buoys and nets and with lobster traps stacked nearby, have become synonymous with the culture of the New England area. Not far from Cape Cod, at Plymouth, the Pilgrim fathers of the ship *Mayflower* established their colony in 1620. It was this toehold, made by British religious dissenters, that began the settlement of the New England region by Europeans.

The largest city in New England is Boston, and as we pass overhead on our imaginary flight we marvel at the ancient, crooked streets in the North End, and we see the old landmarks of American independence, Faneuil Hall, Bunker Hill and the Old North Church.

The "Boston Tea Party," an act of civil disobedience which spurred America's rebellion against England, took place in this harbor in 1773. Modern Boston is a land of skyscrapers and urbanity. The people of Boston are fiercely loyal to their city, their heritage and their sporting teams. High populations of immigrants, particularly Italians and Irish, as well as African Americans, dominate the city. Across the Charles River is Harvard University, one of the oldest and most prestigious institutes of higher learning in the United States, one of many in New England, an area which has always prided itself on education. Moving inland from Boston one sees a vast megalopolis of interconnected towns, many stretched along the highway—the "beltway"—which encircles the city. Modern businesses, especially involving the computer industry, have clustered here. Signs of history abound. We see Lexington and Concord with their cozy little houses and churches, the communities where the American Revolution began with "The shot

heard round the world." Later, men and women of American letters like Ralph Waldo Emerson, Henry David Thoreau, Henry Wadsworth Longfellow, and Louisa May Alcott lived and worked in Concord. Further to the west we begin to see more of the quaint little towns for which New England is rightly famous. The older buildings, made of wood and covered with clapboards, are most often painted white. They are clustered about congested town centers. usually with a village green and one or two churches with huge white gothic steeples pointing upward toward us. Many of these towns once made their livelihood from the old red brick factory buildings we see below us, hugging the rivers. These buildings are often empty now, and have a forlorn look of decay about them.

Autumn is the most spectacular time in New England, when the trees put on an incredible show of reds, oranges and yellows. The festive colors of the leaves stand in stark contrast to the bright white of the houses, buildings, and the trunks of the beautiful birch trees. Flying over the mountain chains, the Berkshires in Massachusetts, the White Mountains in New Hampshire, and the Green Mountains of Vermont, is a never-to-be forgotten treat. Patches of rock can be seen protruding forth from among the trees at the very tops of these old, low, rounded humps of granite. In the winter, the mountains are usually covered with snow, the now-bare deciduous trees standing in contrast to the evergreens which line the busy ski slopes. This delightful region is a pleasure to fly over at any season of the year.

The waters of the Hudson river wind through cliffs and mountains and arrive at the core of New York, Manhattan Island.

West of New England lies upstate New York. For those who think that New York is just a city with tall buildings, flying over the northern regions of the state can come as quite a shock. Instead of an urban jungle, the visitor is presented with a beautiful pastoral landscape of rivers, lakes, fields and mountains. Dairy farms with grazing cows are interspersed with orchards specializing in apples. When crossing over from New England, one first sees the Hudson River Valley, one of the most picturesque rivers in the world. The waters of the lower Hudson wind through cliffs and mountains which seem to spring upward from both sides of the river. Perched upon the western shore at a strategic spot is the U.S. Military Academy at West Point.

Further west we pass over the Catskills, and heading north see the Mohawk River Valley running east to west, with the Adirondack Mountains beyond. The Adirondacks, a state forest preserve since 1892, boast 2.4 million acres of mountains, glacial lakes and rivers which form a recreation paradise. Lake Placid, one of many towns in the region, hosted the Winter Olympic Games in 1932 and 1980. The Adirondacks,

beside the power and terror of the spot where the falls make their plunge. Beautiful day or night, Niagara Falls continues to attract tourists.

On the southern extremity of New York State is the city for which the region is known. New York City is like a nation unto itself. Its own geography has been sculpted not by nature as much as by the hand of man. Huge buildings reach for the sky, creating "canyons" of marble, steel and glass into which we can peer as we glide overhead. Many of the tallest buildings, the World Trade Center, the Empire State Building, Rockefeller Center, the United Nations Headquarters, the Brooklyn Bridge and the Chrysler Building, are all recognizable landmarks which make this unmistakably New York. New York City is the center of the U.S. financial world, a bustling international trade mart, the focus of theater, opera, and a portion of the music, film and television industries in the United States. In short, it is one of the most important urban areas in the United States, and continues to be the most populous. The neighborhoods are filled with people from every corner of the globe,

attracted to New York like metal filings to a magnet. For many, achieving success in New York City means that they have reached the top of their profession. Others are from families who have lived for generations in "the city"—for them, there is no other way of life. The streets are filled with the bustle of traffic, never ending. The docks are often vacant now, but this port continues to be one of the world's most important.

The core of New York City lies on Manhattan Island, but the city itself and its suburbs comprise a larger area. New York would not be New York without its other boroughs—the Bronx, Queens, Brooklyn and Staten Island. Flying away from Manhattan toward the ocean, we see the Statue of Liberty holding her torch aloft, while boats ply the waters below. On a rectangular isle of land between lady Liberty and the city we see the buildings of the former immigration center on Ellis Island, the portal through which millions of people from other lands entered the United States. Further on we see the huge span of the Verrazano-Narrows Bridge, the longest single-span suspension bridge in the world. The entire scene of New York City and its harbor reminds one of an anthill from this vantage point. Nothing seems to be at rest in New York, and a kind of nervous energy pervades the whole.

composed of igneous and metamorphic rock, are geologically some of the oldest mountains in the world. The tree-covered humps form the borders of clear blue lakes dotted with islands of green. In the winter months, the weather can be harsher than Alaska or the Great Plains, yet wood smoke pours from the chimneys, while deer make their way through the high drifts of snow. Central New York was once the land of the Iroquois Indians. Today, central New York is a region of abandoned factories and diminishing population. Due to the brutal winter weather, many businesses have relocated to the southern part of the country.

On the far western border of New York State, we pass low over incredible Niagara Falls, which drops 167 feet to the river below. Niagara is mightily impressive for its width (1,001 feet on the American side, plus 2,592 feet on the Canadian side), and the noise of its rushing waters. The water courses and roils through rapids and around islands and rocks as it approaches the falls, then suddenly drops into a roaring cauldron from which a flume of spray emerges, rising nearly as high as the falls themselves. There are few places where one can stand

16-17 The buildings of midtown Manhattan are bathed in the light of sunset. Many of the most recent skyscrapers can be seen in this photo. The "post-modern" era of architecture is said to have begun with Philip Johnson's AT&T Building, seen to the left of center. Looming above it and to the right is the 59 story Citicorp Center, while at the far right the Art Deco Chrysler Building continues to grace the skyline.

16 bottom Lower Manhattan is seen in this photo. Near the center foreground the arch in Washington Square Park can be seen at the head of Fifth Avenue. The park is in the heart of Greenwich Village, with New York University on the south side. At the tip of the island is the financial district, with the World Trade Center and the Statue of Liberty on her island to the right in the bay.

17 top left A corner of Battery Park nestles up against the skyscrapers of lower Manhattan. The Battery has been the site of a fort since colonial times. New York City was settled by the Dutch in 1624 as New Amsterdam, then taken by force by the British in 1664 and renamed New York. Originally the little village at the tip of the island was surrounded by a wall which offered protection and kept livestock from straying. The street built on the site of the wall became Wall Street, located at the foot of the tall, squat building at the center of this photo.

17 top right The Empire State Building was the tallest building in the world for 41 years. Just to the left of the Empire State Building in this photo is the Pan Am Building, which rises above Grand Central Station on Park Avenue.

17 bottom The twin towers of the World Trade Center dominate lower Manhattan, known world-wide as a financial center.

Washington, D.C. was specially created in the 1790s as the nation's capital, and first occupied by the government in 1800.

Turning to the southwest, we cross New York City once more and then fly over the hills and plains of New Jersey and eastern Pennsylvania. In the summer this region is verdant with green trees and pastures. Many international corporations have located their headquarters here, to escape the crowding of New York yet still have easy access to the city. The suburban "campuses" of these corporations blend with a seemingly endless stretch of homes and towns, growing in a semicircular fashion outward from the city. This area, although only a suburb of New York City, is part of a thriving hive of activity in a population belt which begins in Boston and ends south of Washington, D.C. This region is the most urban and populous in the United States. A flight at night over this area allows us to understand more clearly, by the huge number of lights, the multitude of people who live and work here.

Continuing across the hills of New Jersey to the southwest, we soon arrive over Philadelphia. The

fascinating downtown was laid out in a rectangular grid pattern in the 1600s by the city's founders, the Quakers. Today, new skyscrapers punctuate the skyline, while far below them history beckons in the form of older brick buildings such as Independence Hall, where the Declaration of Independence and the Constitution were debated and signed. Stretching in all directions from the city center on the waterfront are streets lined with rows of neat little three or four story red brick homes. Proud residents of every ethnicity enjoy this predominantly working-class city.

The huge harbor is full of historic water craft, while further south the Navy Yard hosts current and decommissioned ships of war. Unlike New York, Philadelphia has a different pace, still vibrant but capable of rest and reflection. Its heritage has been preserved in the downtown area, and its streets have a friendly, intimate feeling to them.

Flying to the west away from the city and over the state of Pennsylvania, one finds that Philadelphia's suburbs give way to beautiful rural areas, including

one of the centers of America's Amish population. The rolling hills lead to the little town of Gettysburg, where one of the most important battles of the American Civil War took place. North and west of Gettysburg we soar over a very mountainous area, with long, curving ridges which look like a giant of ancient times ran a huge comb through them, sweeping them in an arc to the northeast. The mountains, much higher than those in New England or New York, are particularly beautiful in the autumn. On the far western side of this huge, rectangular state lies Pittsburgh. A very industrial city, we notice immediately the smokestacks from the steel mills and other industries which clustered here at the confluence of two rivers—the Allegheny and the Monongahela, which meet at Pittsburgh to form the Ohio River. Parts of Pittsburgh are black with the soot of industry, while the environs of the city are gorgeous with their steep tree-covered hills and magnificent views of the river valleys.

Before leaving the east for the midsection of the country, we return from Pittsburgh to the Atlantic coast over Maryland. Soon we see the urban area of Baltimore, another industrial town and one of the busiest ports in the United States. Today Baltimore is best known as a research center for the pharmaceutical industry and marine biotechnology. Founded in 1729, Baltimore, along with the colony of Maryland which surrounds it, became a haven for Roman Catholics in an age of little religious tolerance. As we travel over Baltimore's brick homes, we notice that they are much like those we saw in Philadelphia, except for their famous white marble stoops, or front steps. Flying over downtown Baltimore we notice a revived inner harbor area with many tourist attractions, including the star-shaped Fort McHenry. Besieged by the British during the War of 1812, the

18 top left The idea of a memorial to President Thomas Jefferson was championed by Franklin D. Roosevelt during the Great Depression. The result, completed in 1943, borrows from Jefferson's love of the dome as an architectural feature.

18 bottom left East Potomac Park is a peninsula which stretches from the Jefferson Memorial in the center background to Hains Point at the far left of the photo. The body of water in the foreground is the Washington Channel of the Potomac River, the main channel of which can be seen in the background at the upper left. On the far distant skyline, to the left of the Washington Monument can be seen the National Cathedral.

18 right The National Cathedral in Washington, D.C. is an Episcopal Church open to all, and one of the largest church structures in the world. Italian stone carvers have painstakingly fashioned gargoyles of every imaginable shape and style for its towers. Even Darth Vader, movie villain of the Star Wars films, has a place on the tower at the suggestion of a young student.

fort and its huge garrison flag were the inspiration for the national anthem of the United States, *The Star Spangled Banner*, written by a lawyer named Francis Scott Key to an old British drinking tune.

A short flight southwest from Baltimore brings us to Washington, D.C., the capital of the United States. The city was specially created in the 1790s as the nation's capital, and first occupied by the government in 1800. The center of the city, where the business of government is conducted, is filled with some of the most famous landmarks in the world. We soar above the Capitol Building, the White House, home to the American presidents, and the many monuments, including those to presidents Jefferson, Washington and Lincoln. We also see the buildings of the Smithsonian Institution, where many of the treasures of the nation are kept and displayed. Surrounding this spectacular central core of gleaming white memorials, however, live thousands of poor people. Indeed, Washington, D.C. exemplifies the extremes of American society—affluence and poverty, power and powerlessness. Its unique, planned grid design of streets interspersed with long avenues which run at diagonals, sometimes make it a

nightmare for drivers. Luckily, the city has a wonderful mass-transit system which links nearly all of its important sites.

Continuing southward we enter the beautiful state of Virginia, flying over Arlington National Cemetery, a memorial to the nation's military veterans and war dead. A little farther on we see Mount Vernon, George Washington's famous home on the Potomac River. Leaving the suburbs of Washington, D.C. behind, we begin to note the end of the crowded conditions of the Boston-to-Washington population belt. We note with pleasure the beautiful beaches along the Atlantic Ocean and the huge blue Chesapeake Bay, punctuated by the white sails of pleasure boats.

Turning inland we begin to see the horse farms of the piedmont region, interspersed with monuments to hundreds of Civil War encounters, for this region contains some of the fiercest battlefields of that conflict. Beyond this, on the western side of Virginia, are the beautiful Shenandoah Mountains. Gorgeous at any time of the year, the Shenandoah Mountains and valley constitute a region rich in history and scenic beauty.

18-19 This photo of the Washington Mall looking east shows some of America's most-cherished and familiar buildings. Laws are made by the U.S. Congress at the Capitol Building in the top left center, while the 555 foot tall Washington Monument, dedicated to the memory of the first President, is on an axis with the Lincoln Memorial at the end of the reflecting pool. At the far left center at the edge of the trees is the Vietnam Veterans Memorial.

19 bottom The Basilica of the National Shrine of the Immaculate Conception in northeast Washington, D.C., constructed of Italian marble, covers 77,500 square feet. Begun in 1920, construction was delayed by the Great Depression and World War II, and the church was not finished until the 1960s.

Atlanta is famous as the setting for Margaret Mitchell's novel Gone with the Wind, *but very little of its ante bellum past can be seen, dominated by steel and glass towers.*

20 *The Interstate Highway System, seen here near Atlanta, Georgia, was inaugurated by a law passed in 1956 at the urging of President Dwight D. Eisenhower.*

21 top left *The Georgia State Capitol Building in Atlanta has a dome much like that of the U.S. Capitol in Washington. The building cost less than a million dollars to construct, and was completed in 1889.*

21 top right *The modern buildings of Atlanta, Georgia's downtown are indicative of the new, modern South, the "Sunbelt."*

21 bottom *The huge exposed granite boulder called Stone Mountain rises above the Atlanta suburb of the same name. Stone Mountain has become a tourist destination, not just for the Confederate Memorial on its side, but also for the state park surrounding it.*

Proceeding south along the Shenandoah Valley we watch as the elevation rises as the Shenandoah Mountains become the Great Smokies in the state of North Carolina. The Great Smoky Mountains comprise one of the oldest upland regions in the world. Although they rise only to a maximum height of 6,642 feet, they are nonetheless an impressive mountain range. The peaks are often obscured by fog or clouds, which gives them their name. The Great Smokies are the tallest mountains in the Appalachian chain, which parallels the entire Atlantic coast, from Maine to Georgia.

Circling back to the Atlantic coast once more we come to the sandy stretches of Cape Hatteras along the shoreline. Shoals and frequent gales and storms make navigating these waters treacherous, and the wrecks of many boats lie beneath the crashing waves offshore. On these sandy beaches man first flew in a heavier-than-air machine, when the Wright Brothers made their historic flight in December 1903. The British first tried to plant a new world colony in this area in 1585, but the colony failed and its citizens mysteriously disappeared by 1590. The first successful British colony in America was founded north of Cape Hatteras in Virginia, at Jamestown in 1607. Today, we can see the remnants of Jamestown, and fly over the re-creation of colonial American life at Williamsburg, just 10 miles north.

As we continue our journey southward down the Atlantic coast, we notice a drop in the overall population. The Carolinas, Georgia, and Florida have, however, become prime areas for the growing number of retirees in America, and an expanding number of new homes, retirement homes, and recreational homes can be seen, especially along the coastline. As we enter South Carolina, we notice the change in vegetation and the flat countryside, traditionally an area where rice and indigo were grown. Here and there old plantation houses, some of which have been restored, can be seen from our aerial vantage point. We have entered the old south, a land once quite different from the industrial north, once dependent upon thousands of small farms and a smaller number of large plantations with a labor force of black slavery. The weather in this region is much hotter and more humid than in the northeast, with

temperate winters and rare snowfalls. From our vantage point, we can still see damage from some of the hurricanes which sweep into this area each autumn.

Up ahead, we see the city of Charleston perched between the Ashley and Cooper Rivers inside a protected harbor. It has been a major port since its founding in 1670. In 1861, it was in this harbor that the slaveholding southern states began a rebellion against the northern states by firing upon the U.S. Army fortification called Fort Sumter. The old fort is preserved today on an island in the middle of the harbor, a

reminder of the war which once divided this mighty nation. Today, Charleston is a charming city of characteristic "shotgun" houses with wide verandahs. It is a vibrant city, as is its neighbor to the south, Savannah, Georgia. These cities offer the best in "southern charm" to all who visit them. Today Charleston continues to be an important port city. It manufactures petrochemicals and is a center of learning, with several universities and the Citadel Military School within its borders.

Flying inland from Charleston we cross the Savannah River to arrive in the upland region of Georgia, and spot the skyline of Atlanta, a symbol of the "new South." Atlanta is the business capital of the southeastern United States. We marvel at the tall buildings of the center city while we notice the huge sprawling mass of the suburbs. Atlanta is famous as the setting for Margaret Mitchell's Civil War novel *Gone with the Wind*, but very little of its antebellum past can be seen in its downtown area, which is dominated by steel and glass towers. Today, the city is famous as the home of the martyred civil rights leader Dr. Martin Luther King, Jr., and has earned worldwide attention as the site of the 1996 Summer Olympic Games.

Florida belonged to Spain, and for a short time to Great Britain, during America's colonial era. It did not become part of the United States until 1819.

coast are interrupted by the bustling and vibrant city of Miami with its proud Hispanic population, including a large number of Cuban refugees and their descendants. Miami maintains strong ties with Latin America, not only because of the ancestry of the city's people, but also because of its placement so close to the Caribbean, Central and South America. North of Miami we notice the huge structures of the John F. Kennedy Space Center at Cape Canaveral, where the United States has launched rockets, satellites and other vehicles into space for nearly forty years Americans flew to the moon from here, and continue to travel into space on the Space Shuttle.

As we fly over southern Florida, we notice that once again, the climate has changed, becoming semi-tropical. The palm, pine and palmetto trees and other plants we see below us confirm that we are in a hot, humid zone. We see water everywhere across the incredibly flat landscape; the Gulf of Mexico on the west side of the peninsula, the Atlantic on the east, and rivers, lakes and swamps in between. The beautiful blue of the water compliments the white sands, the green vegetation and the festive pastel colors of the homes and buildings.

22 top Water is the key resource in Florida, where a Miami golf course features pond after pond. Once the land of the Tequesta Indians and later the Seminoles, Florida was settled extensively by Europeans long after the other states of the Atlantic coast.

22 bottom left The Art Deco hotels of Miami Beach were built in the 1920s by Dixon and Hohauser, who wanted to change the overall look of the city from its original Mediterranean Revival style to something more contemporary. What they ended up with are architectural gems from one of the last eras of ornamentation on public buildings.

22 bottom right The northward sweep of Miami Beach echoes the similar barrier islands along Florida's shores, with recreation complexes and hotels. During the period of Art Deco hotel building, large numbers of French-Canadian and Jewish people built a community to the north called Surfside, one of many ethnic communities in the area. Each area of the state, like each area of the nation, reflects the polyglot heritage of the United States.

23 Water parks, hotels, go-cart courses, and massive piers characterize Daytona Beach, Florida. One of the major industries of the state is tourism and providing leisure activities for the huge international tourist trade.

Turning southward once more, we reach the huge, 400 mile long peninsula of Florida. The population of this state nearly tripled between 1960 and 1990, as an enormous influx of retired people made their homes here. The region was one of the first explored by Europeans, as the Spanish conquistador Juan Ponce de Leon surveyed its shores in 1513. St. Augustine, the oldest continuously-inhabited Euro-American city in what is now the United States, was founded in 1565.

Florida belonged to Spain, and for a short time to Great Britain, during America's colonial era. It did not become part of the United States until 1819.

Modern Florida is a burgeoning area of retirement communities, bustling cities, historic sites, beaches, recreation complexes such as those in Orlando, and agriculture, particularly oranges and tomatoes. There are also vast and fascinating natural areas, such as the nearly 5,000 square mile area of swamp, savannah and virgin forest called the Everglades, and the Florida Keys, islands stretching in a chain below the southern tip of the mainland for 225 miles into the Gulf of Mexico. Florida's barrier islands along the Atlantic

Today, the Mississippi River is central to life in the Midwest— although at one time it formed the western boundary of the United States.

Traveling north-westward from Florida, we leave the Atlantic coast and enter another, different region of the United States on the far side of the Appalachian mountain chain. We are now in the area Americans call "the Midwest," a vast, mostly flat plain coursed by the tributaries of the Mississippi River. Industrial cities such as Detroit, Pittsburgh, Cincinnati, Louisville, St. Louis and Chicago punctuate an otherwise pastoral region of farms and small towns. The flat, square farm fields of Illinois and Indiana stretch northward into the Great Lakes region, with its rolling hills and smaller lakes sculpted by glaciers. The Midwest is a huge region, and it is a land of great contrasts.

We begin by flying over the bustle of Chicago and its ethnic neighborhoods, its radio stations broadcasting in Polish, Czech, Spanish and other languages, its steel and glass towers crowding up to the vast inland sea of Lake Michigan, its vibrant African American community and seemingly endless summer festivals. Chicago is also a city with a tradition of dynamic architectural achievements. Among the modern skyscrapers we can see some of the original tall buildings designed by the firm of Louis Sullivan in the 1890s. Beginning as Sullivan's apprentice, Frank Lloyd Wright burst onto the international architectural scene in the early 1900s with his "prairie style houses," many of which we can see in Chicago's western suburb of Oak Park. Wright based his architecture around the predominant geographical features of the region, especially the flat horizon, and incorporated as decorative elements the natural prairie plants. Chicago is a city packed full of culture, dominated by beautiful museums and libraries. It exhibits much of the same hustle and bustle as New York, but with a Midwestern twist. Winter weather in Chicago is not for the timid.

have captured the imaginations of readers around the world. The river itself is rarely so romantic. In reality it is a slowly moving, muddy "highway" which winds for 2,348 miles from Minnesota to the Gulf of Mexico and the delta below New Orleans. It is fed by over 250 tributaries, and drains an area of over 1.2 million square miles. Today, the Mississippi River is central to life in the Midwest—although at one time it formed the western boundary of the United States. After the American Revolution, Americans began looking westward. It was the dream of every American, and of many of the nation's political thinkers, that each citizen would be a landowner. Thomas Jefferson in particular was a firm believer in a nation of enlightened "yeoman farmers," people with a direct stake in preserving a democratic form of government. Expansion to the west of the Appalachian Mountains could make this dream a reality. But the rush to settlement by Americans ignored the rights of Native American people and tribal groups. Treaties were signed by unwary Indians which deeded away huge tracts of land, while others fought wars until they were subdued by American armed forces. Defeated tribes had no choice—they either had to try to assimilate into the new Euro-American culture or move further west before the wave of settlement engulfed them.

By 1800, Americans were swiftly settling the region east of the Mississippi River, and casting glances toward land on the west side claimed by Spain and ceded to France. In 1803, circumstances forced Napoleon Bonaparte to sell the 800,000 square mile Louisiana Territory (all the land between the Mississippi on the east and the Rocky Mountains on the west, Canada on the north and the Gulf of Mexico on the south) to the United States for just $15 million dollars.

It is a cold region which is often hit by huge snowstorms. Chicago is a place which begs to be explored.

As we move away from Chicago we are struck by the large "patchwork quilt" of farm fields which stretch off in all directions beneath our wings. This was once the land of prairie Indians and the buffalo. But the original forests and prairie grasses are now gone, replaced by fields of corn, soybeans, wheat and other crops. At one time Indian villages of conical-shaped wigwams dotted the landscape, punctuated here and there by mounds of earth build by the ancient peoples of the region. Today, we see a land of small towns and cities dominated by grain elevators, with huge city halls and county courthouses (many of them architectural gems) which can be spotted from miles away across the flat prairie.

Through it all runs the Mississippi River, a river of legend and literature. The romance of the era of the steamboat was captured by one of America's greatest authors, Samuel Langhorne Clemens, who used the pen name Mark Twain. Twain's vibrant characters, drawn from boyhood memories of growing up along the river,

The 19th century, beginning with the Louisiana Purchase, ushered in the final act in the "conquest" of the West by the U.S.

26 Modern buildings surround St. Louis' Old Courthouse. The former city courthouse is today administered by the National Park Service. The Old Courthouse was built between 1839 and 1862, and was the scene of the Dred Scott case, which began in 1846.

27 top left The Missouri Botanical Garden in St. Louis is one of the world's premiere showcases of plant life. In addition, the Garden is an internationally known research facility on botany and medicines derived from wild plants. One of the most impressive parts of the garden is the Japanese Garden, located around the lagoon at the upper left.

27 top center Downtown St. Louis west of the Arch shows off a hodge-podge of architectural styles, including the City Hall in the center foreground, built in the 1890s as a faithful copy of the Hotel deVille in Paris, France.

27 top right The Gateway Arch reflects sunlight off its stainless steel legs into the Mississippi River at St. Louis. The Arch was built to symbolize St. Louis' role in westward expansion, but has gone on to become a symbol of the city itself and to revitalize the once-decaying downtown.

27 bottom St. Charles, a suburb of St. Louis, has several casino boats as attractions. St. Charles is also famous for its wineries, and a museum dedicated to the Lewis and Clark Expedition which began in the St. Louis area.

Today, flying over the Mississippi River, it is difficult to imagine that era, even though it was only a little less than 200 years ago. The 19th century, beginning with the Louisiana Purchase, ushered in the final act in the "conquest" of the West by the United States. For the next 100 years, Americans moved westward to inhabit the farthest reaches of the continent. In every location they settled in such great numbers that they soon outnumbered the people of any other nation, Indian or European. By 1846, the Oregon Treaty with Great Britain ceded the Oregon country south of the 49th parallel to the United States. The nation finally stretched

from ocean to ocean; but this was not enough for many Americans, who used the new catchphrase "manifest destiny" to claim ownership of all the land from Florida to California. A war was engineered with Mexico, and in less than two years the Americans had achieved their goal; the boundaries of the "lower 48" states assumed their modern configuration (with the small exception of the purchase from Mexico in 1853 of sections of southern Arizona and New Mexico for a transcontinental railroad right-of-way). Americans now had a huge land, millions of square miles to be settled and exploited. In 1848, on the heels of the departure of the Mexicans from California, gold was discovered, making the United States a wealthy nation. A huge migration of overland pioneers in wagons braved the rough topography of the West to stake out homesteads or mining claims in Oregon, California and Washington state.

The centers of this epic westward expansion were located in Missouri. St. Louis, on the east side of the state, was the last major city in which pioneers could outfit themselves for an overland journey. The Kansas City area, on the west side of the state, was where the Oregon and California trails began. The Santa Fe Trail originated in central Missouri, while the Mormon Trail began in Iowa and Nebraska. All these trails, and the

railroads which soon followed, enabled the swift settlement of the American West by Euro-Americans.

Flying over modern St. Louis, it is difficult to see remnants of its heyday as a fur trade center. The 630 foot tall Gateway Arch, designed by Finnish-American architect Eero Saarinen, dominates the city's riverfront and skyline, symbolizing its role as the "Gateway to the West." Below the Arch, copies of historic steamboats hearken back to the city's illustrious past. The Mississippi and Missouri Rivers meet just 18 miles north of St. Louis, mixing their muddy waters as they flow irresistibly toward the Gulf. Today St. Louis continues to be a manufacturing and corporate center, with large parks, beautiful museums and industrial headquarters. It is a small city, easy to navigate. It remains a transportation hub near the center of the nation, and dominates the river from which it rises and the flat, beautiful country which surrounds it.

Turning southward to follow the river, we parallel its muddy progress as it flows by the states of the deep south. As we fly over Arkansas, Mississippi and Louisiana, we see fields of cotton, sugar cane, rice and sweet potatoes, along with other crops. As we enter Louisiana, we note the river, agricultural fields, and a large number of wetlands. We also observe that the state is a major chemical manufacturing area. A striking feature of the landscape are the levees, that is, earthen walls which hold back the waters of the river. Over the years, the Mississippi has deposited so much silt that its bed is actually higher than the surrounding land. As a result, over 2,000 miles of earthen levees protect the region from flooding. Passing over Louisiana, we are once more in a semitropical climate, with mild winters and hot, sticky summers.

The Great Plains states were converted to the plow by Euro-Americans, and today produce enormous amounts of wheat, corn, alfalfa and sorghum, as well as contributing to cattle raising.

We soon arrive at the state's largest and most famous city, New Orleans, founded by the French in 1718 and built in the shape of a crescent around a bend in the river. New Orleans is actually below sea level, and is protected from flooding only by its levees. The city's interesting mix of cultural roots contributes to its utter uniqueness. Africans from the Caribbean, French refugees from Canada, Hispanic settlers from the West Indies and Spain, Native Americans from throughout the South, and a host of other peoples made New Orleans an early "melting pot" of cultures. The beauty of the Garden District, Tulane University, and the above-ground burial plots of the cemeteries add to our enjoyment of the city. As we fly over the city's famous French Quarter, we can hear jazz, blues and zydeco

As we continue to move westward along the coast, we enter Texas and note a series of barrier islands of sand and surf. The modern city of Houston lies just inland. Houston, the nation's fourth largest city, is also the fastest-growing city in the United States. It is the center of the nation's petroleum industry, electronics manufacturing, and the home of the NASA (National Aeronautics and Space Administration). We see the city with its steel-and-glass skyscrapers rise above the coastal

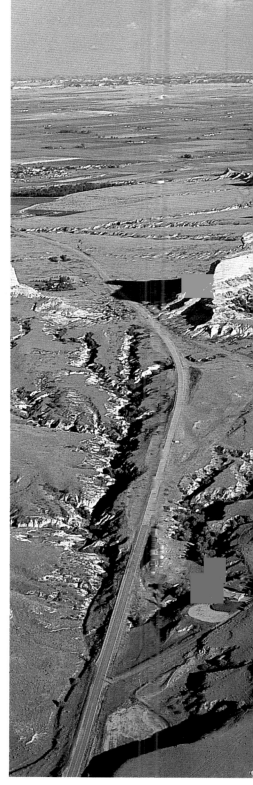

played hot and raw, day and night, while we can almost smell the Cajun cuisine, served blackened to one's taste. We see the old buildings, three and four stories tall, fronted by black cast iron balconies and railings, the louvered window shutters on each level open to the scents of a hot summer night. The crowds are always thick on Bourbon Street, some drunk, others amused, many finding their way from one new experience to the next. The French Quarter is the epicenter of the Mardi Gras celebration, the most famous in the United States, when New Orleans is filled to capacity with revelers from around the nation and the world. From Bourbon Street, all the world seems like a never-ending party.

We leave the revelry to see the green bayous to the south of the city, swampy areas which are home to alligators, muskrats and snakes and are dominated by cypress trees growing in the muddy water, their roots looking like the fingers of a hand resting in a bowl of water. Flying westward along the coast of the Gulf of Mexico we see the enormous delta of the Mississippi River. Proud people live in this region, making their living from fishing and hunting alligators and snakes.

plain and its bayous, and marvel at the juxtaposition of nature in its subtlety and man's overwhelming need to build and transform the landscape.

Proceeding due north we cross Oklahoma, a state once set aside exclusively for American Indian tribes. It is a part of the United States which is still home for large concentrations of Indian people. North of Oklahoma lie Kansas, Nebraska, and North and South Dakota. These states, along with eastern Colorado and Wyoming, constitute the "Great Plains," enormous areas of flat land once home to an ecosystem of animals dominated by the buffalo. During the late 18th and most of the 19th centuries, the region was inhabited by nomadic Indian tribes who lived in tipis and placed enormous value on the horse, which they acquired in the 1700s. Horses enabled them to have the mobility to follow and hunt the enormous herds of buffalo, once estimated at 40 million animals. The proud Lakota (Sioux) exemplified this lifestyle. They are the Indians most often immortalized (or trivialized) by Hollywood. Today, many of these people live on reservations in South Dakota, some under very poor conditions.

28 top The strange topography of Badlands National Park exemplifies the difference between the eastern portion of the U.S. and the West. Exposed rock formations dominate a large share of the states west of the Mississippi, which led explorers and later pioneers in covered wagons to marvel at a landscape that seemed otherworldly.

28 bottom The Midwest and far West display a great range of topographical features. A wheat harvest like this one near Cut Bank, Montana gives the viewer an idea of the massive but essential job accomplished each year, day in and day out, by the American farmer.

28-29 Water, and the lack of water, are the chief factors in farming in the American West. These fields near Scotts Bluff, Nebraska are irrigated with water from the arroyo shown and from the distant Platte River. Agribusiness makes up 13% of the commerce and trade of Nebraska. Because of the arid quality of the region, crops are rotated each year.

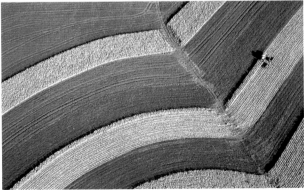

As with the former prairies east of the Mississippi, the Great Plains states were converted to the plow by Euro-Americans, and today produce enormous amounts of wheat, corn, alfalfa, sorghum, as well as contributing to cattle raising. Many of the towns in Kansas, like Abilene and Dodge City, became famous in the late 19th century as the rail centers to which cattle were driven by real-life cowboys. Today, ranches still dot the landscape, with huge feed lots constituting a non-traditional but more expedient way to fatten cattle for market.

Flying over the Great Plains, one sees seemingly endless fields, either square or circular in shape depending upon the method of irrigation, stretching off toward the horizon. Rivers and streams etch their way through the flat landscape in irregular lines, while roads continue the strict grid pattern of the fields. The roads are so straight and the land so flat that one can see for miles ahead, even while traveling on the ground in an auto. From the air the incredible geometric lines of the roads form the borders of the huge mosaic pattern of the fields below. The roads are not straight. Every few miles, the roads jog a bit to the north, then continue onward along their original trajectory. These jogs are "corrections," necessary to keep the straight lines of the roads compatible with the curvature of the earth!

On a summer day over the Great Plains, we see tints of green and brown in the "patchwork quilt" of fields. Each flat field is different than the last, and the fields continue onward in a seemingly endless march toward the west. But on the horizon we can see the purple outline of a mountain range ahead. Steady flying will bring us to it—and the end of the Great Plains.

29 bottom left The Midwest is a major producer of corn, as seen in this view of a Wisconsin field at harvest time. Corn is one of several species native to the Americas which Indian people taught the Europeans how to plant and use.

29 bottom right A small, fairly typical Western town, Fort Laramie, Wyoming was one of the most important stops for fur traders beginning in 1834 and later for pioneers on the Oregon Trail. A restoration of the U.S. Army fort just outside of town commemorates the military occupation of the area as well as two key treaties with plains Indian tribes, signed in 1851 and 1868.

The Great Plains stop abruptly at the badlands in the Dakotas, and where the Rocky Mountains rise in Wyoming, Colorado and New Mexico. Towering dramatically up from the plains, many of the snow-capped peaks of the Rockies are over 14,000 feet tall. Leaving the flatlands behind, it is hard to believe that we are suddenly among such gorgeous mountains, covered with evergreen trees and surrounded by the waters of streams happily dancing their way out of the highlands. Soaring in and among the Rockies, one gets a sense of how powerful the forces of our earth really are. These mountains, in contrast to the Appalachians, are geologically quite young. They rose

continue to make a living through mining and harvesting timber, in addition to tourism.

The quintessential area in which to experience the Rocky Mountains is, paradoxically, not very representative of the mountain region at all. It is that extraordinarily unique area known as Yellowstone National Park. The world's first National Park, founded in 1872, Yellowstone began the process of government-sponsored conservation, preserving unique areas for future generations through legislation. Covering nearly 3,500 square miles, Yellowstone has mountains, dramatically beautiful waterfalls, placid mountain lakes, and the world's largest geyser field, with over 3,000 active geysers and hot springs. Abundant animal life includes bison, bear, elk, mountain goats, mountain sheep and wolves, recently reintroduced to the region in a controversial government program. Yellowstone summarizes all that is good and bad about the conservation movement.

from the earth through uplift only in the late Cretaceous period, less than 100 million years ago. In shape reminiscent of the Alps, the Rocky Mountains constitute a chain 2,000 miles long and a barrier which creates the Continental Divide; that is, the tops of the mountains form the division of the rivers which flow east and south to the Atlantic and those which flow west toward the Pacific.

The early American explorers, including Lewis and Clark, Zebulon Pike, Stephen Long and John C. Fremont, were at first unprepared for the vastness of the Rocky Mountain region and the rugged nature of the peaks themselves.The queen city of the Rockies is Denver, Colorado, beautifully situated at the edge of the Great Plains with the magnificent mountains in view. Other, smaller towns, many of them founded because of the discovery of metal ores like silver, gold, lead and copper, host recreation-minded visitors who come to be amazed by and challenge the mountains on a year-round basis. The Rockies are, for the most part, sparsely populated, and the people of the region

Today, it is a combination of the natural environment and an environment created by park managers over the past 125 years. Huge crowds of people traverse the park in the summer and early fall, damaging fragile resources and disturbing animal habitat. Paradoxically, the National Park Service is asked to preserve the area while allowing access to all, a problem which will only grow in complexity as the 21st century approaches. Beyond the Rockies lies the Great Basin and the arid "desert country" of Arizona, New Mexico, Utah and Nevada. Flying first into the Great Basin, we observe a large, flat area formed just 2 million years ago. The desert itself often seems barren from the air, with little plant life and no water to be seen. Large stretches of gray sand stretch off in all directions, while the silhouettes of purple mountains can be seen in the distance. Water from the Great Basin does not flow to the sea, but dissipates in the desert. Moving further into the Great Basin, we soon notice the huge Great Salt Lake in Utah, one of a number of landlocked saline lakes in the region. To the south of the lake is Salt Lake City, the famous home of the Church of Jesus Christ of Latter-Day Saints, better known as the Mormons.

The Mormon religion was founded in upstate New York by Joseph Smith, a martyred prophet who, along with his outcast flock, was driven from town to town and state to state for several decades. In the late 1840s, Mormon leader Brigham Young brought his people to Utah, where they made the desert bloom, built a temple and founded universities which are today respected around the world. It was a story typical of America—a people plagued by injustice who found a safe haven where they could worship and live as they pleased. Well, almost as they pleased—the U.S. Government fought the Mormon practice of polygamy for over 40 years, finally winning a concession of a church ban on plural marriage. This concession led to Utah's statehood in 1896.

The queen city of the Rockies is Denver, Colorado, situated at the edge of the Great Plains.

30-31 The Yellowstone River, in the foreground, flows into Yellowstone Lake in this photo taken in Yellowstone National Park. Yellowstone Lake is the largest natural freshwater lake above 7,000 feet in the United States. It is 20 miles long by 14 miles wide, with a shoreline perimeter of 110 miles.

31 top People swept westward during the mid-19th century looking for free land, for riches like gold and silver, and also for religious freedom. It was the latter motivation which caused the exodus of the Mormon people to Utah and resulted in their founding Salt Lake City, pictured here. The Mormon Tabernacle with its white towers can be seen in the middle ground.

South of the Great Salt Lake we fly over beautiful desert and canyon country, much of it preserved in National Park areas. The incredible colors of the rock—pink, tan, white, red in places streaked with black, all sandwiched in layers along the walls of the canyons, have drawn visitors to this region for over 100 years. Visitors have also been fascinated by the area's preserved remnants of ancient cultures. Cliff dwellings at Mesa Verde and Canyon de Chelly, and semicircular towns built on the desert floor like those at Chaco Canyon, indicate advanced societies upon which we can only speculate. Remnants of these cultures can be seen today in the pueblos of the Hopi, Zuni, Acoma, Taos and other tribes of Arizona and New Mexico. The Navaho also live in northeastern Arizona. The Navaho and pueblo Indian people strive to preserve their traditional ways. The exquisite jewelry, pottery, woven rugs, paintings, kachina dolls,

Grand Canyon of the Colorado River, winding for nearly 200 miles from Lake Powell to Lake Mead, for at least 90 of those miles dropping a vertical mile into the ground from the rim to the river, and averaging ten miles across from the north rim to the south rim. Near the western end of the Grand Canyon a modern city, Las Vegas, Nevada, city of a billion lights, illuminates the night in the middle of the ghostly quiet Mojave Desert. Although colonized by the Mormons as early as 1857, Las Vegas did not begin its rise to glory until 1930, with the construction of nearby Hoover Dam. In 1946 the first casino opened, and in a short time Las Vegas became a popular resort "playground." Gambling revenues in Las Vegas are reputed to top several million dollars each day. The improbable nature of the town's livelihood and its juxtaposition with the desert environment that surrounds it exemplify one more instance of something which could happen "only

32 top left Glen Canyon Dam was completed in 1966, blocking the Colorado River above the Grand Canyon and creating Lake Powell behind it.

32 top right Monument Valley, in Utah and Arizona, is an area of incredible beauty encompassing 2,000 square miles.

32 bottom The Grand Canyon of the Colorado River in the state of Arizona is one of nature's masterpieces. President Theodore Roosevelt ensured that it would remain unmarred as a National Park, which it became in 1919.

33 Homes are built in and among Saguaro cactus near Saguaro National Park in southern Arizona, outside Tucson. The park preserves about 131 square miles of the Sonoran desert ecosystem, including the cacti called Saguaro. The Sonoran desert itself covers about 120,000 square miles.

34-35 The Glen Canyon Dam holds back the waters of the Colorado River, creating Lake Powell. Winding through the once-dry Glen Canyon washes, the lake creates hundreds of inlets and coves.

and other works of art for which these people are justly famous draw many visitors to the area. Individual tribes also have business deals with companies which mine coal, and other natural resources within the boundaries of the reservations. All of these activities bring visitors and money to the area. In short, flying over this region we can observe the ancient, the traditional, and the modern Indian way of life from our aerial vantage point.

The Sonoran Desert of Arizona has a beauty all its own. Sometimes the endless stretches of rock, low-lying vegetation and flat landscape wear on the visitor, but the sharp-eyed traveler can see the variations in rock type, color and form, the changes in vegetation, and the ever-changing pattern of the distant horizons. Punctuated by deep canyons and buttes, arches and other shapes sculpted by eons of wind and erosion, the desert never loses its fascination. At night, millions of stars light up the sky, so many that they make one think that there is more light than darkness in the heavens.

The most magnificent feature of this landscape lies in northwestern Arizona. Its beauty and immensity even dwarf such extraordinarily gorgeous areas as Bryce Canyon, Zion, Arches and Rainbow Bridge. It is the

in America." The wasteful use of limited hydroelectric and coal-produced power in the middle of the desert to enable this strange monument to mankind's pursuit of pleasure to exist defies logic, yet there it stands. Huge hotels of steel and glass dominate the skyline as we pass over the city toward the mountains on the north.

Flying onward, we reach the border of California. In the south, California's desert blends with that of Arizona, split only by the Colorado River. It is south of

California's Sierra Mountains that we encounter Death Valley, the lowest point in the U.S. The desert is much more barren in this region than in Arizona. Further north, the Sierra Nevada Mountains form a ridge higher than the Rockies. This huge range must be crossed before we can reach the Pacific. Continuing north, we see Sequoia-Kings Canyon National Park followed by Yosemite.

36-37 Rising 8,852 feet, Halfdome, beloved of John Muir, Ansel Adams, Theodore Roosevelt and millions of other less famous visitors, protrudes through the cloud cover over the Yosemite Valley. The valley is a wondrous place with incredible waterfalls, cliffs and rock formations. It was set aside by Abraham Lincoln in 1864 with the proviso that it be managed by the State of California; in 1890, after long years of agitation by Muir, it was made a National Park.

37 bottom The Don Pedro Reservoir is located west of Yosemite National Park, and was created by the damming of the Tuolumne River as it flows into California's fertile Central Valley, above Modesto. To the south of the Don Pedro, Lake McClure is created by damming the Merced River, which also flows from the mountains in Yosemite.

Yosemite is another major destination for visitors to the United States. Few have not heard of its incredible scenery, and few can resist wanting to experience the park for themselves. Yosemite is most famous for its picturesque valley, seven miles long and about a mile in width, dominated by granite rock formations which suddenly rise over 4,000 feet from the valley floor. A series of dramatic waterfalls plunge from the tops of the rocks; most famous are the Upper and Lower Yosemite falls, with a combined drop of over 2,000 feet. Unlike the red desert sandstone and tinted limestone of the southwest, Yosemite is dominated by the grays of its massive blocks of granite, the green of its ponderosa pine with its sweet vanilla scent, and the crystal blue clearness of its mountain pools. From the air we can see that Yosemite is far more than the famous valley, however. Stands of Giant Sequoia trees, beautiful alpine meadows, over 1,300 species of flowering plants, and marvelous hiking and skiing opportunities await those who venture into the vastness of this 1,189 square mile preserve.

Turning westward we leave the Sierras and pass over areas once mined for gold by the famous "forty-niners." It was gold that led to California's rapid settlement by Americans after 1849, and they quickly

and ruthlessly supplanted the native Indian and Hispanic residents. California became a state in 1850. Today, it is the most populous in the United States, with over 32 million residents. It is also the most urbanized, with 93% of its people living in ever-growing cities and their suburbs. In addition to these statistics, however, California is also known for its incredible natural wonders. In geographical area California is the third largest state in the union at 158,869 square miles. National Parks such as Yosemite, Sequoia-Kings Canyon, Death Valley, Muir Woods, Point Reyes and Santa Monica Mountains share the honors of preserving California's wilderness areas with the largest state park system in the U.S. One of the longest coastlines of any state forms the western border of California, beloved for its spectacular Pacific sunsets. Forty percent of all indigenous U.S. plant species are native to California. The coast redwoods, the world's tallest trees, grow there, as do the bristlecone pines, the world's oldest living things; one of these trees is estimated to be 4,000 years old.

In short, California is like a nation unto itself. It has developed its own unique lifestyle which has been parodied and imitated around the world. The public image of hippies, communes, surfers, motorcycle gangs, backcountry "dropouts" and other carefree, laid-back lifestyles has been exaggerated by

Hollywood, but these types can be found by those who look for them. Stereotypes are quickly dispelled, however, as one travels the state and gets to know its residents. In fact, Californians are as diverse if not more so, than the residents of other areas of the United States. Most Californians are extremely health-conscious, committed to environmental issues, and avidly interested in outdoor recreation of all kinds. They seek excellence in all things, and are sometimes prone to follow fads and set trends. But like all "countries," California and its people cannot easily be pigeon-holed. Besides, California is growing so quickly that a large share of its residents are from elsewhere—chances are that the Californian you meet was not born in California.

Yosemite is dominated by the grays of its blocks of granite, the green of its ponderosa pine with its sweet vanilla scent, and the crystal blue clearness of its mountain pools.

San Francisco is famous for its rosy-red steel bridges, and fog-shrouded evenings punctuated by the blasts of fog horns.

Continuing our flight out of the Sierras, we drop in elevation as we reach California's Central Valley, where mile upon mile of irrigated fields punctuated by canals contain all manner of crops. The state's long growing season makes it an ideal agricultural area, amounting to about 11% of the nation's produce. To the north, the vineyards of Napa and Sonoma Counties produce world-famous wines, and to the south the Imperial Valley also provides hundreds of square miles of farm land.

Continuing eastward we soon reach San Francisco, with its tall hills, roller-coaster streets, precariously perched homes, rosy-red steel bridges, incredible vistas, moderate weather, and fog-shrouded evenings punctuated by the blasts of fog horns. Nearly surrounded by water, the Pacific Ocean on the west and the San Francisco Bay on the east present a backdrop of blue behind the vistas of the city. Over all the laid-back fun and slow pace of San Francisco lies the constant threat of earthquakes posed by the San Andreas Fault, upon which the city is built. The city was devastated by a major earthquake and fire in 1906, and again in 1989 extensive damage was caused by another quake. San Francisco is famous for its "Beat Generation" landmarks in North Beach, the Haight-Ashbury district of the hippie era, an extensive Chinatown with stores and restaurants, and the famous cable cars which strain up and roar down the hills of the city, to the delight of tourists and residents alike. The National Park Service manages Golden Gate Park, the Presidio, San Francisco

Maritime, and the former prison on Alcatraz Island, providing plenty of recreational and tourist opportunities. The city is home to large populations of Asians (including one of the largest Chinese populations outside China), Hispanics and African Americans. Flying above it all, we see a jumble of buildings seemingly thrown like dice onto a carpet which has been wadded into an irregular, deeply furrowed ball, all of which is surrounded by water. A great variety of buildings, dominated by the Transamerica pyramid, Coit Tower, Fisherman's Wharf and other landmarks, saves San Francisco from the boringly repetitive edifices of other large cities. The beauties and contrasts of this amazing city are endless. We point the nose of our aircraft southward from San Francisco, soon passing over the gorgeous scenery of the Big Sur country, its huge cliffs overlooking the pounding surf of the Pacific. Next, Monterey Bay, a sweeping arc of water, looms before us. One of the deepest regions of ocean water so close to shore, the bay is an excellent place to study marine life. The canneries are now shops, but fishing and the maritime life remains an important part of the regional economy.

Passing down the coastline we notice the many missions which were established by Franciscan priests in the late 18th century. In that long-ago era, California was sparsely settled by Europeans, with a chain of 21 missions, four presidios (forts) and three pueblos (or towns). In contrast, the Indians enjoyed a carefree life and an abundant population before the advent of the Europeans. The first mission was founded in 1769 by Father Junipero Serra in San Diego. The missions grew slowly, and European population was never great before 1849. In the 1820s the Mexicans won their independence from Spain and secularized the missions. Not long afterward the Americans, looking for riches, invaded California and used the buildings for other purposes. In the 1860s most of the mission structures and churches were given back to the Catholic Church by the U.S. Government, and a program of restoration during the early 20th century brought most back to their glory.

Southern California boasts an authentic Mediterranean climate.

Los Angeles appears on the horizon next, as we fly first over Malibu and the Santa Monica Mountains. We see the sprawling city, low in stature because a law once prevented residents from building structures taller than 150 feet. Today a few earthquake-proof skyscrapers have been built, but the city has retained its character of short buildings spread over a wide area. Los Angeles is a

horizontal city, and is noted for its balmy climate and its reputation as the motion picture and recording capital of the States. Los Angeles is also famous for its universities. It is the second-largest U.S. city, after New York. In area, Los Angeles covers 465 square miles, and is tied together by a system of "freeways." Because of California's love affair with autos and an inadequate mass transportation system, Los Angeles is plagued with air pollution. Over 38% of its residents were not born in the States, and it has large African American and Hispanic communities. Its rise has been meteoric: in just 90 years, Los Angeles has grown from a small city of just 100,000 people to over 3.5 million (without counting the suburbs). Leaving the smog-covered stretches of the city, we head southward along the coast, noting the Los Angeles harbor at San Pedro and Long Beach. Suddenly, the urban area stops at a fenceline and the natural desert and canyon terrain of the area emerges. We are flying west of Camp Pendleton, a U.S. Marine Corps base which preserves the natural areas of coastal southern California. On the far side of Camp Pendleton we fly over the town of La Jolla, and then arrive over San Diego. One of the fastest-growing cities in the United States, San Diego boasts a Mediterranean climate, cultural attractions, beautiful beaches, an incredible harbor, and defense-related industries and military bases. From the air, the harbor looks as though it is protected by two arms which fold in on themselves. The tidepools

and lighthouse at Cabrillo are on the end of one arm, while the other is a long ribbon of sand called Coronado, capped by the Hotel Del Coronado. Our flight above this city concludes when we reach the Mexican border, a few miles south. Over the fence lies Tijuana, but we have reached the southwestern limits of the States.

We continue our journey at the north-westernmost point in the lower 48 states, the Pacific Northwest state of Washington. We cross over the San Juan Islands and Puget Sound. Olympic National Park is on our right, where we see a wonderland of evergreen trees. Snow capped mountain peaks such as Mount Adams and Mount St. Helens are to the south. Not all of the state has topography like this, however. East of the Cascade Range in both Washington and Oregon, desert-like conditions prevail. Chief industries of the region include logging, fishing, mining and growing wheat. Manufacturing have lured a burgeoning population in the 1990s, and as we pass Seattle we see evidence of this growth. Turning southward we reach the Columbia River, 1,245 miles long, exploited for its salmon and the hydroelectric power it produces. Crossing the river we reach Oregon, and follow along the coastline, where we see rock-islands which spring upward from the ocean waters. The nature of the Pacific Northwest coast is obscured by the weather, however, which is often rainy. Few coastlines on earth can compare with the view, though, as we take leave of the continental States.

40 *The California Coast runs for much of its length in an undeveloped state. As the traveler approaches Santa Barbara, as seen in this photo taken near Lompoc, more beachfront development has taken place. Natural areas have been preserved near Los Angeles in several locations, including Santa Monica Mountains National Recreation Area.*

41 top left *Long Beach, California was incorporated in 1888, and its large port began to rise to prominence in 1909. Discovery of offshore oil in 1921 promoted yet another industry, while its wide beach continues to attract recreationists.*

41 top right *The city of Seattle, Washington was founded in 1852, but grew slowly until the late 19th century, when the railroads reached it from the East. The city is dominated by the 605 foot Space Needle, built for the Century 21 Exposition in 1962. The area at the base of the Space Needle constitutes a cultural center for the city, with opera, ballet, theater and symphonic music.*

41 center right *A sailing ship plies the waters off San Diego. The clear, deep offshore waters are perfect for sailing.*

41 bottom *The Coronado Peninsula, off San Diego, mixes military functions, recreation and civilian communities along its narrow length. In the upper left-hand corner can be seen the community of Coronado, with the road called the Silver Strand winding along the ocean shoreline toward the viewer. The protrusion from the peninsula to the upper right is the community of Coronado Cays, with the U.S. Naval Amphibious Base to its left. In the foreground is the Navy Radio Station at Imperial Beach.*

Alaska and Hawaii, the 49th and 50th states, show the greatest differences of the United States.

42-43 Volcanic cliffs rise precipitously from the ocean on the northern coast of Molokai, one of the Hawaiian Islands. It was also on the north shore that Roman Catholic missionary Father Damien set up his hospital and retreat for victims of leprosy in the 19th century.

42 bottom Part of the Alaska Mountain Range near Mount McKinley, the highest point in North America. Land of snow and glaciers, Alaska is a final frontier for Americans, where questions of wilderness and its preservation or wise use continue to be argued strenuously. Over 10% of Alaska's population is composed of Native Americans.

43 top Mount Cook rises over Cook Inlet, southwest of Anchorage, Alaska. Mount Cook is part of the Aleutian Range, a series of volcanoes which extend outward along the whip-like Aleutian archipelago.

Alaska is no stranger to aircraft, as they are by far the easiest mode of transport for a good portion of the state. As we fly over Alaska, we can see that about a third of the state is heavily forested, while the remainder is composed of treeless tundra.

Alaska became the 49th state in 1959. It is surrounded by the Arctic Sea, the Bering Sea, and Canada's Yukon Territory and the province of British Columbia. It is the northernmost state and easily the largest of the 50 states. Nearly 70% of the state's land is owned by the federal government. Mt. McKinley, at 20,320 feet, is the highest peak in North America, and part of the spectacular Denali National Park. The National Park Service and National Forest Service manage large areas of the state. The population of about 600,000 people is the least dense of any state in the union. Native Americans of the Tlingit, Haida and Athabaska tribes, as well as Aleut people, compose the descendants of the original inhabitants. The Russians claimed Alaska in 1741 and exploited it primarily for its furs. It was purchased by the United States for $7.2 million in 1867, a controversial move at the time. Since that time Alaska has proved its worth many times over, with a gold strike in 1897–98 and petroleum resources discovered in the 1970s. The area's chief resources continue to be crude oil, mining, lumber and fishing.

What a contrast between the huge subarctic regions of Alaska and the balmy shores of the 50th state, Hawaii! Like Alaska, Hawaii became a state in 1959. And, also like Alaska, an airplane is a very handy thing to have when one wants to get around the islands. Hawaii is composed of eight main islands and 124 islets, reefs and shoals. Temperatures remain moderate year round at about 75 degrees Fahrenheit in this delightful tropical climate. One of the smallest states in the union, Hawaii is a land of incredible physical beauty. The islands rise up from the ocean, in the case of the peak of Mauna Kea, dramatically to over 13,000 feet. The islands are actually the tops of shield volcanoes (those that are formed from lava floes and not explosions). The original Polynesian inhabitants of the Islands were first contacted by British explorer James Cook. Later, American influences on the islands grew, and American missionaries and sugar plantation owners attempted to control their culture. In 1893 the last native ruler, Queen Liliuokalani, was deposed, and in 1898 the United States annexed the islands. The most famous incident in Hawaiian history was the Japanese aerial attack on the American naval base at Pearl Harbor on December 7, 1941. The sudden strike propelled the United States into World War II. Through the clear

blue waters of the harbor, we can still see the sunken hulk of the *U.S.S. Arizona* below, where she lies with her crew. She is topped with a graceful pearl-white memorial, visited by large numbers of American and Japanese tourists. As we fly above the islands, we are immediately struck with their lush greenery and the black volcanic soil and sand. Today, tourism, the American defense industry, raising sugar cane, and growing pineapples compose the major sources of income for the islands. The over one million inhabitants of the islands constitute the most racially and ethnically mixed population in the entire United States. In short, as we end our imaginary aerial tour, Hawaii marks a fitting conclusion to the cultural and topographical mosaic that is the United States.

43 center left and right The Hawaiian Islands form a lovely Pacific paradise, extemely different than anywhere else in the United States. A polyglot mixture of people, as complex but unified under the American flag as New York City, Chicago, Florida or Los Angeles contributes to the uniqueness and strength of the States. In the photos one can admire two different views of Oahu Island.

43 bottom Naturalist John Muir came to Glacier Bay, Alaska, in 1879 to see nature creating itself in the wake of glaciers. He was not disappointed. Today the visitor can see moving glaciers falling into the bay, while a mature forest beckons at Bartlett Cove, the final result of a glacier's retreat. Scientists continue to study and be fascinated by the push and pull of nature as exhibited at Glacier Bay, including the patterns of plant competition and animal rehabitation in the wake of a glacier.

The total picture of the United States is often hard to see close up. One has to stand back to see the grandeur of its geographical features.

44 top The marina of Santa Barbara, California recalls the Spanish explorer Sebastian Vizcaino, who anchored near here on the feast day of Saint Barbara in 1602, giving the town its name. The lovely town is a popular resort 92 miles from Los Angeles.

44 center left Irrigation has made California a year-round producer of a large portion of the nation's food supply.

44 center right The skyscrapers of downtown Los Angeles, California, stand above an old town founded in 1781 by the Spanish. Today it is a city of 3.5 million.

44 bottom The shoreline of Daytona Beach, Florida is peopled by residents of many parts of the U.S. and many overseas countries.

45 An interchange of the Interstate Highway System across the Mississippi River from St. Louis in Illinois. As the number of people in the U.S. increases, the demand for smoothly-functioning services grows along with it.

46-47 Chicago's Near North Side, dominated by the black John Hancock Building at the center, looks out on the wide expanses of Lake Michigan.

Today, the United States remains a compendium of the forces from which it was created. Amerindiańs, blacks descended from slaves, Hispanics descended from Conquistadores, people whose ancestors came to its shores on the Mayflower in 1620, and others who became American citizens just last week, all share space in a remarkably abundant land. Not only is the United States a nation of immigrants, it is also a restless nation in which large numbers of people have shifted the location where they choose to live. This trend continued to accelerate during the latter half of the 20th century, with the farmlands and small towns of America shrinking as the cities and their suburbs grew ever larger. Beginning in the 1960s and growing ever after in pace, the move from the older factory towns of the northwest to the "Sunbelt" in the south created major manufacturing and entertainment areas in Texas, Alabama and Florida, and changed each of the states of the Old South dramatically. The rush to urbanization, coupled with the rise of ubiquitous chain franchise stores and restaurants, as well as the immediacy and homogeneous quality of mass entertainment, particularly television, has tended to erode regional cultures across the United States. In many areas regional accents and holidays are gradually disappearing, overwhelmed by an influx of people from other parts of the nation or other countries. And so the story of the United States is not yet over. It remains affluent as it continues to produce less in the way of goods and more in the way of entertainment, information and technology. It uses huge amounts of the world's resources, more per person than any other nation on earth. At the same time, it struggles to protect its own national resources in the face of a growing population and the continual battle between use and conservation. The patchwork quilt of its landscape has changed greatly over 200 years—from tallgrass prairie throughout its midsection to endless farm fields, from vast areas of virgin timber to largely clearcut regions. Much has been reforested by conservationists, like the Blue Ridge and Great Smoky Mountains. West of the Rockies a more fragile landscape is threatened by the encroachments of urbanization, especially in California. Meanwhile, the mosaic effect of its

population only grows more diverse as more and more people become part of the nation. Ironically, however, these diverse groups grow more homogeneous as the nation is united through popular culture.

The total picture of the United States is often hard to see close up. One has to stand back to see the grandeur of its geographical features. One has to look at the crowds of people from afar to understand how so many diverse individuals can compose a unified nation capable of greatness. The landscape and the people are united to form the mosaic of a vast nation, but it is only from the air that the visitor—or the reader—can begin to understand the true scope, complexity, beauty and power of the United States.

48 top *A small puff of steam from the active volcano Kilauea can be seen in this view of the Island of Hawaii, just above the brighter white band of clouds which cling to its eastern coast. Black lines running to the right, or north, are the routes of lava flows. Hawaii is the largest of the six main Hawaiian Islands.*

48-49 *The dark form of the Florida peninsula is highlighted by the reflected sunlight bouncing off the Atlantic Ocean and the Gulf of Mexico. A series of small lakes can be detected in the middle portion of the state, near Orlando, while to the south the large form of Lake Okeechobee can be seen. The bay along the west coast marks the Tampa-St. Petersburg area.*

AMERICA FROM Space

49 top The tail surfaces of the Space Shuttle fill the bottom of this view of the Pacific Northwest. The picture is about 180 degrees out of alignment with a map, with north on the bottom. In the lower right-hand corner is Vancouver Island in Canada's British Columbia. The Strait of Juan de Fuca runs between the island and the coast of Washington, which leads toward Puget Sound and the City of Seattle in the upper center.

49 bottom This view of the Earth was photographed by the Apollo 16 astronauts in April 1972. The Pacific Coastline from Mexico and Baja California to California in the United States can be seen clearly, as can the continent's backbone along the Rocky Mountains. Just visible between weather systems near the edge of the Earth's horizon are lakes Superior and Michigan.

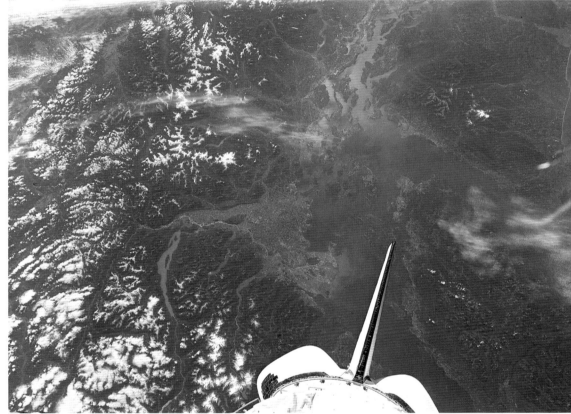

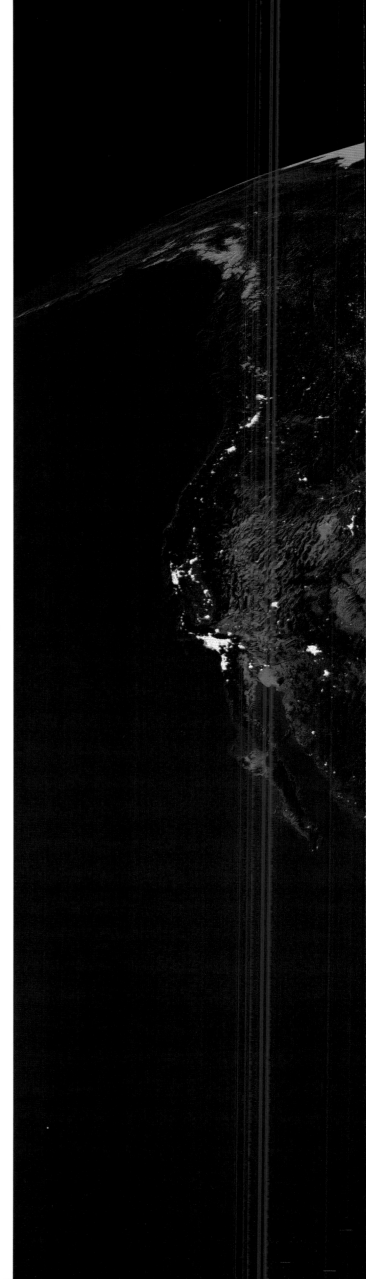

From the very beginning of human thought, people have wondered what it would be like to leave the Earth, to look back upon their home planet from a distance.

50 and 50-51 Satellite views of the United States at night reveal the positions of all the major metropolitan areas, which are aglow with light. Throughout the 20th century the use of electric power and the growth in population has increased the number of lights visible from space. The photograph at top left shows the multitude of lights of the City of New York.

The furrowed wrinkles of a land shaped by wind, water, tectonic forces and volcanoes are laid out below like the features of a gigantic map. But this is not a paper re-creation—this is real! The spacecraft floats serenely over the rugged land, moving at speeds unimaginable on Earth, above the clouds, the atmosphere itself.

Far below the landscape changes beneath the cloud cover from blue to green, from red to yellow, from brown to white, as the ship passes over water, forest, desert, plains, mountains and snow.

There is no oxygen or gravity outside the spacecraft, and human bodies without protection would be subject to danger from micrometeorites, extreme cold and other threats. In this environment the spacecraft becomes our home, our cocoon, the only place we can survive. It is a rare privilege to be able to see the earth like this, high enough to see the sweeping arc of the sphere we call Earth, a small, fragile refuge for life as we know it in the vastness of the universe.

In many ways our spacecraft can be compared to Earth, for the Earth is really just a larger version of the refuge we enjoy here. The Earth provides us with the proper temperature and atmospheric mix of gasses, not only supporting human life but the other life forms which we depend upon as food sources.

Yet from the very beginning of human thought, people have wondered what it would be like to leave the Earth, to look back upon our home planet from a distance, or perhaps even to travel to another heavenly body. Space flight is part of an ancient dream, only fulfilled in the 20th century.

Satellite photos of Earth show our planet's complexity and beauty as never before.

52 This marvelous view of New England is accented by snow. At the bottom of the view are the islands of Martha's Vineyard and Nantucket, with the familiar hook of Cape Cod above them. The indentation on the mainland inside Cape Cod's sickle pinpoints Plymouth Bay, where English colonists popularly known as the "Pilgrims" founded a colony in 1620. Further north, the next large bay is Boston Harbor, with Gloucester and Cape Ann on the far right. The bay to the left is Narragansett Bay, with Newport, Rhode Island near its entrance and Providence at its head.

53 top This dramatic view of Cape Hatteras, North Carolina clearly shows the long line of barrier islands formed by swift ocean currents and storms. The Gulf Stream passes the coastline, here seen looking toward the south, at three to five nautical miles per hour. This movement can be seen in eddies within the Sun's glare. The glare also pinpoints the thin stretch of island where the pioneering Wright Brothers made man's first powered flight in 1903.

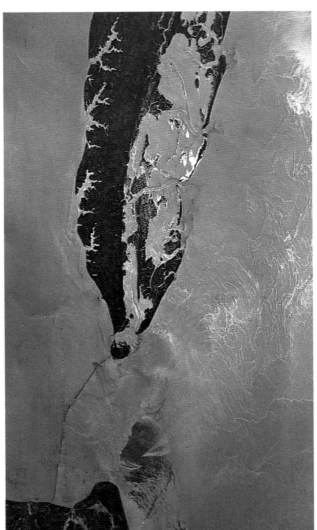

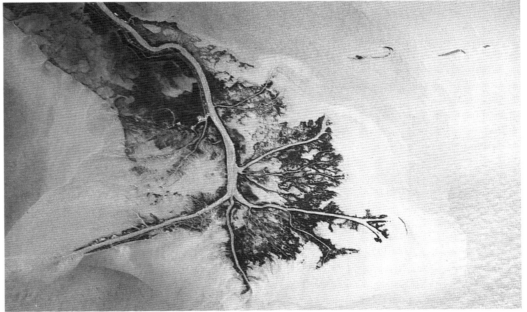

53 bottom left A major gateway to the East Coast of the U.S., the entrance to Chesapeake Bay is seen in this view, with the Atlantic Ocean on the left. The peninsula protruding from the top culminates at Cape Charles and Fisherman's Island, while the Chesapeake Bay Bridge Tunnel connects it with the mainland. The rounded peninsula at the lower center is Cape Henry, the first landfall of the English Jamestown settlers in 1607; to the left are the cities of Norfolk and Hampton. The areas in the glint of the sun reveal eddies where the waters of the bay mix with ocean currents.

53 bottom right Looking like the fossilized branch of a tree, this view of the Mississippi River Delta from space shows the mighty river's last gasp as it empties itself into the Gulf of Mexico. Since tides and waves are not extensive in this area of the Gulf, the Delta can continue to grow as silt from 31 upriver states is deposited here. The town of Venice, Louisiana can be seen on the river, just before the Delta branches into its three main shipping channels.

54 top Galveston, Texas can be seen in this view, in which north is to the bottom of the photo. The line of barrier islands moves down the Gulf Coast. In the center of the photo on the mainland is Texas City, while above it on the barrier island is Galveston. This image taken from the Space Shuttle Endeavour is so clear that Interstate Route 10 can be seen in the lower right corner, as well as Galveston's two jetties, the Interstate 45 Causeway, the San Luis Pass Bridge and the Baytown Bridge.

54 bottom The hook of Cape Cod, Massachusetts can be seen in this view. The curved tip of the cape points west toward the City of Boston and the indentation of Boston Harbor, while to the south of the cape lie the islands of Nantucket and Martha's Vineyard. The unusual glare of the sun is helpful in picking out detail. The darker ocean areas delineate calmer waters. "Internal waves," traveling many feet below the surface in a denser layer of water, can also be seen.

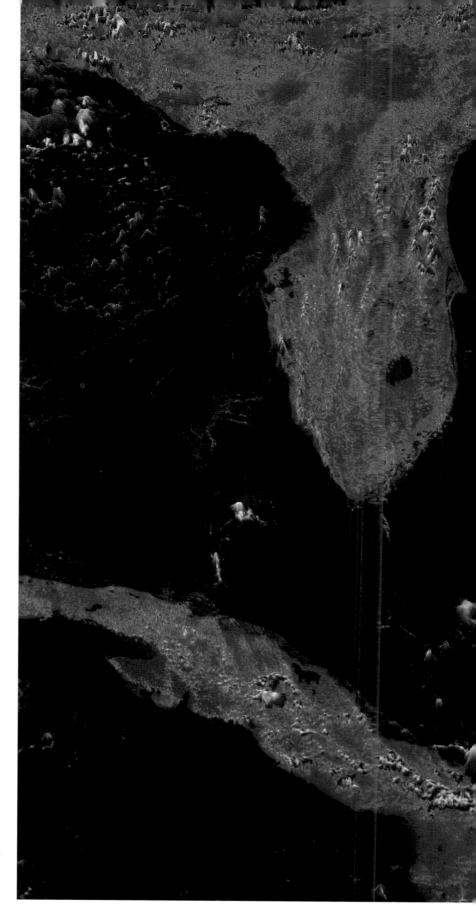

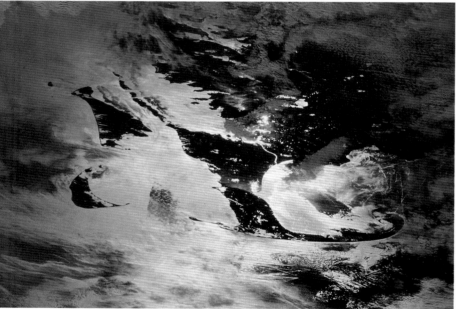

It hearkens back to the story of flight itself, a story rooted in the dreams of Leonardo DaVinci, the Montgolfiers, Octave Chanute, and Otto Lilienthal, a story brought to full reality by the experiments of two American brothers named Orville and Wilbur Wright between 1899 and 1903. These Americans were the first to achieve powered flight successfully in a heavier-than-air machine, and in later experiments became the first airplane pilots—that is, they learned to control their craft in the air, to turn and to land safely. The people of other nations quickly embraced powered flight, so quickly that the English Channel had been flown within five years of the Wright Brothers' first uncertain hops off the North Carolina sands. In five more years, airplanes were being used in combat over the skies of Europe in the First World War, shooting bullets at one another's fragile wood

and canvas machines. By 1927 another American, Charles A. Lindbergh, captured the imagination of the world by flying nonstop across the Atlantic Ocean. World War II showcased the terrible and awesome destructive power of war from the air, with rockets, jet aircraft and the atomic bomb becoming a part of global consciousness. Immediately following the war still another American, Chuck Yeager, became the first human being to fly faster than the speed of sound. The world was brought closer together by the advent of powered flight, yet we learned to mistrust one another even more deeply, to fear other nations more than ever before.

The surprise attack on Pearl Harbor on December 7, 1941 left a scar on the American psyche, insuring that such an act would never be repeated. After World War II, with nuclear arsenals

Modern satellite technology has affected the lives of people the world over, but probably its most beneficial aspect is the prediction and reporting of the weather.

54-55 and 55 top Modern satellite technology has affected the lives of people the world over, but probably its most beneficial aspect is the prediction and reporting of the weather. In the large view, 1996's devastating Hurricane Fran appears to be menacing the Florida peninsula, although it was the Carolinas which were hit instead by its 115-mile-per-hour winds.

55 bottom This view shows four of the five Great Lakes from the vantage point of space. North is at the lower right hand corner of the image. Lake Ontario is seen at the lower left, with Lake Erie to its right, Lake Huron to the lower right and Lake Michigan along the horizon on the right. Lake Superior would be off the upper edge of the photo. Niagara Falls is located on the narrow band of water between Lakes Ontario and Erie.

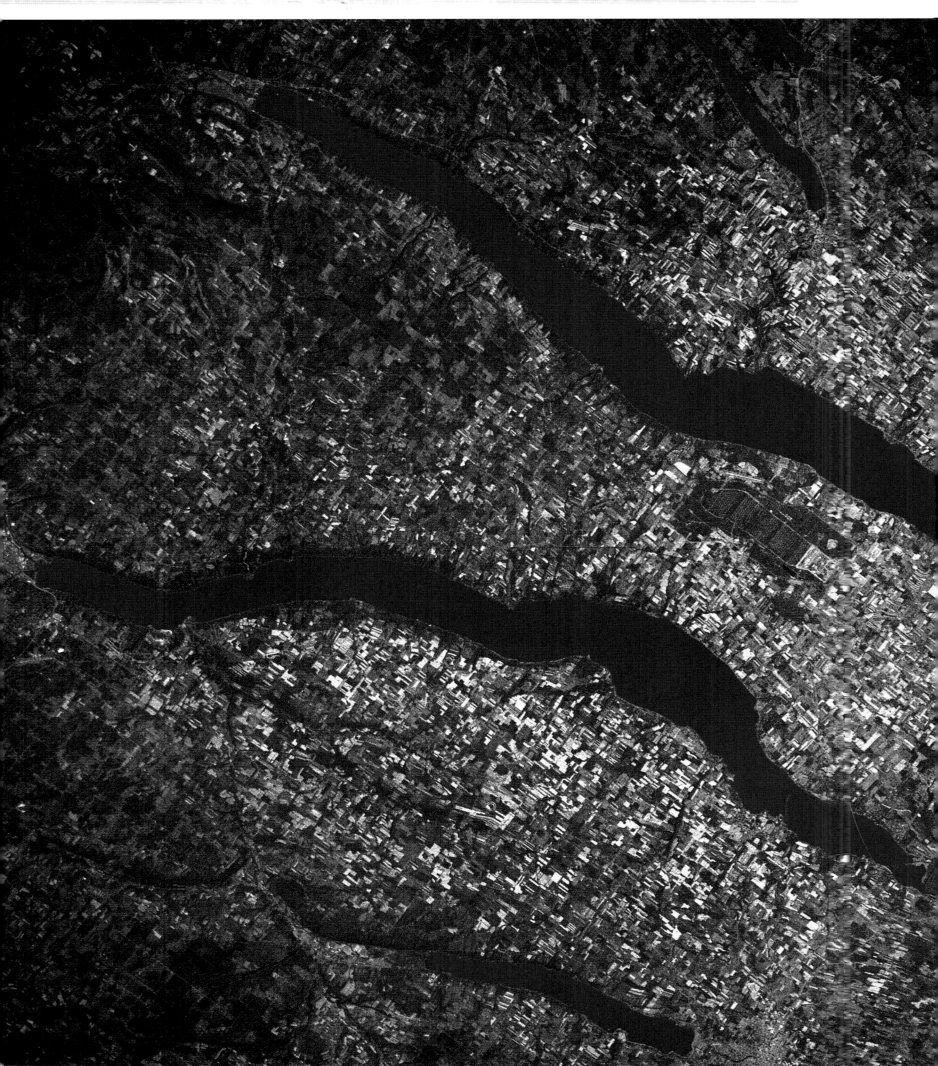

President John F. Kennedy challenged the nation in 1961 to put a man on the moon by the end of the decade.

in the hands of the United States, the Soviet Union and China, mutual distrust led to a worldwide fear of mass destruction which might rain from the skies at any moment.

In 1957 the United States was once more surprised and fearful, fear caused by a tiny round sphere fired into space by the Soviet Union called "Sputnik." This, the world's first artificial satellite, profoundly disturbed the nation of the first powered flight and early rocket experiments. The United States felt that it had lost its edge, lost its preeminence in science, lost in the race for the high ground, for the Soviet Union had achieved the highest perch of all, space. And they had gotten there first. The United States tried vainly to catch up.

President John F. Kennedy challenged the nation in 1961 to put a man on the moon by the end of the decade. Once again, Americans rose to the challenge, and in just eight years the first two human beings to set foot on another celestial body were sent there by the United States. On July 20, 1969, Neil Armstrong and Edwin "Buzz" Aldrin landed on the moon, stating that they "came in peace for all mankind." In the subsequent years, tensions between the United States and the Soviet Union eased enough to allow joint space projects, including Skylab, Space Shuttle missions and a Russian space station. Resisting the militarization of space, the National Aeronautics and Space Administration (NASA), a civilian agency, tried over the years to promote the peaceful joint exploration of space with scientists from other nations. Today, cameras can be turned toward Earth to provide dramatic photographs of unbelievable clarity, which can show topographical features in detail and context unimaginable to early explorers.

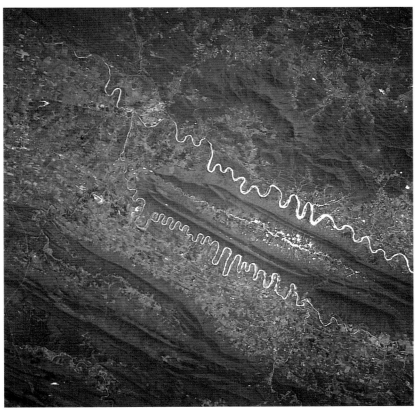

56-57 The glacially-carved Finger Lakes of upstate New York are shown surrounded by farm fields in this view, in which north is to the bottom right. The lakes are located just southwest of Syracuse. In the photo, the two northern spurs of Keuka Lake are on the top, followed by the 35 mile long form of Seneca Lake. Next comes Cayuga Lake, followed by the Owasco Lake at the bottom.

57 left The power and fury of an erupting volcano can be seen in this view from space of Mount St. Helens in Washington State. On May 18, 1980, an earthquake helped explode molten rock and gasses out one side of the mountain, reducing its height by 1300 feet. The route of this explosion and landslide can be seen in this photo of the mountain, on the side facing the bottom of the photo. The explosion killed a total of 57 people, and destroyed a forest covering 230 square miles.

57 top right The confluence of two of the nation's mightiest rivers is shown in this photo of St. Louis, Missouri. The city's downtown is located inside the bend of the river at the center, while its suburbs spread outward toward the west. The Mississippi, the wider of the rivers which runs from the top of the photo, joins the Missouri, the river running from the left, 18 miles above the city.

57 bottom right In this view of the Shenandoah Mountains, the north and south forks of the Shenandoah River flow toward their junction at Front Royal, Virginia. North is on the left side of this view, with the rivers separated by the ridges of Massanutten Mountain. At the upper right, the dark brown area is 3368 foot Mount Marshall. The fertile valley along the rivers has been known as prosperous farmland for 200 years.

58 A startlingly map-like image of uptown Manhattan shows the waters of the Hudson River on the left and the East River on the right, with the long expanse of Roosevelt Island floating in the river like a ship. The entire length of Central Park is shown, with the Metropolitan Museum of Art midway along the east side and the Museum of Natural History almost directly across the park on the west. North of the museums is the newly-named Jacqueline Kennedy Onassis Reservoir, a favorite place of the former First Lady. To the northwest of the park are Columbia University and Harlem.

59 top This high altitude photo of the greater New York area shows New Jersey on the left and New York on the right, divided by the Hudson River. Manhattan Island is nestled to the right of the Hudson inside the bay, while Long Island with its barrier islands runs off to the east. The large island that huddles close to the New Jersey shoreline in the left center is Staten Island, one of the boroughs of the City of New York. The long peninsula pointing northward at the lower center is Sandy Hook, which protects the Raritan Bay near Staten Island. Much of New Jersey and Long Island serve as a bedroom community for New York City.

59 center left San Francisco is located on the tip of the peninsula at the lower center of the photo. The expanse of San Francisco Bay runs northward to the rounded San Pablo Bay at the upper center. Urban development can be seen as San Francisco moves southward toward San Jose and the "Silicon Valley," while across the bay are Oakland and Berkeley. On the left side of the photo are Golden Gate National Recreation Area and Point Reyes National Seashore, the finely-delineated white line of sand at the lower left.

59 center right In this view of San Diego, north is to the left. The waters of San Diego Bay are enclosed within the embracing arms of Cabrillo, on the coast, and the long peninsula enclosing the bay, Coronado. To the north of the bay lies the smaller Mission Bay, and the city of La Jolla.

59 bottom This view of Washington, D.C. shows the National Mall, White House, Capitol and government buildings, at the center. In the foreground is Arlington, with the Pentagon to the center right. In the lower left is Georgetown, with the waters of Rock Creek Park winding down to the Potomac River, which runs from the lower left to the upper right of the picture, where it is joined by the narrower Anacostia River.

Today, cameras can be turned toward Earth to provide photographs of unbelievable clarity, which can show topographical features in detail.

59

Satellites carry communications around the world, enabling people to view an event on the other side of the Earth while it is taking place.

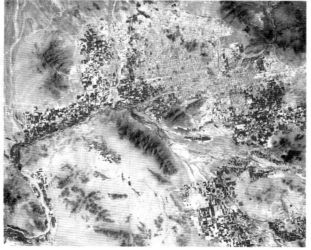

60-61 An infrared view of the California coastline, from San Diego to San Francisco. Los Angeles can be seen at the center of this view, with the Channel Islands offshore. The fertile San Joaquin Valley is to the upper right, while the expanse of the Mojave Desert trails off to the right center.

60 bottom The Phoenix, Arizona metropolitan area is seen in this infrared view, with urban areas showing as bright red and the cooler mountains surrounding the city showing as blue and black. The City of Phoenix is in the upper center, with part of the Tonto National Forest in the upper right corner. Sun City is near the upper left.

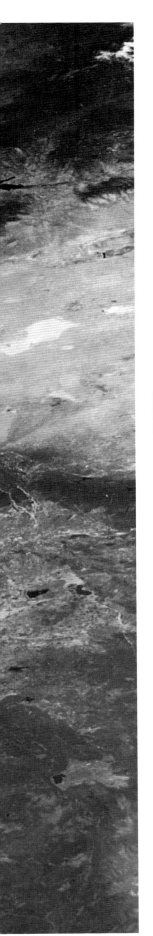

Satellites carry communications around the world, enabling people on one side of the earth to view an event on the other side via television while it is taking place.

The weather can now be predicted with far greater certainty than ever before in history, warning people about storms, floods and other destructive phenomena and saving countless lives in the process. Of course, there is always a negative side. Satellites can be used for spy purposes, and technology has advanced to the point that a headline on a newspaper can be read from a photograph taken from Earth orbit. Nations including the United States have spoken of taking weapons into space, particularly in the "Star Wars" program of the Reagan Administration.

But exciting advances continue. One of the world's oldest dreams, a dream of science fiction stories, has now become a reality. Americans have flown piloted, reusable spacecraft, the Space

Shuttles, for nearly 20 years. Space probes have investigated the outermost planets of our solar system, and landed on Venus and Mars to send back geological and meteorological data. A plan is now discussed seriously for a voyage to carry human beings to Mars. The orbiting Hubble Space Telescope sends back photos of deep space, other star clusters and galaxies, in a search for some of the secrets of the cosmos. And satellite photos of our own world show our planet's complexities, beauties and defects as never before.

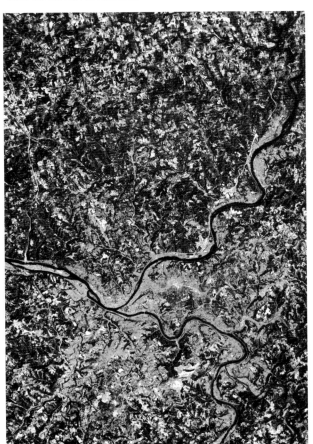

61 top The City of Houston is at the upper left of this photo, with the waters of Galveston Bay leading out to the Gulf of Mexico.

61 center left In this infrared view of Ocean Park, Virginia, north is on the lower left hand corner. Ocean Park is on the Chesapeake Bay just east of Norfolk. The body of water in the center of the picture is Lynnhaven Bay. The Chesapeake Bay Bridge Tunnel begins east of Ocean Park, along the bottom edge of the photo.

61 center right The City of Sacramento is the capital of the State of California. Located on the American River near the gold rush diggings of the 1840s and 50s, Sacramento later became the destination for the Pony Express and the first Transcontinental Railroad.

61 bottom left The Allegheny and Monongahela rivers join at Pittsburgh to form the Ohio, which flows west, to the left of this picture. The rugged mountain terrain surrounding the city shows up well in this photo.

61 bottom right This view of the city of Des Moines, Iowa shows this state capital surrounded by farm fields. The city is located in the center of Iowa on the Des Moines River, seen entering this view on the top and exiting on the right. Des Moines is the largest city in the state.

61

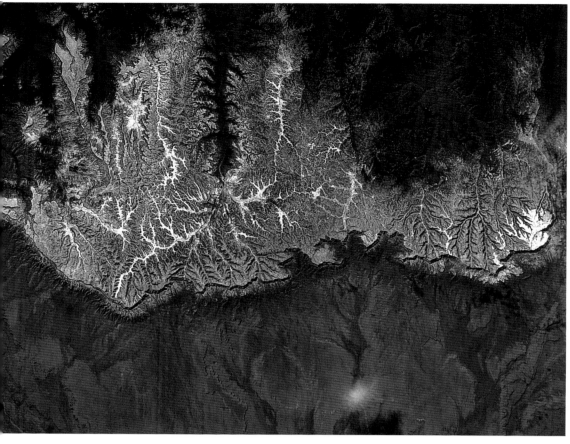

What does one see as one looks down from the lofty height of the space shuttle or a satellite as it flies over the United States? A land blessed by nature with extreme beauty, variety of topography and fertile land. A nation with its billions of lights left ablaze each evening, flaunting its wealth - and its ability to waste energy. A nation of forests grasslands, mighty rivers, farm fields, mountains, lakes, deserts, wild lands and crowded cities, nearly surrounded by the beautiful azure blue of the Atlantic and Pacific Oceans. Looking down on the United States from the lofty perch of space, one realizes the immensity of the nation, the diversity of its people, and the awesome beauty of its land forms. It is an alluring land in which to live or to travel, an intriguing land of diversity to explore and enjoy, whether one is on the ground, in the air, or in the unbelievable vastness of space.

Looking down on the United States from the lofty perch of space, one realizes the immensity of the nation, the diversity of its people and the awesome beauty of its land forms.

62 top The colors seem off in this view of Black Mesa in Arizona, but they are correct, for the tops of the mesa are covered with white snow. The mesa is located on the Navajo Indian Reservation, and its rich coal deposits are fed through the world's longest coal-slurry pipeline which leads to a power station in Nevada. The Navajo people have made a good deal of money from leases to coal companies at Black Mesa.

62 center North is roughly at the upper right corner of this photo of Utah's Great Salt Lake from space. In the center of the photo is the Great Salt Lake Desert, while to the lower left is Salt Lake City. The Grouse Creek Mountains can be seen in the upper right corner of the photo.

62 bottom White Sands, New Mexico, the world's largest gypsum dune field, covers nearly 300 square miles and lies at the center of this photo. To the lower left are the San Andres Mountains, while the city of Alamogordo nestles in the Sacramento Mountains at the upper right. About 40 miles to the north of the area of the photo was the "Trinity Site," where the first atomic bomb was exploded in 1945.

63 The Grand Canyon can be seen in this view of the Arizona and Utah deserts, taken from space in 1994. North is roughly to the left of the photo, with the dark ribbon of the Colorado River and Lake Powell in the center. The river winds past Glen Canyon Dam and down through the magnificent Grand Canyon to the lower right.

64-65 This satellite view shows the Mojave Desert between the Grand Canyon to the east and Death Valley to the west. The lake in the center left is Lake Mead, formed from the Colorado River by the Hoover Dam at the lower center. Just to the left of the dam at the right center, Las Vegas appears. To the right of the lake are the Virgin Mountains, while above Las Vegas the Sheep Range can be seen.

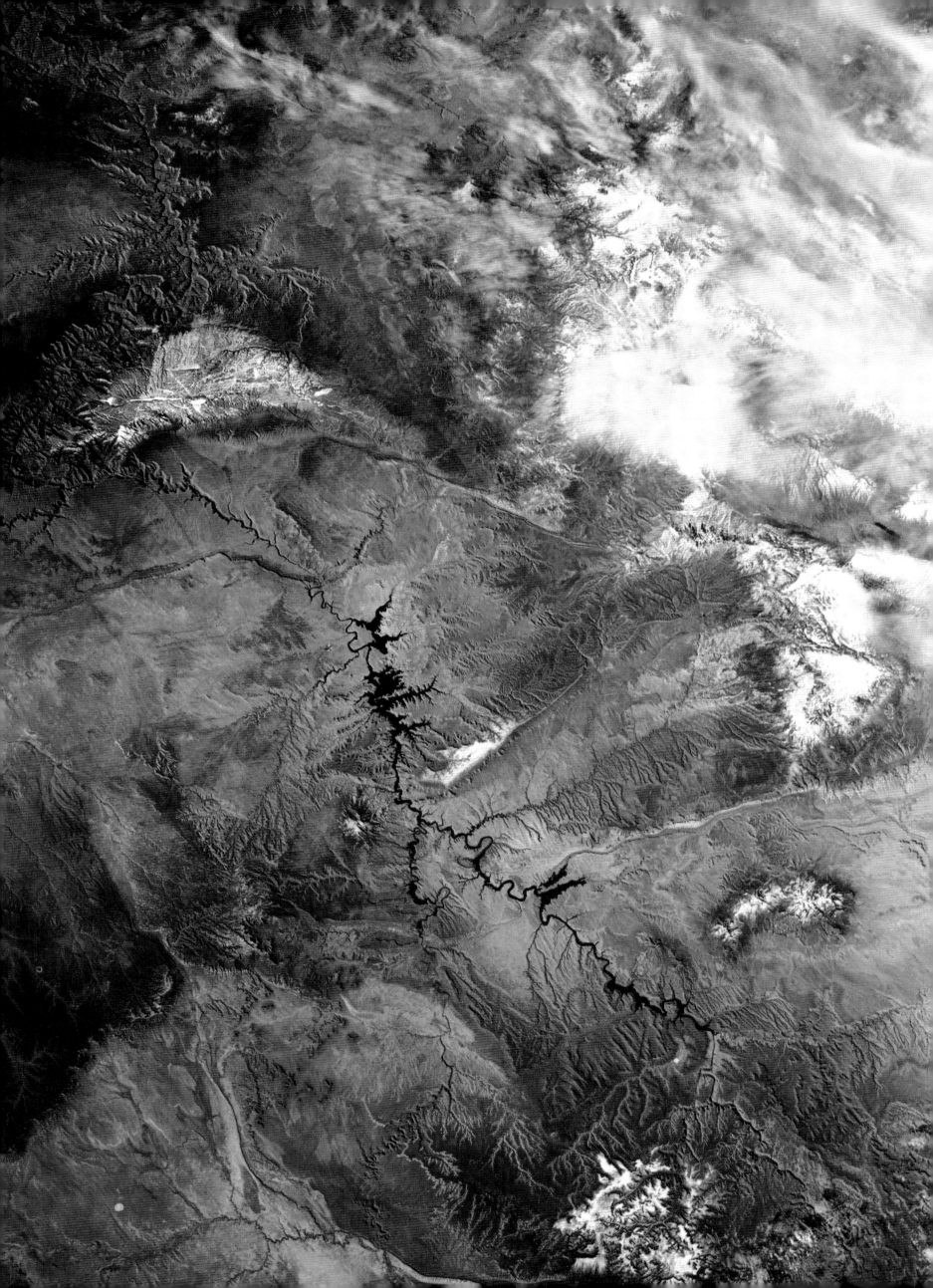

66 top The southwestern coast of Alaska is seen in this view. The Aleutian Island chain begins in the lower center. Most of the area of the photograph is part of the Togiak, Cape Newenham, and Yukon Delta National Wildlife Refuges. The confluence of the Yukon River with the Bering Sea can be seen at the large indentation of the shoreline in the lower right of the photo.

66 center The entire chain of the Hawaiian Islands can be seen in this view, with north at the bottom of the image. The islands, starting in the lower right-hand corner, are Nihau, Kauai, Oahu, Molokai, Lanai, Maui, Kahoolawe and Hawaii.

66 bottom The Island of Oahu is seen in this image, with north to the bottom. At the upper left of the island is Honolulu and Pearl Harbor. Clouds cluster over the Koolau Range of Mountains along the island's northeastern face.

Americans have flown piloted spacecraft, the Space Shuttles, for nearly 20 years, and space probes have investigated the outermost planets of our solar system.

66-67 Glaciers flow toward the sea in Glacier Bay National Park in a photo with north to the right of the image. Mount Fairweather, upper right, is just over the Canadian border in British Columbia. It is the highest point in that province at 15,300 feet tall.

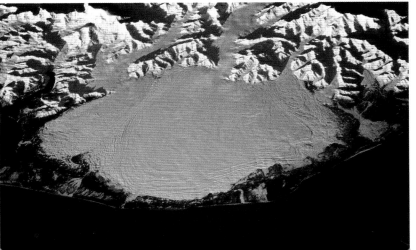

67 bottom The Malaspina Glacier in Alaska is located along the south shore of the state, near the junction of the Alexander Archipelago and the mainland. Most of the glacier is located within Wrangell-St. Elias National Park. Glacier ice can be seen moving along several routes to feed the ice near the shore.

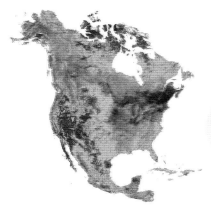

68-69 A beautiful autumn day awakens the peaceful town of Pittsfield, nestled in the Berkshire Mountains near the western border of Massachusetts. The Berkshires average 1,000 to 1,500 feet in height, and culminate on 3,491 foot tall Mount Greylock, the tallest point in Massachusetts, which commands a view of five states.

The Northeast

68 bottom Yellow taxi cabs line up at
an intersection on busy Fifth Avenue
in New York City. The city has been
a commercial, shipping and
manufacturing center since its founding
in 1624 by the Dutch. Today, over
seven million people live within the
city limits of New York, the largest
urban area in the United States.

69 Sailboats dot the harbor of Newport,
Rhode Island, one of the wealthiest
communities in the United States.
Founded in 1639 by religious separatists
from Massachusetts Bay, Rhode Island
attracted Quakers, Sephardic Jews, and
a large number of free blacks and slaves
during the 1600s. Today, the community
of about 29,000 people plays host
annually to the Newport Jazz Festival.

*Five hundred twelve miles from the spires of Manhattan,
the Atlantic Coast is sprinkled with forested islands
and accented by quaint fishing villages.*

*70-71 Five hundred twelve miles from
the spires of Manhattan, the Atlantic
Coast is sprinkled with forested islands
and accented by quaint fishing villages
like the one in this photo, taken near
Acadia National Park in Maine.*

*70 bottom Maine's oceanside villages
provide recreational opportunities
and a peaceful, laid-back atmosphere.
People who earn their living on the sea,
including commercial fishermen and
tour boat operators, make their homes
here year-round.*

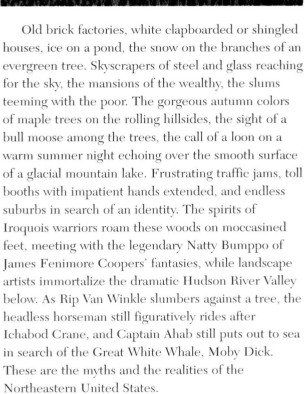

71 top left Acadia National Park is located on Mount Desert Island, Isle au Haut, and the Schoodic Peninsula in Maine. The park preserves native forests, coastal mountains, offshore islands, tidepools and wildlife habitat along New England's rocky coast.

Old brick factories, white clapboarded or shingled houses, ice on a pond, the snow on the branches of an evergreen tree. Skyscrapers of steel and glass reaching for the sky, the mansions of the wealthy, the slums teeming with the poor. The gorgeous autumn colors of maple trees on the rolling hillsides, the sight of a bull moose among the trees, the call of a loon on a warm summer night echoing over the smooth surface of a glacial mountain lake. Frustrating traffic jams, toll booths with impatient hands extended, and endless suburbs in search of an identity. The spirits of Iroquois warriors roam these woods on moccasined feet, meeting with the legendary Natty Bumppo of James Fenimore Coopers' fantasies, while landscape artists immortalize the dramatic Hudson River Valley below. As Rip Van Winkle slumbers against a tree, the headless horseman still figuratively rides after Ichabod Crane, and Captain Ahab still puts out to sea in search of the Great White Whale, Moby Dick. These are the myths and the realities of the Northeastern United States.

A land carved out by glaciers, the Northeastern United States offers the visitor nearly every type of vista and recreational experience, from ocean beaches to quiet mountaintops, from one of the world's greatest cities to forest and animal preserves. This is a land of history, where some of the most organized and powerful American Indian tribes met some of the earliest European colonizers. It was the land of the Mayflower Pilgrims, the early historians, poets and authors of the United States, the growth of industrialism. Historic sites, markers and museums dot the entire region with an awareness of the past which is impossible to ignore. Immigration from far-flung lands touched the region early, and has never abated. A temperate climate allows a wide range of agriculture, including dairy farming, the cultivation of corn fields and apple orchards. But the rocky soil and the undulating landscape prevented farming on the large scale demanded by the machine age. As a result, many of the early inhabitants lived off the sea, fishing in the ocean waters and enjoying the recreational opportunities of sand and surf.

71 top right The French explorer Samuel de Champlain, who named Mount Desert Island in 1604, ran aground on its rocky shoreline, the first of many seagoing mishaps in the area. After the Civil War, foghorns and lighthouses were installed to make navigation safer. There are four lighthouses maintained by the U.S. Coastguard in the area of Acadia National Park.

71 center right The clear, cold ocean waters, the lure of nature and the area's physical beauty draw vacationers each summer to Maine. Deep-sea fishing, whale watches, boating, swimming and other recreational activities are a healthful tonic for stressed-out urban dwellers.

71 bottom right The views surrounding Acadia National Park, like these lush, green islands, have inspired artists, writers and lovers since the 19th century, when Mount Desert Island became a fashionable summer resort.

The explorer Samuel de Champlain, who named Mount Desert Island, ran aground on its shoreline, the first of many seagoing mishaps in the area.

72 top left Acadia National Park covers some 30,000 acres, and shares Mount Desert Island with villages, museums, and proud local people who love the Maine coast. This sunrise near Acadia National Park provides a notion of the beauty and serenity of this gorgeous natural area.

72-73 A beautiful four-masted schooner sails a serene sea after sunrise near Acadia National Park. Sights like this recall the heyday of Mount Desert Island and its early role as a shipbuilding center.

72 bottom Bald Porcupine Island and its breakwater point toward Bar Harbor, the largest town on Mount Desert Island. Bar Harbor is located just below 1,530-foot Cadillac Mountain. The island in the upper right corner of the photo is Bar Island.

The other side of life in the northeast is one dictated by the fast pace of urban areas and a great concentration of population. The northeast has traditionally been the most populous region of the nation, and continues to be so today. Individual towns along the Boston to Washington corridor may have retained their historic names and borders, but they often run together with no distinguishable demarcation other than highway signs denoting the transition. A trip through suburban New Jersey, for example, reveals one large urban area in a line from New York City to Philadelphia, with little pause between housing developments, strip malls, fast food restaurants and gas stations. The only

variety comes in the different sequence of each cluster of businesses as one town follows on the heels of the last.

It is an urban world formed by the hand of the architect, engineer and construction worker. In city after city, concrete, steel, asphalt, brick and glass combine to create a scene often devoid of the natural world, or at best where nature only exists to provide a counterpoint to the work of human beings. Buildings, shopping areas, churches, bridges and monuments, some inspired and many mundane, are crowded together to create an urban landscape where man-made structures tower like trees, and streams of traffic substitute for rivers. The pace is hectic, and the bigger the city, the faster it gets.

73 top left The town of Bar Harbor, on the far right, with Champlain and Cadillac Mountains behind it, on a foggy summer morning. The three small islands, from left to right, are Bald Porcupine, Sheep Porcupine and Bar.

73 top right The English settled Mount Desert Island following the victory of British forces over the French in Canada in 1759. Abnaki Indians inhabited the Maine coast, and fished around the island. Farming, lumbering, shipbuilding and fishing became the major occupations of residents. In the 1850s, steamboats began to bring artists, writers and America's newly wealthy to Mount Desert.

73 bottom Cadillac Mountain and nearby Champlain Mountain are seen near sunrise in this photo. These peaks, like Mount Desert Island, were carved by an ancient glacier, in places two miles thick, which created the long valleys, lakes and rounded hills seen by the modern visitor.

74 top The rocky New England shoreline preserves many of the homes of sea captains, topped by "widow's walks" like the one on the tip of the peninsula in this photo. The wives of these seamen often kept a vigil in these tower perches, waiting for their husbands to return from the sea.

74-75 Boston, located at the top center of the photo, clings to the Atlantic Coast along with its suburbs. In the foreground is Cohasset, with Nantasket Beach, Allerton and Hull located on the long peninsula in the center of the photo. To the left is Quincy, home of two Presidents, John and John Quincy Adams.

74 bottom A winding road leads to adventure along the rocky New England coastline. Beautiful scenery and an abundance of marine wildlife make walks, bicycle rides and picnicking favorite summer pastimes. In the photo one can recognize Cape Ann.

75 left The Cape Ann Peninsula north of Boston lies at the northern limit of Massachusetts Bay. Cape Ann is also known for its stone quarries.

75 top and center right The city of Gloucester, Massachusetts, is world-famous as a fishing port. The schooners that put forth from Gloucester were immortalized in Rudyard Kipling's Captains Courageous. Settled in 1623,

its protected harbor features a bronze statue of a fisherman, where an annual memorial service is held each year to honor men lost at sea.

75 bottom right The New England coastline is an area rich in opportunities. It offers scenic views, whale watching and quaint towns with art colonies, old fishing wharves and historic buildings.

Many talk of escape, of one day owning a "little house in the country" and "getting away from it all." Few make it. In fact, the proportion of urban-dwelling Americans continues to rise, while the rural population declines.

Luckily, there is escape, even if it is only temporary—the fringes of the urban megalopolis offer calm. Southern New Jersey, for instance, is sparsely populated compared with the northern section of the state, and offers beautiful rural areas and beaches for those weary of crowds. Long Island, for all of its crowding, also offers superb beaches along its southern shore, with abundant wildlife, recreational fishing and the delighted shouts of children swimming in the ocean and playing on the

beach in the summer. The mountains of New York State and eastern Pennsylvania beckon with refreshing clean air and streams, as well as winter skiing. New York's St. Lawrence River and glacial lakes provide boating and swimming for all. And further up the coast lies Maine, less densely populated and a vacation haven for many. Perhaps much of the area's natural importance is summed up by the lands within the 41,000 acre Acadia National Park in Maine. Lichen-covered rock, windy summits with a mist-shrouded profusion of colorful trees, Acadia hugs the coast while displaying the lovely extremes of nature in the northeast.

In contrast, the landscape of the city involves man-made landmarks. New York City, with a population of 7.5 million, is the largest city in the United States. Its metropolitan area extends into neighboring upstate New York, Long Island, Connecticut and New Jersey, and comprises nearly 20 million people. But the heart of New York continues to be Manhattan Island and its well-known landmarks. Many of these landmarks are bridges since Manhattan must be connected to the mainland and its other boroughs. Transportation needs and

Settled in 1623, Gloucester's protected harbor features a bronze statue of a fisherman, where an annual memorial service is held each year to honor men lost at sea.

Famous for its Italian community, Boston's North End also has the Old North Church, famous for two lanterns which informed Paul Revere that the British were coming in 1775.

76 top Downtown Boston, with the Charles River in the background, is not entirely composed of brand-new structures. Examining this photo carefully will reveal, among other historic buildings, Faneuil Hall, a brick building with a gold-topped cupola near the lower left hand corner. Faneuil Hall, built in 1742, serves as a market and was a historic meeting hall for American patriots. Another gold-domed building near the center of the photo is the State House and Archives, built in 1795.

76 center The inner harbor of Boston, looking southward, reveals the way in which water divides the city. On the left of the photograph are Logan Airport and East Boston, at the lower right the Charlestown Navy Yard, and at the upper right downtown Boston, with the North End in the foreground. Famous for its Italian community, the North End also has the Old North Church, the steeple of which can be seen at the very right-hand edge of the photo. It was in this steeple that two lanterns were hung in 1775, informing Paul Revere that the British were coming by sea.

the wide water spans in New York have placed unique demands on civil engineers for over 100 years. The most notable results are the Brooklyn Bridge (1884), the George Washington Bridge (1931), and the Verrazano-Narrows Bridge, but each New Yorker has their favorite. The island environment has also necessitated tall buildings, since space is at a premium and must be used as efficiently as possible. As time went on, the buildings got taller: the Flatiron Building (1902), the Woolworth Building (1915), the Chrysler Building (1931), the Empire State Building (1931), Rockefeller Center (1935), and the twin towers of the World Trade Center (1977). Again, each New Yorker has their favorite skyscraper. Many, however, prefer smaller buildings, those more in scale with the human experience. These might include the New York City Hall, Frank Lloyd Wright's Guggenheim Museum, the Plaza Hotel, Federal Hall, the New York Public Library, Grand Central Station, or any one of thousands of structures within the city. Perhaps more than any building, however, New York and its harbor are symbolized by a statue—the 305 foot Statue of Liberty, a gift from France, erected in 1886.

Although weights and measures remain constant, distances are perceived differently in the various sections of the United States. For a northeasterner, a destination farther than 50 miles seems a long way off, while a westerner might drive 50 miles or more each week just to pick up groceries. Northeasterners

76 bottom The Charles River cuts through the center of this photo, with Boston on the left and Cambridge on the right, or north side. Cambridge is renowned for its institutions of higher learning. In addition to Harvard, it also boasts the Massachusetts Institute of Technology, near the center of this photo, and Radcliffe, near the upper right-hand corner.

76-77 The heart of downtown Boston, pictured here, reveals a city composed of both old and new. In the foreground along the harbor is the Aquarium. To the left of center at the top of the picture is the green park called the Boston Common, where British troops marched in the 1770s.

77 bottom left The buildings of the Massachusetts Institute of Technology in Cambridge, including the dome of the university's famous Maclaurin Building. Just upriver, Harvard, founded 1636, is the oldest institution of higher learning in the United States. Notable alumni include William James, Ralph Waldo Emerson, Henry David Thoreau, Robert Frost, T.S. Eliot, and U.S. Presidents John Adams, John Quincy Adams, Theodore Roosevelt, Franklin D. Roosevelt, and John F. Kennedy.

77 bottom right Some of the old, storied residences of Boston in the Back Bay area near the Prudential

Tower recall the prosperous past of the city. The Back Bay area, once a marshy creek, was drained and filled between 1858 and 1886. Today, Boston is the largest city in New England, with a population of people of over 5.5 million.

78 top Cambridge, Massachusetts was named after the city of Cambridge, England in 1638. Like its historic forebear, the New World Cambridge has became a world-renowned center of learning and scientific inquiry. Stephen Daye published the first book in the English Colonies, the Bay Psalm Book, *in Cambridge in 1640.*

Cambridge, Massachusetts was named after Cambridge, England in 1638, and like its namesake became a renowned center of learning.

are more apt to use modes of transportation other than autos for long trips, but love to take short trips into the country. A drive through the countryside of the Northeast can be very rewarding, no matter how short the distance. Historical sites and natural vistas abound. The entire Northeast was a battleground for hundreds of years, first for American Indians, later for European powers vying for colonial supremacy. Wars between the French and English, and later the American revolutionaries and the British, were fought throughout the region. A legacy of historic forts and battlefield sites, as well as homes dating back 200 to 300 years, dot the landscape.

The northeast was important historically because it was a crossroads of travel. Boston and New York offered excellent port facilities where many entered the United States from Europe. Numerous river valleys enabled travel from Canada and the northeast into the interior along the St. Lawrence River, from north to south along the Hudson River—Lake Champlain corridor, and from east to west along the Mohawk River to Lakes Ontario and Erie. This east to west route was improved by 1825 when the Erie Canal was completed, bypassing the Appalachian Mountain chain and making New York State the first "Gateway to the West."

Today, these traditional travel and trade routes are still in use. Beside the still-functioning (but much-improved) Erie Canal are railroad tracks and an interstate highway, all following the historic paths first worn by the Iroquois Confederacy hundreds of years ago.

The northeast is an area of contrasts, with the various amenities of city and country living allowing a vast number of choices for recreation and entertainment. History blends with an awesome but subtle natural world which awes visitors and delights residents alike. The northeast, with its natural and man-made beauty, offers something for everyone.

78-79 The Harvard Business School in Cambridge, with the Charles River running through the center, presents a nostalgic scene in the winter, with the snow clinging to the roofs of the graceful brick Georgian-style structures. It was in Cambridge on July 3, 1775 that George Washington took command of the Continental Army, standing under an elm tree on the common.

79 top Dorchester Heights in South Boston culminates at the memorial to the Revolutionary War fortifications which drove the British out of Boston after a year-long siege on March 17, 1776. It was George Washington's first military victory as a commander. In the background is Boston Harbor and the circular Marine Park.

79 bottom Houses and apartments along Massachusetts Avenue provide a view of city living in Boston. The city's industries include banking, insurance, printing, publishing, medicine and medical research.

The docks of Newport front the historic district, which evokes the city's heyday as a rum production center in the 18th century.

80 left This photograph of a sailboat on Narragansett Bay, Rhode Island, recalls the maritime history that made Newport a wealthy town even before the advent of millionaire summer residents in the late 19th century. Newport was host to the America's Cup yacht race from 1930 to 1983.

80-81 At the end of the 19th century, Newport, Rhode Island became a fashionable summer locale for America's millionaires. Making fortunes in railroads, shipping, manufacturing, steel, oil and other commodities, the richest of the rich built "cottages" like these along the shore of Aquidneck Island.

80 bottom The Massachusetts shore south of Boston and west of Cape Cod includes many peninsulas and islands, as well as beautiful little fishing towns. Cities like New Bedford, famous for its whaling ships of the 19th century, and Fall River, known for its textile mills, are located in this area.

81 bottom The Newport Bridge is one of two connections of Aquidneck Island to the mainland. Newport is known as a boat and electronics manufacturing area, as well as the home of the U.S. Naval War College, founded in 1885.

82-83 The docks of Newport front the historic district, which evokes Newport's heyday as a rum production center in the 18th century. Ships brought molasses from the West Indies which was converted into rum in the town's 22 distilleries.

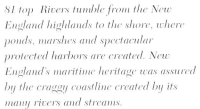

81 top Rivers tumble from the New England highlands to the shore, where ponds, marshes and spectacular protected harbors are created. New England's maritime heritage was assured by the craggy coastline created by its many rivers and streams.

81 center The ocean breakers near Newport, Rhode Island evoke the peaceful and temperate nature of the area. With a population of about 28,000 people, the area has an attractively relaxing pace.

Nantucket was famous in the 19th century for its whaling industry. Its modern economy is based on recreation during the vacation season.

84 top Provincetown, with its excellent harbor, is one of the most popular vacation spots on Cape Cod. In the distance is the sandy beach of the National Seashore and the Atlantic Ocean.

84 center right Summer houses and hotels line the inner shore of Cape Cod, while the cape's famous beach runs along the Atlantic side of the peninsula.

84 center left This long peninsula, called Great Point, protrudes north westward from the shores of Nantucket Island, south of Cape Cod. Nantucket was famous in the 19th century for its whaling industry, commemorated today by a museum on the island. Nantucket is 14 miles long and from 3 to 6 miles wide. First settled in 1659, its modern economy is based on recreation during the vacation season.

84 bottom left The east coast of Cape Cod sports sandy beaches that face the Atlantic Ocean. Route 6 winds its way around the 75 mile sickle-shaped arm of the cape. The popular resort area provides swimming, fishing and boating opportunities. The Cape Cod National Seashore, administered by the National Park Service, covers much of the northeastern part of the peninsula.

84 bottom right The protected harbor of Nantucket Village on Nantucket Island is seen in this photo, which looks to the north toward Great Point. The Nantucket Whaling Museum is located on the peninsula on the left.

85 The blue water off the summer shores of Cape Cod has attracted vacationers for well over a century. The cape was named in 1602 by Bartholomew Gosnold for its great numbers of codfish. First came the fishermen, then the Pilgrims to settle, and eventually the tourists who make this sickle-shaped peninsula a haven for recreation.

86-87 "The Breakers," a 70-room "cottage" which cost $4 million when completed in 1895, was a summer home for Cornelius Vanderbilt, one of America's richest men. Designed by William Morris Hunt, it became a mecca for high society at the turn of the 20th century. Today it can be toured, along with several other Newport "cottages."

86 bottom One of the earlier Newport mansions is Chateau-sur-Mer, built in 1852 for William Wetmore, who made his fortune in the China trade. In 1872 Richard Morris Hunt redesigned and enlarged the house, which reflects the high Victorian taste.

Newport is famous for its marvelous "cottages," like "The Breakers," designed by William Morris Hunt.

87 top Rosecliff was built in 1902 with elegant Louis XV styling. Its marble facade reflects the waning light near sunset.

87 center top left The Beechwood estate of the Astor family in Newport. The Astors made their fortune in the fur trade in the early 1800s, then diversified their interests. The name Astor became synonymous with wealth, taste and class.

87 center left The homes of wealthy Americans are still congregated along Ocean Drive in Newport, where this modern mansion is located.

87 center right Another of Newport's "cottages" on Bellevue Avenue. Many of the rooms and details of such houses were fabricated in Europe, then taken apart, shipped across the Atlantic, and reassembled in America. The finest wood, marble, brick and other materials were used to build these expensive but wonderfully ostentatious reminders of an American past of unbridled business opportunities— and no income tax.

87 bottom Marble House, another of Newport's fabulous mansions, was built in 1892 and included this Japanese tea house along its ocean walk.

88 top The neat frame houses of Pittsfield on a perfect autumn day. A city of about 49,000 people, Pittsfield was settled in 1761. It is a winter and summer resort, and is also important in the development of plastics, as well as paper manufacturing.

88-89 and 89 top left The tree-shrouded Berkshire Mountains of western Massachusetts accent white-framed homes like the ones pictured, some modest and others grand.

89 top right Autumn leaves reach their peak along the Mohawk Trail, a stretch of the Berkshires in northwestern Massachusetts on Route 2. The trail passes below Mount Greylock, highest point in the state, near the town of North Adams. Just over the border to the west is New York State.

89 center Autumn touches part of the city of Pittsfield, Massachusetts, with the Berkshire Mountains in the background. Pittsfield's neighbors included a colony of Shakers beginning in the 1890s at Hancock, and author Hermann Melville who lived in the area from 1850 to 1863. At nearby Tanglewood the annual Berkshire Music Festival began in 1937, and has been a tradition ever since.

89 bottom Jams, jellies, juice and sauce will be the result of the cranberry harvest in Carver, Massachusetts, a small town about 8 miles southwest of Plymouth in the eastern portion of the state. The large American cranberry grows on low vines and is cultivated in sand-covered bogs which can be flooded or drained at will. The water protects the berries from frosts and insects.

90-91 A quiet autumn day on Onota Lake near Pittsfield, Massachusetts, looking northward toward the Berkshires. Within a couple of months snow will fall, and ski enthusiasts will begin to arrive to enjoy the white-covered hills, now devoid of their spectacular color.

The change in leaf color comes about when the leaf dies and accessory pigments, called carotenoids, become visible.

92 left and 92-93 A helicopter (right) approaches the raging torrent of Niagara Falls, on the Canadian side across the western border of New York State. The raging torrent of water (left) flows over the escarpment at the rate of 194,940 cubic feet per second. The Canadian, or "horseshoe falls" are eroding at the rate of five feet per year. The American Falls, which carry a smaller volume of water, are eroding at only 6 inches per year.

The falls formed about 12,000 years ago, when water from Lake Erie began flowing over the Niagara Escarpment.

92 bottom The reason for the name "horseshoe" is evident in this high shot of the Canadian side of Niagara Falls. The Canadian side of Niagara forms a horseshoe shape 2,592 feet long, and drops 160 feet to the river below. The American side is slightly higher, but is only 1,001 feet along the escarpment.

93 right A helicopter pilot hovers above the Niagara River, upstream from Niagara Falls. The falls may be viewed in a variety of ways from several different vantage points. Parks on each side of the falls allow visitors to stand close to the thundering edge, observation towers allow a view from above, while boats maneuver in close for a view from below.

93 bottom The Canadian side of Niagara Falls, and Goat Island which separates the American from the Canadian side, can be seen in this view. Niagara Falls occur almost midway along the Niagara River, which flows from Lake Erie into Lake Ontario. The falls formed about 12,000 years ago, when glaciers retreated northward and water from Lake Erie began flowing over the Niagara Escarpment, a ridge which runs from Wisconsin to New York through the Great Lakes region. Erosion has since pushed the falls 11 miles upstream, forming the spectacular Niagara River Gorge.

94 *A visitor snaps a picture from a window inside the crown of the Statue of Liberty. The statue, which stands 306 feet 8 inches tall from the bottom of the pedestal to the top of the torch, was a gift to the United States financed by popular subscription from the people of France. A similar subscription drive in America paid for the pedestal, designed by Richard Morris Hunt. The statue, sculpted by French artist Frederic-Auguste Bartholdi, was dedicated in 1886.*

The Statue of Liberty stands on Liberty Island, where she is seen by every ship entering and leaving New York Harbor.

95 top right *The Statue of Liberty stands on Liberty Island, where she is seen by every ship entering and leaving New York Harbor. She was the first sight to greet immigrants to America, who after 1892 were landed at the Ellis Island Immigration station, in the left background. She also was the last and first sight of America for many departing and returning servicemen in World Wars I and II.*

95 top left *The main building on Ellis Island saw some 20 million immigrants pass through its doors between 1892 and 1954, where they were quarantined until their entry into the States was approved. An overwhelming majority of Americans alive today has at least one ancestor who passed through Ellis Island. Today the area is a museum, which underwent an eight year renovation to open in 1990.*

95 center left *The Staten Island Ferry plies the waters of New York Harbor in this view of Manhattan Island as seen from the south. On the west side of the island along the left of the photo, the Hudson River winds down to the ocean. On the right of the photo is the East River and its bridges which connect Manhattan to Brooklyn and Queens. The island in the lower right corner is Governor's Island, the home of Fort Jay, a U.S. Coast Guard Base.*

95 center right *The east side of Manhattan Island is seen in the foreground, with the Williamsburg Bridge crossing over to Brooklyn in the background. The "Lower East Side," as the area is called, was the home of teeming immigrant ghettoes in the early 1900s for large numbers of Italian, Irish and Jewish immigrants and smaller numbers of people from untold other lands.*

95 bottom *The Brooklyn Bridge, in the foreground, was completed in 1883, linking lower Manhattan Island with the mainland for the first time. For its time it was an incredible engineering feat, and for many years the longest suspension* bridge in the world. It was joined by the Manhattan Bridge, which runs parallel to the Brooklyn Bridge, in 1909 and the Williamsburg Bridge, further north and around the bend of the island, in 1903.

96-97 *The sun sets on Central Park, a delightful "natural" area in the middle of the largest city in the United States. Designed in 1857 by Frederick Law Olmsted and Calvert Vaux, Central Park consists of 840 acres of winding paths and roads, statues, points of interest, hills and ponds, as well as the large reservoir seen in this view. In the background is the Triborough Bridge and Queens.*

The skyscrapers of Manhattan loom over the East River, and the Empire State Building once dominated the landscape. It stands 102 stories tall and was completed in 1931. It was made famous worldwide in movies such as King Kong and An Affair to Remember

98 left and 98-99 Dominating the skyline of lower Manhattan, the twin towers of the World Trade Center rise 1,350 feet at 110 stories. Designed by Minoru Yamasaki, the World Trade Center was opened in 1973, with four million square feet of office space.

98 bottom The skyscrapers of Lower Manhattan loom over the East River in this photograph. New York City is never dull and has something for every taste and budget. Whether one wants to see a Broadway play, stroll through an art museum, watch itinerant performers on the street, or enjoy fine food from all over the world, from escargot to blintzes and egg creams, New York is the place to be.

99 top left This photo of midtown Manhattan near sunset shows areas of the garment district and the beginning of the theater district at the left hand side. At the lower right is Madison Square Garden, a round building in counterpoint to its name. The tall skyscraper in the middle right is of course the Empire State Building, while to the left can be seen the Cathedral-like spire of the Chrysler Building.

99 top right The classic Art Deco spire of the Chrysler Building was completed in 1930 as the corporate headquarters of the automobile manufacturers. Huge, shining gargoyles in the form of falcon's heads can be seen protruding from the base of the spire.

99 bottom right The Empire State Building stands 102 stories tall and was completed in 1931. It was the tallest building in the world for 41 years, and was made famous world-wide in movies such as King Kong and An Affair to Remember.

99 bottom left The tall buildings of lower Manhattan glow in the foreground, while thousands of apartment buildings and row houses throng the Lower East Side in the background. In the immediate foreground of the picture is the Woolworth Building, completed in 1913. At 60 stories tall it is one of Manhattan's older skyscrapers. The 34 story Municipal Building, highlighted to the right of the Woolworth spire, was designed by McKim, Mead and White and completed in 1914.

100 top left Lower Manhattan is seen in this night shot looking downtown toward the World Trade Center and the towers of the financial district. The streams of automobile lights on the lower left side form a V shape where Broadway crosses Fifth Avenue. The dark form rising within this V is the Flatiron Building, with the lighted spire of the Metropolitan Life Building at the far left.

100 center left Lower Manhattan can be seen clearly in this night shot looking uptown. In the center is the lighted tower of the Empire State Building, while to its left can be seen the lighted strands of the George Washington Bridge crossing the Hudson River into New Jersey. The area in the foreground is Tribecca, a revitalized portion of the city. The S-curve formed by the auto lights on the lower left side shows the approach to the Holland Tunnel, which takes autos under the river to New Jersey.

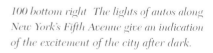

100 bottom right The lights of autos along New York's Fifth Avenue give an indication of the excitement of the city after dark.

100-101 This photo of New York Harbor at night looks toward New Jersey from the World Trade Center. Jersey City is immediately across the Harbor, while Newark Bay and the city of Newark are seen beyond. In the foreground are Ellis Island to the right and Liberty Island, with a lighted Lady Liberty, in the center.

101 bottom Jersey City, New Jersey, across the Hudson River from Manhattan, can be seen in this night view. Just to the north is Hoboken, birthplace of Frank Sinatra, home of the Clam Broth House and Stevens Technical Institute, and the setting of the film On the Waterfront. Still further north Weehawken sits high above the river, a former dueling ground where Aaron Burr killed Alexander Hamilton in 1804.

Night lights illuminate Manhattan so that the city looks like a precious jewel of uncomparable beauty.

102-103 *The south shore of Long Island is seen in this pleasant view. Barrier islands like this stretch for over 100 miles along the south shore, providing beautiful sand dunes, salty surf, nature trails and ocean sports. Fire Island National Seashore protects a 32 mile stretch of this shore.*

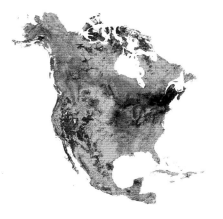

104-105 *The rolling piedmont of North Carolina can be seen in this view. Not far to the west, the Great Smoky Mountains rise from the surrounding country. Primarily an agricultural region which grows corn and tobacco, the farms of the piedmont were settled by Scots Irish immigrants in the 1700s.*

The Mid-Atlantic States

104 bottom In this general view of the heart of Washington, D.C., viewed in the mellow light of an autumn sunrise, many of the nation's most important structures can be seen. In the foreground, the White House, first occupied in 1800, has been the home of every American President except George Washington. To the left of the White House is the U.S. Treasury Department building, to the right the Executive Office Building; the 555-foot tall Washington Monument and the Jefferson Memorial can be seen in the distance.

105 A sprawling suburban area surrounds metropolitan Washington, D.C., which extends into the states of Maryland, Virginia, West Virginia and Pennsylvania. Quaint older and historic homes like these blend with newer ranch-style houses in towns famous for their part in the American Revolution and the Civil War. Commuting from these restful suburbs has become a chore, particularly when traveling by car along often-clogged highways. Extensions of the Washington Metro train system have alleviated part of this problem.

The U.S. Capitol Building was enlarged over a period of many years, culminating with the completion of the cast iron dome in 1864.

106 top A view of East Potomac Park along the Potomac River south of Washington, D.C. Hains Point is to the left of the photo. The park is used for recreational activities, and is part of a large system of city parklands in Washington. The city of Arlington, Virginia can be seen across the river in the distance to the left center. The city of Washington is accented by the Washington Monument to the right.

106 center The John F. Kennedy Center for the Performing Arts is located along the Potomac River near the Arlington Memorial Bridge. The center's facilities include an opera house, a concert hall, a performing arts library, restaurants, the American Film Institute Theater, and the Eisenhower Theater.

106 bottom Located on a nicely-landscaped tidal basin in Washington, D.C., the Jefferson Memorial honors the nation's third President and author of the Declaration of Independence. The memorial, designed by John Russell Pope to reflect Jefferson's own architectural tastes, was completed in 1943. Inside, a large statue and the words of Jefferson express his personal and political philosophy. In the distance the Ronald Reagan National Airport and the city of Arlington, Virginia can be seen.

The endless curves of the ancient mountains of Pennsylvania in autumn are accented by the billowing smoke of steel mills, as deer hunters creep on silent feet with ready gun in hand. This is a region of history, which echoes with the voices of the Revolutionary patriots and the death cries, smoke and confusion of the Civil War. Wood smoke pours alike from the log cabin of a mountain family and a shingled fishing shack on the Atlantic Ocean. On a hot July night, fireworks light the landmarks of American liberty in the nation's capital, the stark obelisk dedicated to George Washington, the imitation Greek Temple which houses the statue of Lincoln, and the White House, residence of U.S. Presidents. Ice sheathes part of a roaring waterfall in the Great Smokies, as springtime tries to bud forth on neighboring trees. Ocean waves pound the beach near

a black and white striped lighthouse, while dolphins play in the surf offshore. And at Monticello, the architectural masterpiece in the Virginia foothills, the ghost of Thomas Jefferson paces the floor, pondering the direction of his nation. History, nature and commerce mix in the unique Mid-Atlantic region.

The Mid-Atlantic States are filled with history and scenic wonders. In the heart of the region's largest city, for instance, Philadelphia's most important colonial buildings have been preserved and restored for tourists. Administered by the National Park Service, the enclave of precious structures is called Independence National Historical Park. Among other buildings, it preserves Independence Hall. Built between 1732 and 1756, this building was the scene of the drafting of the Declaration of Independence in 1776 and the United States Constitution in 1787.

106-107 The U.S. Capitol Building dominates this view of central Washington, D.C. Part of the massive building was first used in 1800. It was enlarged over a period of many years, culminating with the completion of the cast iron dome in 1864. The white Greek temple-style building in the foreground is the U.S. Supreme Court. Looking down the grassy mall to the right of the Capitol dome, one can see several museum buildings of the Smithsonian Institution, including the National Air and Space Museum.

107 bottom The Watergate Apartment
Buildings in Washington, D.C. seem to
attract scandal like a magnet. In 1972,
thieves hired by the Nixon
Administration broke into the
headquarters of the Democratic
National Committee located in the
building. Their capture and arrest led
to a political scandal which eventually
involved the President himself. Richard
Nixon resigned from the Presidency in
August 1974 as a result of the affair
still known simply as "Watergate."

*108-109 The largest office building in the
world, the Pentagon covers 29 acres of land
and employs 23,000 people in Arlington,
Virginia. The home of the U.S. Department
of Defense, the building received its name
from its design. The Pentagon was
designed by George Edwin Bergstrom and
built between 1941 and 1943.*

*109 left Robert F. Kennedy Memorial
Stadium, in Washington, was formerly the
home of the Washington Senators baseball
team and the Washington Redskins football
team. The Senators no longer exist and the
Redskins have moved to a larger stadium.
Today, the stadium is the scene of Washington
Uniteds soccer games, and concerts.*

*109 top right A portion of Arlington
National Cemetery, probably the best-
known cemetery in the U.S. The cemetery
includes over 253,000 burials, primarily of
military servicemen and their spouses.
President John F. Kennedy and his brother
Robert F. Kennedy are buried here. The
cemetery was established in 1864 on the*

*former estate of Confederate General
Robert E. Lee. Behind the colonnaded
white amphitheater at the center of the
photo is the Tomb of the Unknown Soldiers.
Just to the upper right of the amphitheater
is a large sandy-colored building resting
low on the horizon—the Pentagon, office
building for the U.S. Department of Defense.*

Arlington National Cemetery was established in 1864 on the former estate of Confederate General Robert E. Lee.

The outbuildings of the hall served as the official meeting place of the U.S. Government between 1790 and 1800. The famous bell later known as the Liberty Bell is also preserved within the park for all to see. The great founders of the United States, Thomas Jefferson, George Washington, Benjamin Franklin, John Adams, Alexander Hamilton, George Mason and a host of others come to life in this section of the city, their memory preserved in exhibits, original buildings, and through the skills of park rangers who give public talks.

Just to the west of Philadelphia visitors can find Valley Forge, the legendary winter encampment of George Washington's army in 1777-78. And not 90 miles further west lies a great battlefield of the Civil War, Gettysburg. The costliest single battle of that war, at Gettysburg over 51,000 men were killed, wounded or captured during the three days of

fighting. President Abraham Lincoln dedicated a national cemetery there three months later with one of the most famous speeches ever given, speaking of a nation "dedicated to the proposition that all men are created equal" and of the battles being fought between the nation's separated sections as a test of whether American liberties and democracy "could long endure."

History continues further to the south in the nation's capital, Washington, D.C. Clustered in the center of Washington are many of the United States' most cherished buildings, memorials and institutions. The U.S. Capitol, the White House, the Lincoln Memorial, the Washington Monument, the Jefferson Memorial, and the Vietnam Veterans Memorial are all larger than life symbols of what the United States stands for as a nation, as well as the trials and tribulations of its past. Museums lining a grassy mall between the government buildings, most of them part of the Smithsonian Institution, interpret the rich history, culture, art and politics of the nation.

But the Mid-Atlantic region is far more than cities, architecture and monuments. For instance the beaches of Maryland, Virginia, and North Carolina are spectacular. These beaches are dominated by the

109 center right The National Cathedral is a Protestant Episcopal Church built on the highest point of land in the District of Columbia in the 14th century English Gothic style. Begun in 1907, the cathedral is still unfinished, primarily because it is being built in the manner of the classic cathedrals of Europe, stone upon stone, with no structural steel. At 514 feet in length, the National Cathedral is the sixth largest cathedral in the world, the second largest in the United States. In addition to religious imagery, the cathedral contains works of art commemorating important individuals and events in U.S. history.

109 bottom right The suburbs of Washington D.C. include many attractive homes in an area surrounded by history and nature. Such communities as Manassas, Fairfax, Leesburg, Monocacy, Frederick and Harpers Ferry all felt the sting of battle or occupation during the Civil War. The area's many parks and riverways are inviting to wildlife and recreationists.

110 top The Potomac River winds through some of the most historic areas of the U.S., recalling its rich natural and cultural legacy. Old farmsteads are mixed together along its 287 mile length.

110 center The monuments of Gettysburg National Battlefield recall one of the Civil War's bloodiest battles. "Little Round Top," the low hill on the horizon, proved to be the key to the battlefield for the Union.

110 bottom The city of Charlotte, North Carolina is the largest urban area in the Piedmont region, 20 miles north of the border with South Carolina. The city was founded in 1768 and was named for Queen Charlotte, wife of King George III of England. In 1775 a group of local patriots signed the Mecklenburg Declaration, protesting British rule.

110-111 George Washington's home at Mount Vernon, located south of Washington, D.C. along the Potomac River in Virginia, preserves an 18th century plantation beloved by the nation's first President. Today, the restored plantation's 500 acres includes the original main house as designed by George Washington, outbuildings and barns, formal flower and kitchen gardens, an "orangery" (greenhouse) and slave quarters, a bowling green, and the graves of Washington and his wife, Martha.

Outer Banks, a broken strand of islands which curves outward in a horseshoe facing the Atlantic. For thousands of years these barrier islands have survived a continual onslaught of wind and sea. Some of these beaches can be very lonely, a place where one can walk along and contemplate shore birds and the tide in solitude. Others spring to life, especially during the summer months, with millions of people seeking recreation. Storms sometimes batter this shoreline with fierce winds and waves. In the fall and spring large flocks of migrating seabirds travel through the area. Salt marshes tucked behind the barrier islands of the Outer Banks are a source of food for these birds and other animals year-round. Tides come and go twice each day, replenishing the nutrients of the marshes. The barrier islands are also famous for wild herds of horses which roam freely over them.

111 top George Washington inherited the Mount Vernon estate in 1754 when he was 22 years old. He enlarged the house on the property and farmed its then-2100 acres. Tobacco and other crops grown in the fields were shipped to European and American ports via the Potomac River. Washington loved his home at Mount Vernon, yet was forced to remain away during the 8 years of the American Revolution and later during the 8 years of his Presidency. Washington died at Mount Vernon in 1799. The estate was preserved by the Mount Vernon Ladies' Association in 1858 in one of the first restoration projects in U.S. history.

111 bottom Little Round Top at
Gettysburg looks down upon the "Valley
of Death" where many brave soldiers
lost their lives on July 2, 1863.
Confederate forces attacked Union lines
in the valley and tried vainly to take the
high ground of Little Round Top. The
Union position held, forcing Confederate
Gen. Robert E. Lee to make a vain
frontal assault a mile to the north on
July 3. The Confederate loss at
Gettysburg is generally acknowledged as
the beginning of the end for the southern
cause, but the war dragged on for nearly
two more years.

112 top On Philadelphia's Penn's Landing on the Delaware River, the U.S.S. Olympia rides at anchor. The Olympia is a reminder of the entrance of America upon the world stage in the Spanish-American War. Beside the Olympia is the U.S.S. Becuna, a submarine which saw service in World War II, Korea and Vietnam.

112-113 A gigantic statue of William Penn, Quaker founder of Philadelphia stands atop the Philadelphia City Hall, the tower of which is clad in scaffolding in this view. The Walt Whitman Bridge can be seen arcing over the Delaware River in the background.

Old and new are contrasted in the heart of the historic district of Philadelphia, which is dominated by a gigantic statue of William Penn, Quaker founder of Philadelphia.

But the waters here are hazardous. Violent storms provoked by winter "nor'easters" or tropic-bred hurricanes have claimed over 600 ships off the Outer Banks alone. Storms were not the only hazard of the region, which was famous in history as the lair of notorious pirates such as Edward Teach, better known as Blackbeard. In addition, war took its toll of ships, most recently during World War II, when German U-boats sank so many that the waters off the Outer Banks were given the name "Torpedo Junction." To make the shoreline safe for shipping, a system of lighthouses was built, including the 1870 Cape Hatteras Lighthouse, at 208 feet the tallest in the United States. In addition to the lighthouses, local residents joined the U.S. Life Saving Service in the late 19th and early 20th centuries, forming a special corps of men to assist in the rescue of persons from ships in peril off the coast.

At the western edge and at the opposite extreme of the Mid-Atlantic states lie the Appalachian Mountains, remnants of ancient peaks that rose over 300 million years ago when the continent of Africa was still bumping into North America. Most of the rocks which form these mountains are ancient granitic and metamorphosed volcanic formations, some over a billion years old.

113 top Old and new are contrasted in the heart of the historic district of Philadelphia. In the foreground is the Greek Revival style Second Bank of the U.S., which now serves as an art gallery of portraits of early American leaders. Beyond, the older brick buildings of the American Philosophical Society house treasures of culture and science. Beyond lies Independence Hall, the brick building with the white clock tower, in which the Declaration of Independence and the Constitution were adopted.

113 bottom The Philadelphia Museum of Art dominates this view of the city, looking eastward toward the Delaware River. The thoroughfare heading from the museum toward the City Hall is the Ben Franklin Parkway, named for Philadelphia's most famous citizen.

The Blue Ridge Mountains form the eastern wall of the Appalachians between Pennsylvania and Georgia. This range runs southward from Virginia to the Great Smoky Mountains in North Carolina. American Indians lived in the region for at least 9,000 years before the first Englishmen from Virginia crossed the Blue Ridge in 1716.

The region was settled in the 1800s, and heavily logged. Beginning in 1926 with the establishment of

Shenandoah National Park, the area was returned to its former natural beauty. Now inhabited by deer, bobcats, bears, wild turkeys, chipmunks, raccoons, skunks, opossums, squirrels and other native animals, including 200 bird species, the park gives visitors an idea of what eastern North America was like before the heavy hand of man fell upon it.

Unlike the dominant conifer trees of western forests, the eastern forest areas of the southern Appalachians are dominated by hardwoods, like the majestic yellow (or tulip) poplar. Old growth trees of this species thrive in the shady coves of the mountains and can grow up to 150 feet tall.

Abundant rainfall, between 50 and 80 inches each year, makes these mountain regions havens for plant and animal life with few parallels anywhere in the world. For instance, the Great Smoky Mountains National Park contains 130 species of trees, 1,200 species of flowering plants, 2,000 species of fungi, and 300 kinds of moss within its boundaries. Spring in the mountains begins in March with the blooming of red maple, serviceberry, and hepatica. The green of leafing trees moves up the ridges about 100 feet each day, reaching the peaks in late May. Wildflowers like the large-flowered trillium carpet the forest floor. Summer covers the region with deep greens, from the ridges to the hollows, which echo with the sounds of the region's verdant waterfalls.

114-115 *Founded in 1682, Norfolk, Virginia is a port city, home to the world's largest naval base. It is the second-largest city in the state of Virginia, after Richmond. Looking across Portsmouth (in the foreground of the photo) and the Elizabeth River to Norfolk, one sees the Festival Marketplace at the white building in the left center. Norfolk is also home to a National Maritime Center and an art museum.*

115 bottom *Chattanooga, Tennessee, is a scenic city nestled in the green hills of eastern Tennessee. The area surrounding the city was the scene of two crucial battles during the American Civil War, which opened the road to Atlanta. Chattanooga hosts downtown festivals along the Tennessee River, which winds around its northern and western sides.*

English settlement began in America on Cape Hatteras in the 1580s, and the Wright Brothers discovered the secrets of powered flight on nearby dunes between 1900 and 1903.

place of blue smoke," for the wispy blankets of soft mist that rise about them. But the Cherokee were cruelly evicted by the U.S. Government in the 1830s along the Trail of Tears; only a small remnant was able to hide in the mountains and escape removal. The mountains were next inhabited by proud Euro-Americans with a unique culture of their own. Log homes, churches, barns and mills tell of a life of hard work and devotion, of people who lived off the land and its regional abundance. Today the descendants of these people, in North Carolina and throughout the Mid-Atlantic region, from German farmers to Scots-Irish highlanders, from tobacco plantation owners to the descendants of slaves, from those who tilled the soil to those who worked in mines, all share a common love of their homeland and its unique history and beauty.

Nesting birds and little fawns can be seen, and rhododendrons bloom. The clear, crisp days of autumn arrive in September and October, with the height of the beautiful leaf season bursting in gold, rust and fiery red in mid-October. Winter brings a somber beauty to the forest, with the brown and gray trunks of the trees protruding from the crisp white snow. Shenandoah, the Blue Ridge and Great Smoky Mountains parks can be toured by automobile from strategically located road systems, but of course are better seen from over 1,000 combined miles of backcountry trails which reveal the truly incredible nature of these areas. The parks also preserve the history of the region. First, the Cherokee Indians lived here—they called the mountains Shaconge, "the

116 Vehicle tracks line the sand of a peaceful North Carolina beach near sunset, as breakers from the Atlantic Ocean roll in. Spectacular scenery and recreational opportunities exist along seventy miles of such beaches within Cape Hatteras National Seashore. English settlement began in this area in the 1580s, and the Wright Brothers discovered the secrets of flight on nearby dunes between 1900 and 1903. Swimming, ocean fishing, and quiet contemplation draw thousands of visitors each year to this ocean paradise.

117 top and center right The Great Smoky Mountains form the apex of the Appalachian Mountains, and the park established in their midst is a wildlands sanctuary which preserves the world's finest examples of temperate deciduous forest. The name smoky comes from the smoke-like haze which often envelops the mountains, as in this photograph. The park boasts unspoiled forests such as those enjoyed by Native American tribes and the early European settlers.

117 center left This placid lake in the North Carolina piedmont provides a calm environment for a weekend swim, picnicking, or fishing. Many rivers in the South have lakes created by dams.

117 bottom The farmland of North Carolina has traditionally been used for tobacco farming, as well as for growing foodstuffs like corn and milo.

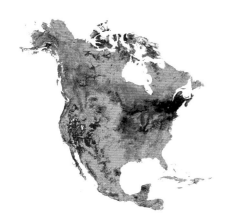

LAND OF OLD, LAND OF NEW:

118-119 Located on the Atlantic Ocean between Daytona Beach on the north and the John F. Kennedy Space Center on the south, Canaveral National Seashore near Titusville, Florida has 24 miles of beaches, wooded areas and salt marshes, where visitors can swim, fish, surf and walk on pristine trails. An abundance of wildlife includes waterfowl, bald eagles, alligators and sea turtles. The salt water estuary along the top and right of the picture is called Mosquito Lagoon.

The Sunbelt

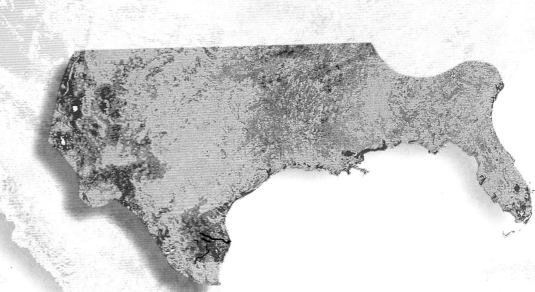

118 bottom On the side of Stone Mountain, Georgia, a memorial to Confederate soldiers, 90 feet tall and 190 feet wide was commissioned in the 1920s, and begun by sculptor Gutzon Borglum, who later carved Mount Rushmore. Borglum had a falling-out with his sponsors, and so the enormous work was not completed until the 1960s. Confederate President Jefferson Davis and generals Robert E. Lee and Stonewall Jackson are depicted on the memorial.

119 Orlando, Florida is a growing city of nearly 200,000 persons. Orlando is currently working to diversify its business enterprises, which are almost solely wrapped around the entertainment industry in such venues as Walt Disney World, Sea World and Universal Studios. Orlando has beautiful parks, lakes, lush landscaping, a pleasant climate and friendly neighborhoods.

The Old South, now often referred to as the "Sunbelt," is a mixture of tradition and progress, of incredibly beautiful natural areas contrasted with some of America's most modern cities.

Mickey Mouse steps from behind a clapboard fence to welcome visitors to his Magic Kingdom. Beautiful women laugh from the cast iron balcony of a New Orleans house on a sultry summer night. Stock cars vie with one another around a slippery Daytona track, while not far off a space shuttle is being safety-checked for a launch. A woman hawks her beautifully woven baskets in front of a Charleston church, while a young couple sips pina coladas outside one of Ernest Hemingway's Key West haunts. The gleaming walls of a corporate headquarters in downtown Atlanta present a contrast to the stately columns of the preserved plantation homes off the cities' beltway. The cries of birds ring through a forest hung with Spanish moss, as alligators loll on the shore near cypress trees. Steamboats, now run on diesel fuel and most often in the guise of casinos, still ply the muddy Mississippi River of Mark Twain. This is the land of B'rer Rabbit and B'rer Fox, of Scarlett O'Hara and Rhett Butler, of William Faulkner and Tennessee Williams, and most recently of Anne Rice's vampire Lestat. It was once the land of the Cherokee, Creek, and the other so-called "Five Civilized Tribes" of Indians, forcibly removed westward over the "Trail of Tears" in the 1830s.

The Old South, now usually referred to as the "Sunbelt," is a mixture of tradition and progress, of incredibly beautiful natural areas contrasted with some of America's most modern cities. Vestiges of America's Civil War can be found throughout the South—in fact, the war and its aftermath once seemed to define the area. Today, all that has changed. But to understand the region, one has to have an understanding of the war, its causes, and the lingering animosity it engendered.

120 bottom right Downtown Charleston, South Carolina is a city steeped in tradition. Many of the old homes are built of stuccoed brick, and have steep slate roofs. Known locally as "single houses," their sides include wide, airy verandahs. The city was founded in 1670, and continues as an important seaport and naval base.

120-121 Georgia provides many recreational opportunities on its rivers and the lakes formed by dams. The northern part of the state, with an elevation of over 1,000 feet above sea level, is blessed with a far milder climate than in the southern lowlands, perfect for recreation on its many waterways.

121 top Navigation on many of the rivers
in northern Georgia has been facilitated by
the addition of ship locks beside the dams.
Rivers and reservoirs in the region are used
for recreation by the residents of many states.

121 bottom The lowland rivers of Georgia
move slowly through flat fields and swamps
as they make their way toward the sea.
Okefenokee Swamp, one of the largest in
the United States, lies in the southeast
corner of Georgia along the St. Mary's River.

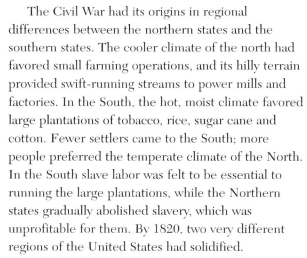

The City of Savannah and the Colony of Georgia were both founded by Englishman James Oglethorpe in 1733.

122 top and center left Birmingham, Alabama was founded in 1871 in an area of rural farms and plantations. It grew quickly during World War II, when it became a center of war industries. During the 1960s, many civil rights protests swirled around the city, a fact commemorated today in the Birmingham Civil Rights Institute.

122 center right Fort Pulaski, located east of Savannah, Georgia, once guarded the entrance to the Savannah River. Built between 1829 and 1847 on Cockspur Island, it is a typically designed fort for its era, surrounded by a water-filled moat and with about 25 million bricks in its stout walls. By the mid-1840s, 69 such forts were in existence or under construction along the Atlantic Coast. Confiscated by Confederate forces during the Civil War, the fort was bombarded by Union guns on Tybee Island in 1862, leaving pockmarks which can still be seen in this photo. Today the fort is a National Monument.

The Civil War had its origins in regional differences between the northern states and the southern states. The cooler climate of the north had favored small farming operations, and its hilly terrain provided swift-running streams to power mills and factories. In the South, the hot, moist climate favored large plantations of tobacco, rice, sugar cane and cotton. Fewer settlers came to the South; more people preferred the temperate climate of the North. In the South slave labor was felt to be essential to running the large plantations, while the Northern states gradually abolished slavery, which was unprofitable for them. By 1820, two very different regions of the United States had solidified.

The South felt threatened by the larger population of the North and its growing economic might, while many in the North questioned how a nation founded on the proposition that "all men are created equal" could let slavery continue within its borders.

Northern abolition groups did little to help the

situation by militantly demanding an end to slavery. Neither side left the other much leeway, and tensions rose perceptibly during the 1850s. With the election of Abraham Lincoln (a man who had condemned the institution of slavery) as President in 1860, the Southern states had had enough. They seceded from the United States and formed their own government which they called the Confederate States of America. Lincoln refused to acknowledge the legality of secession, considered the Southern states in rebellion, and was determined to keep the Union together.

So it was that over the course of four long and bloody years, the nation's citizens fought one another.

122 bottom Lake Sidney Lanier, Georgia, located northeast of Atlanta, was created when Buford Dam was built across the Chattahoochie River between 1953 and 1956. The lake covers 58,000 acres of land and has 540 miles of twisting shoreline. The dam produces hydroelectric power and provides flood control for the Chattahoochie. The lake is a popular recreation area run by the U.S. Army Corps of Engineers. It was named for Sidney Lanier, a 19th century Georgia poet who immortalized the Chattahoochie River.

122-123 *The Savannah River empties into the Atlantic Ocean at Tybee's Island, east of Savannah, Georgia. Many National Wildlife Refuges in the area provide habitat for water birds and native animal species.*

123 bottom *The Savannah River flows from the Appalachian Mountains to the northeast and forms the border between South Carolina and Georgia. Savannah and the Colony of Georgia were both founded by Englishman James Oglethorpe in 1733. He laid out the 2.2 square miles of Savannah's grid of streets, fronting on the river. Savannah's harbor made it wealthy through the export of cotton. Today, an average of 2,200 ships use the river and port each year.*

Atlanta is the primary commercial, transportation and financial center of the Southeastern United States.

The more powerful, industrial-based Northern states were able to blockade Southern ports and prevent foreign aid with a powerful navy. Through a series of water and land borne campaigns they were able to gain control of the South's major trade artery, the Mississippi River. Large armies with superior numbers and weapons marched into the Southern homeland and left devastation in their wake. The Southern states were defeated. Slavery was abolished, but resentments lasted for generations.

Today, plantations recalling an idyllic past—one that never really existed—draw tourists to the South.

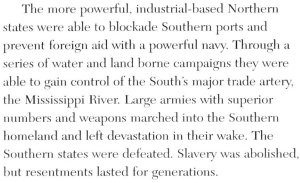

Grand old cities like Charleston, South Carolina revel in their past as a leader of the rebellion, and proudly display Fort Sumter in the center of their harbor, where the first shots were fired in 1861.

The Civil War left its mark upon the entire region, and it was many years before the defeated people were able to bounce back. It was once thought by northerners that the South would forever be defined by the "War Between the States." But recent history has shown that this was a false perception. Beginning in the 1960s, the climate of the region began to appeal to businesses, many of which pulled up stakes and moved from the North. New Southern businesses grew up alongside already established regional companies like Coca Cola. With air conditioning making year-round production possible and comfortable, the South's temperate climate drew labor, industry, technology, tourism and retirees in an "invasion" with few parallels in American history. Today, many native Southerners question whether increased regional productivity and prosperity are worth the accelerated pace and burgeoning population of a second "Yankee invasion." Nevertheless, the new industrial, corporate and recreational image of the "Sunbelt" had redefined the southern United States.

The contrasts between old and new are most visible in places like central and southern Florida, and can be noticed in such things as architecture, especially the abundance of new structures.

It can also be noticed in the growing concern about ecological imbalance.

Unlike much of the East Coast, which is geologically very old, the peninsula of Florida is quite young. South Florida surfaced from the waters of the Atlantic Ocean only after the last Ice Age, and its ecosystem is just 6,000 to 8,000 years old.

124 top left The Atlanta-Fulton County Stadium opened in 1965 is now called Turner Stadium after the owner of the Atlanta Braves baseball team, Ted Turner.

124 bottom left The State Capitol in Atlanta, Georgia was completed in 1889, and stands 272 feet tall. One and a half acres of Georgia marble were used throughout the interior of the building, and the dome is gilt with 60 ounces of 23 karat gold. The exterior building material is Indiana limestone, and the building is capped with a 15 foot tall, 2,000 pound statue entitled "Miss Freedom."

124 right The modern look of a burgeoning city, skyscrapers in Atlanta, Georgia speak of the affluence and progress generated by this corporate center. Rising from the surrounding plain like the City of Oz, downtown Atlanta is the quintessential city of the "New South."

124-125 The Georgia Dome in Atlanta is the largest cable-supported domed stadium in the world, and is capable of holding up to 80,000 people. Located near downtown Atlanta, the stadium hosted the 1996 Summer Olympic Games and is the home venue for the Atlanta Falcons football team.

125 bottom left Stone Mountain, Georgia is an area of geological interest which has become a suburb of Atlanta.

125 bottom right Atlanta is the primary commercial, transportation and financial center of the Southeastern United States. Founded as an early railroad hub in 1836, Atlanta was ranked as the 13th largest metropolitan area in the United States in 1992, with 3,142,875 people.

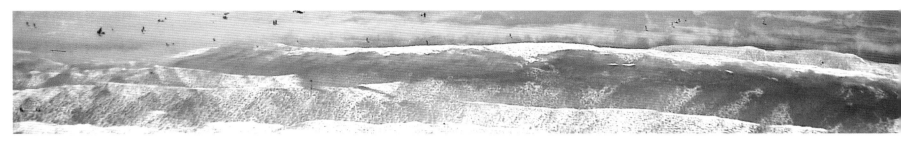

126 Barrier islands south of Daytona Beach, Florida provide an excellent environment for sunny recreation. The shipping channel dividing the islands is the Ponce Inlet, which allows access to the Intercoastal Waterway, which winds for hundreds of miles behind the protection of the coast's barrier islands.

127 top and center left The Ponce Inlet south of Daytona Beach provides an access for small watercraft, including sailboats, to the Atlantic Ocean. Sandy beaches are a year-round haven for lovers of sun and surf. The scenic fishing village of Ponce Inlet includes charter fishing boats and seafood restaurants.

127 center right Catamarans line the shore at Daytona Beach, Florida, one of the best-known beaches in the world. North of Daytona Beach is Ormond Beach, once home to the Rockefellers and the Flaglers. Early automobile magnates tested their cars on the hard-packed beach. Driving on the beaches at Ormond-by-the-Sea is no longer allowed, producing a serene environment enjoyed by its visitors. In mid-February each year, Daytona hosts the Daytona 500 auto race. Known as the "World Center of Racing," Daytona International Speedway hosts eight weekends of racing annually, including NASCAR stock car, sports car, motorcycle and go-cart racing.

Ironically, in a region surrounded by sea water, the fragile ecosystem of the Everglades depends upon fresh water from rivers and rainfall for survival.

That water is being drawn off or fouled by extensive canal and levee systems, the rapid population growth of the state, and toxic waste. Several native species, including the wood stork and the Florida panther, are near extinction. The threats to the Everglades present a danger to the ecosystem of the entire region. Numbers of wading bird nesting colonies have declined 93 percent since the 1930s. Other threatened animals, all of which once flourished in the Everglades and South Florida, include plants like the swamp lily, saw grass and periphyton; water dwellers like the bluegill, Florida gar and largemouth bass; birds like the ibis; and animals like the alligator, crocodile, and manatee.

The National Park Service allows visitors to see this unique ecosystem at Everglades National Park, but spends a good share of its time trying to improve and restore the original habitat which is being lost so rapidly.

Part of the reason for this loss is the regional rise in population and the resulting environmental demands. Central Florida, with Orlando at the midpoint, has become a corporate and entertainment center second to none. The recreation complexes of the area provide a world seemingly unconnected with reality, one which is readily embraced by tourists and conventioneers from around the world.

The Florida beaches run continuously for over 200 miles south to Miami.

127 bottom left The friendly roar of the ocean is always heard at Daytona Beach, where visitors and locals enjoy swimming, snorkeling, surfing, sailing, jetskiing, ocean fishing and other water sports. In addition, historical sites like the Main Street Pier, the Oceanfront Boardwalk and the clock tower in Oceanfront Park add diversity to the area's recreational opportunities. In this photo autos and busses arrive on the beach for another day of frolicking in the surf.

127 bottom right Daytona Beach and Daytona Beach Shores are seen in this photo, which looks northward toward neighboring Ormond Beach. The Florida beaches run almost continuously for 50 miles to the north to the Georgia border, and for over 200 miles south to Miami. Hotels and extreme development in most of the public areas contrasts with the pristine nature of National Wildlife Refuges and National Park areas which are interspersed with them along the coastline.

128 top The entrance courtyard to Epcot Center at Walt Disney World is dominated by the 18 story tall geosphere dubbed "Spaceship Earth." The embracing arms of the "Communicore" are packed full of the latest in computer wizardry, while beyond await pavilions dedicated to the role of the land, the sea, transportation, advances in health, and other aspects of the future.

128-129 The spires of Cinderella's Castle provide an entrance to Fantasyland at Walt Disney World's Magic Kingdom. Opened in October, 1971 twenty miles southwest of Orlando, Florida, Disney World was intended as an improvement over Anaheim and California's Disneyland, which opened in 1955. Fearing the blight of peripheral development, the Disney Corporation bought 27,400 acres of land to buffer the park from outside intrusions.

129 top left Walt Disney World has continued to grow since its debut in 1971. An ever-expanding series of on-site hotels and recreation facilities with the architecture and decor of various nations and time periods ensure that visitors stay within the Disney theme parks for all of their entertainment needs.

129 center right More than an amusement park, Walt Disney World is a complete entertainment experience, including hotels, restaurants, and entertainment venues. Various areas of interest dedicated to fairy tales, Disney cartoons, a "Tomorrowland," an old-fashioned c. 1910 American main street, exotic African and Caribbean locales, and a Colonial American village bring excitement and wonder to children and adults alike.

Walt Disney World is a complete entertainment experience

129 bottom left The success of Walt Disney World and other theme parks has drawn competitors to the Orlando area, such as Sea World, a theme park built around ocean life and live aquatic animal shows. In this aerial view, the popular killer whales, including Shamu, who delight audiences with their choreographed routines, can be seen in their tank.

Unfortunately, despite the efforts of the corporations who founded theme parks in Central Florida, the peripheral population increase and development has given the region a "boom town" atmosphere and greatly affected the area's ecosystem. The growth of Miami and the Atlantic Coast cities have also contributed to the area's problems, as the state's population tripled between 1960 and 1990. Other areas of the South, notably Atlanta, Georgia; Huntsville, Alabama; Houston, San Antonio and Dallas, Texas and the Atlantic Coast of South Carolina have experienced similar runaway growth.

Despite the huge influx of people, the region struggles to preserve its unique character. The charm of its cities, particularly Charleston, Savannah, Mobile and New Orleans continues to delight tourists and residents alike. Splendid gardens, respected cultural

institutions, and magnificent old homes with characteristic Southern architecture grace the region. Additionally, the South is home to some of the nation's leading cultural institutions. Few Americans know that the nation's first museum was established in Charleston at the time of the Revolutionary War, that the nation's first regular railway service began in South Carolina in 1831, and that some of the nation's most respected colleges and universities, as well as military schools, are located in the South. Ironically, research and development facilities for private corporations and the U.S. Government are today headquartered in a region which was often unfairly characterized as long on tradition and short on ideas and common sense.

129 bottom right Epcot Center, the second resort at Walt Disney World to open to the public, was added in 1982. An acronym for "Experimental Prototype Community of Tomorrow," Epcot was intended to show visitors the world of the future. The displays and buildings near the entrance (in the background) accomplish that, but Epcot Center evolved into more of a permanent world's fair after Disney's death, with the pavilions of many nations clustered around a lagoon, shown here in the foreground.

*Beautiful
Art Deco
style hotels
were built
in Miami
Beach
during the
1920s, and
painted in
the pastel
shades of
the tropics.*

Some of the most interesting of these institutions are those founded to educate African-Americans, like Tuskegee University in Alabama and the Atlanta University Center (formerly Morehouse and Spelman Colleges) in Atlanta, Georgia.

Much of the inland region of the American south

is flat, rural and agricultural, but retains a special character all its own. Cotton and tobacco are still grown here, but agricultural pursuits have shifted to raising livestock (particularly chickens), peanuts and soybeans. Economically, manufacturing and government business now overshadow agriculture.

The flat piedmont plateau is crossed by forested ridges, and leads to the Cumberland plateau and up to the beautiful mountains of northern Alabama, Georgia and eastern Tennessee. The Chattahoochee River has become a cherished (and overused) recreation area in the middle of three growing metropolitan areas—Atlanta, Huntsville and Knoxville. And few areas of the world can boast the seemingly endless miles of gorgeous beaches and barrier islands which run down the Atlantic Coast to the tip of Florida, then up and around the Gulf of Mexico to the Texas/Mexico border.

The economic successes of the American South in the last three decades have been tempered by the threats to the area's cultural traditions and ecological treasures by a burgeoning population. It seems clear that the South will never again be considered in its post-Civil War "economic backwater" guise, and equally certain that its strong and vibrant people will find ways to deal with the challenges of the 21st century.

130 bottom A closer view of the more modern Miami Beach hotels gives a flavor of luxury vacation living along the white sands and clear blue waters of the Florida coast. In fact today, Miami Beach continues to be a popular vacation spot, with soaring modern hotels and restored classic hotels vying for the business of a world-wide clientele.

131 top right Cabanas and parasols dot the shore of Miami Beach, where a visitor is likely to see vacationing Germans, British, Jamaicans, Americans from the midwest, New Yorkers, and all manner of other nationalities represented among the vacation-goers.

130 left Miami, Florida is a city of nearly 400,000 people in a metropolitan area of nearly two million. It is an important trading center, and its port serves many steamship lines traveling to and from Latin America. It has large populations of Cuban exiles and Haitian refugees in areas called "Little Havana" and "Little Haiti," respectively. The mild climate of the region has attracted tourists and year-round residents alike.

130-131 A dream of wealthy auto magnate Carl Fisher, Miami Beach, Florida was created in the early 1900s as a playground for the rich. Beautiful Art Deco style hotels were built in the 1920s and painted in the pastel shades of the tropics. In this view Miami Beach, once called "the billion dollar sandbar," is seen from the Atlantic Ocean, with the City of Miami in the background.

131 center left Urban crowding has pushed up to the edge of the ocean at Miami Beach, a year-round vacation destination. This is part of the famous Art Deco District, an eighty square block area of 800 historic buildings including the famous Ocean Drive, a favorite night spot with vibrant restaurants and bars.

131 bottom left A view of Miami Beach (looking south) shows the cluster of hotels in the famous Art Deco District with their pastel colors. Along the shoreline are the Jackie Gleason Theater of Performing Arts and the Miami Beach Exhibition Hall.

131

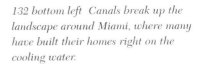

132 bottom left Canals break up the landscape around Miami, where many have built their homes right on the cooling water.

132 right Many homes in Florida are built along canals, some with enclosed patios and pools. Many retired people make their homes in Florida, where the weather is fine year-round. Coral Gables, Florida, south of Miami, was a community planned in the 1920s by a team fostered by George Merrick. The community they created had broad boulevards, lined with palm trees, which intersected at plazas and fountains. The styles of houses varied with each "village" having a distinct style of architecture.

133 The homes of the wealthy are still clustered near Miami Beach, where some can enjoy their own private island.

Many homes in Florida are built along canals, some with enclosed patios and pools.

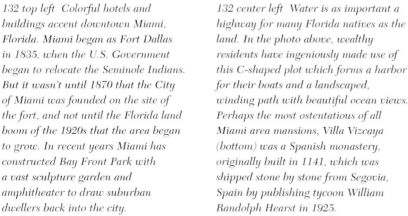

132 top left Colorful hotels and buildings accent downtown Miami, Florida. Miami began as Fort Dallas in 1835, when the U.S. Government began to relocate the Seminole Indians. But it wasn't until 1870 that the City of Miami was founded on the site of the fort, and not until the Florida land boom of the 1920s that the area began to grow. In recent years Miami has constructed Bay Front Park with a vast sculpture garden and amphitheater to draw suburban dwellers back into the city.

132 center left Water is as important a highway for many Florida natives as the land. In the photo above, wealthy residents have ingeniously made use of this C-shaped plot which forms a harbor for their boats and a landscaped, winding path with beautiful ocean views. Perhaps the most ostentatious of all Miami area mansions, Villa Vizcaya (bottom) was a Spanish monastery, originally built in 1141, which was shipped stone by stone from Segovia, Spain by publishing tycoon William Randolph Hearst in 1925.

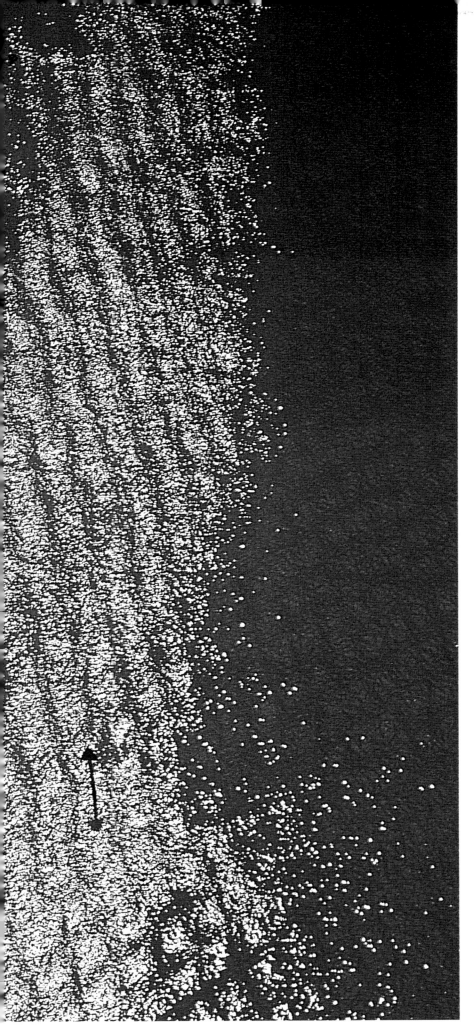

Biscayne National Park encompasses about 180,000 acres, 95% of which is under water.

134-135 and 134 bottom This remarkable house was built on piers in the shallow, sandy water of Biscayne Bay, south of Miami. Nearby Biscayne National Park encompasses about 180,000 acres, 95% of which is under water. Beneath the shallow, nearly transparent waters are living coral reefs burgeoning with 250 species of colorful tropical fish.

135 top The water of Biscayne Bay is warm and clear, and home to sea turtles, dolphins, tropical fish, lobsters and manatees. It is an excellent place to go snorkeling or diving. It is here that the Florida Keys begin, moving southwest past the Everglades on the shoreline toward the open ocean, like ships putting out to sea.

135 center A floating house and docks in Biscayne Bay recall the many profitable businesses of the region which have to do with the ocean, including cruises, deep-sea fishing, and small boat rentals.

135 bottom A sailboat with distinctive red sails glides through the placid waters of Biscayne Bay. The National Park includes the northernmost living coral reef along the Atlantic coast. The Intercoastal Waterway runs along the west of the Florida Keys down to Marathon.

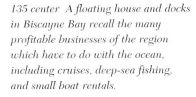

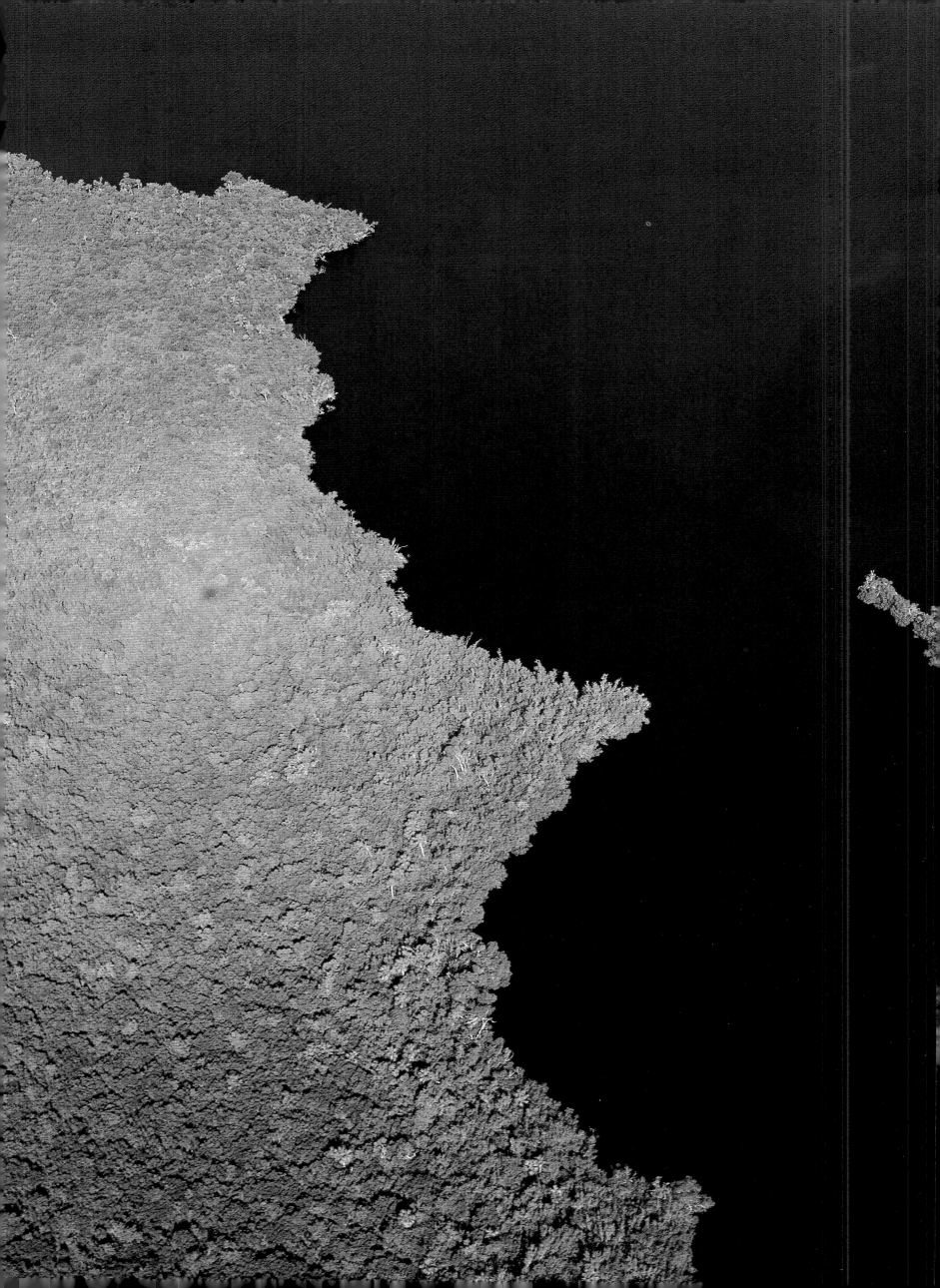

Everglades is the only National Park which also has three international designations: International Biosphere Reserve, World Heritage Site, and Wetland of International Significance.

136 Looking like an abstract painting, the coastline of Everglades National Park protrudes from the Mangrove Swamp into Florida Bay at the tip of the peninsula. Everglades National Park was authorized in 1935 and dedicated in 1947. The park was created with one of the strongest mandates ever given to the National Park Service to preserve a wilderness biosphere. It was the first National Park created primarily because of its wildlife and plant life rather than its scenic or historic value.

137 center right The Gulf Coast area of Everglades National Park includes some 10,000 islands. On a boat trip through the area one might see dolphins jumping from the water, or the snout of a manatee probing upward. The intricate labyrinth of mangrove covered islands shelters birds, plants and marine life.

137 bottom Visitors to Everglades National Park fish, hike, watch birds, snorkel, swim and attend programs given by Park Rangers who interpret the fascinating scenic, natural and historic wonders of the region.

137 top Like the claw of a lobster, peninsulas jutting from Everglades National Park enter the waters of Florida Bay. In addition to the problem of water, the region's other biological conundrums include the intrusion of non-native species introduced from other parts of the world

137 center left A vast flat table of green and blue, Everglades National Park at no point rises higher than eight feet above sea level. Yet it depends entirely upon rainwater for its subsistence, and the battle in recent years has been a losing one, since rainwater is drawn off by canal and levee systems before it reaches the park. Everglades is the only National Park which also has three international designations: International Biosphere Reserve, World Heritage Site, and Wetland of International Significance.

138 top The name Key West was taken from the Spanish Cayo Hueso, meaning "Island of Bones." That is just what explorer Ponce de Leon discovered in 1513 when he visited the island—the bones of Calusa Indians. Today, the community is a melting pot of people engaged in the tourist trade.

138 left Race Week at Key West is part of a year-round calendar of special events, including fishing tournaments, art festivals and the Fantasy Festival, a ten-day Mardi Gras- type celebration held each October.

The small islands of the Florida Keys derive their name from the Spanish Cayo, or Cay.

138-139 Seven Mile Bridge along U.S. Route 1 is a connecting link between the main group of Florida Keys, small islands that derive their name from the Spanish Cayo, or Cay. The highway runs from Key Largo near the mainland to Key West, a distance of roughly 120 miles. The keys continue beyond Key West to the Dry Tortugas.

139 top Key West, Florida is a small island with a big reputation. The population of nearly 25,000 is well-educated and artistic. The natives, many of whom have been residents for seven generations or more, refer to themselves as "Conchs." Internationally known as a haven for artists and writers, Key West has played host to Ernest Hemingway, John Hersey and Tennessee Williams.

139 center Islamorada, a town located on Upper Matacumbe Key, boasts nearby attractions like the Pennekamp Coral Reef State Park with its excellent snorkeling, and the underwater Christ statue at Dry Rocks. The Florida Keys provide a rich environment for land, sea and bird species.

139 bottom Beyond Key West, only water and air transportation can take visitors the 70 miles from Key West to the Dry Tortugas. Lighthouses like this one prevent ships from running aground in shallow water and on coral reefs.

140-141 Fort Jefferson stands on the Dry Tortugas. Built between 1846 and 1874, it was never completed. Today the fort is part of Dry Tortugas National Park. The area is called "dry" because there is no fresh drinking water there; all potable water must be shipped in. Ponce de Leon gave it the name "Tortugas" after he caught 160 sea turtles there in 1513.

142 top *Water vapor trails down a field as a farmer irrigates his crops in Louisiana. The state's abundant water supply makes it one of the wettest in the Union. Moreover the state produces small amounts of hay, sweet potatoes, corn, sorghum and horticultural crops.*

The Mississippi River Delta encompasses an area of about 15,000 square miles formed by alluvial silt washed down the rivers.

142-143 *The shipping channel can be seen slicing diagonally from upper right to lower left across this view of the Mississippi River Delta in southeastern Louisiana. This is where the Mississippi River, along with its tributaries the Missouri and Ohio rivers, finally meets the ocean in the Gulf of Mexico. The Delta forms an area of about 15,000 square miles formed by alluvial silt washed down the rivers.*

143 top *Offshore oil exploration and drilling is seen in this view of the Gulf of Mexico near Louisiana. The towers of these rigs may descend 1,500 to 3,000 feet below the surface.*

143 center *The green fields of Louisiana rest serenely beside the winding Mississippi River. Louisiana produces cotton, sugar cane, soybeans and rice, but agriculture is not one of the state's major industries.*

143 bottom *Harvest time in the Sunbelt means hard work and dedication from thousands of farmers and their hired help.*

144 bottom right A sandy beach along the Mississippi River. Silt deposited by the rivers has formed the incredibly fertile soil of the state over a period of thousands of years.

144 bottom left Cypress trees thrive in the waters of Devil's Swamp, Louisiana, home to many types of aquatic and reptilian wildlife.

144 top left The scattered islands of the Mississippi River delta are the final stop before the ocean.

144 center left Devil's Swamp near New Orleans, Louisiana. All told Louisiana has about 3,400 square miles of inland water. Silt carried by the rivers has raised the level of the river beds above the surrounding land, causing large areas of flooded land where levees have not been built.

144 center right Houses are built on stilts in Louisiana's river deltas. In addition to water from rivers, lakes, bayous and swamps, the state's semi-tropical climate ensures an average of 56 inches of precipitation each year.

145 The famous Louisiana bayous, lakes and canebrakes provide great boating opportunities. A bayou is a shallow, curving channel filled with slow-moving, sometimes stagnant water. The term is used by the people who live in the drainages of the Mississippi in Louisiana, Texas and Mississippi.

Louisiana has about 3,400 square miles of inland water.

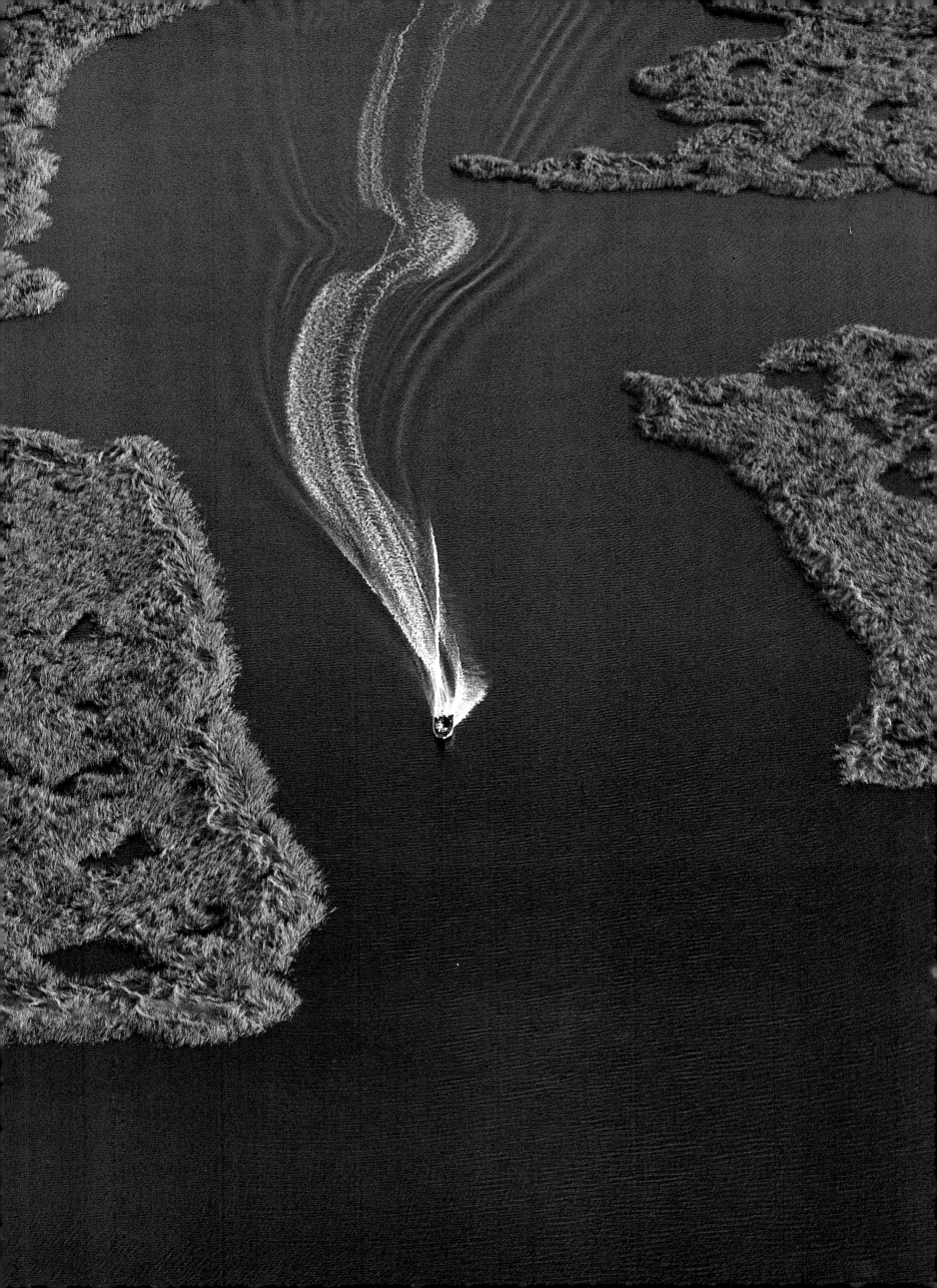

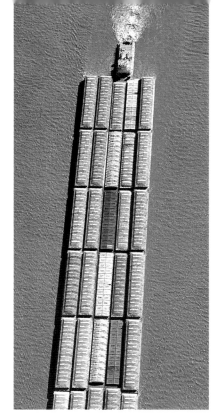

Prior to the deepening of the river channel in the 1870s and the construction of permanent levees along it, cargoes had to be taken in smaller-draft boats out to ships in the Gulf.

146 *Huge barges like these are the primary method of moving goods on the Mississippi River. New Orleans, located near the mouth of the river with access to the industrial and agricultural heartland of the United States, continues to be a major port.*

147 top left *Barges are pushed up and down the Mississippi River by tugboats. Louisiana has more than 5,000 miles of navigable waterways.*

147 top right *A tugboat pushes its cargo up the river under a graceful bridge near New Orleans.*

147 center left *One of the primary cargoes shipped on the river is coal, mined to the north and floated down to New Orleans.*

147 center right *A placid area of the Louisiana bayou country uses roads of water to travel from place to place. Expert hunters and fishermen in the region can be hired as guides to the area's best outdoor sports.*

147 bottom *Prior to the deepening of the river channel in the 1870s and the construction of permanent levees along it, cargoes had to be taken in smaller-draft boats out to ships in the Gulf. Today, seagoing vessels can navigate the Mississippi River to New Orleans and up to Baton Rouge.*

The roughly 91 blocks of the French Quarter are the prime tourist destination for New Orleans, with jazz, blues, cajun food and history available in its narrow streets.

148 top left The white building in the center of this photo of downtown New Orleans is the Westin Canal Place Hotel, which divides the city's modern buildings from the French Quarter, to the right. The roughly 91 blocks of the Quarter, only a portion of which is shown in this view, are the prime tourist destination for the city. Jazz, blues, cajun food and history are available in the narrow streets of the French Quarter.

148 center left One of 42 cemeteries in the New Orleans area, these "cities of the dead" are famous for their above-ground graves and mausoleums, necessary because of the high water table. Many of the grave sites are elaborate and ornate.

In the older cemeteries, the paths between the graves are twisted, with sudden dead ends. Flowers, votive candles and hoodoo money (coins left with the dead for favors) are placed at many of the notable graves.

148 bottom right Baton Rouge, Louisiana's State capital, is in the center of an area of old plantations and river trading. The tall building to the right is the 34-story state capitol building. When completed in 1932, it was the tallest building in the South. Built in the Art Deco Style, the capitol was one of many improvement and modernization projects championed by populist Governor Huey Long during the Great Depression. Long was assassinated in the capitol building in 1935.

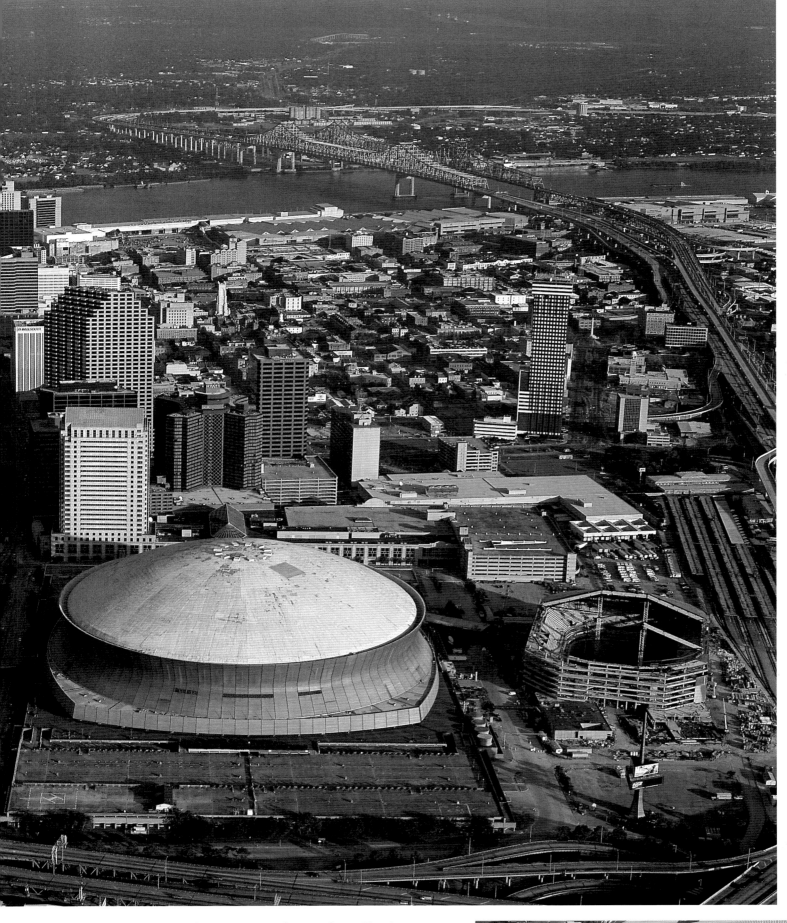

148-149 The Louisiana Superdome stadium is prominent in this view of downtown New Orleans. The curve of the Mississippi River as it winds its way around the community of Algiers across the river can be seen clearly in this photo. The Huey P. Long Bridge, named for the state's most famous governor, can be seen spanning the river. Canal Street and the French Quarter are just to the right of this picture.

149 top The top of one of the most modern buildings in New Orleans, the World Trade Center on the riverfront towers over the old copper roof of the Rivergate building.

149 bottom The gambling boat Casino Rouge in Baton Rouge, Louisiana, evokes the heyday of the paddle-wheeled steamboat on the Mississippi River. Steamboats first appeared on the river in 1811, and within ten years became common sights. Before the advent of the steamboat it could take five to six months to pole and haul a boat up to St. Louis, and less than a week to return. Steam made trips on the river last the same amount of time, no matter what the direction.

149

The largest city in Texas, Houston has become an important financial center.

150 left The Battle of San Jacinto was fought near modern-day Houston, Texas on April 21, 1836. This monument honors the men from Texas, led by General Sam Houston, who defeated the Mexican Army of Antonio Lopez de Santa Anna on that day, thus winning Texas independence. Texas did not become part of the United States until it was annexed by Congress in 1845.

150-151 The largest city in Texas, Houston has become an important financial and petrochemical center. The central business district, seen here, has become an important hub of the national petroleum industry.

151 top The Lyndon B. Johnson Space Center, southeast of Houston, is administered by NASA and is the mission control center for all manned space flights.

151 center top The buildings of downtown Dallas, Texas can be seen in this photo, with Reunion Park and the Reunion Arena in the right foreground, and the Convention Center complex beyond. One of America's worst tragedies occurred at the very center of the photograph, where the three roads come together to form one highway amid a green, grassy park named Dealey Plaza. On November 22, 1963, gunfire was directed at a motorcade driving on the street to the far left, and President John F. Kennedy was killed.

151 center bottom Relative sizes of America's space vehicles are on display outside the Johnson Space Center. A lengthy Saturn Five rocket, like this one which is displayed in pieces, catapulted the Apollo series spacecraft into Earth orbit, sending them on their way to the moon, 1969-1972. The smaller Redstone rocket, standing upright behind the Saturn with a red escape tower mounted to the top, powered the early Mercury flights, 1961–1963.

151 bottom The professionals at the Johnson Space Center have talked many Astronauts through tense situations, most notably during the flight of Apollo 13 in 1970.

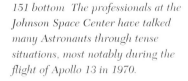

The Houston Ship Channel leads from Galveston Bay into Buffalo Bayou and on to Houston.

152 top The downtown buildings of Houston, Texas include the Civic Center and the Texas Commerce Tower. The downtown area is a center for the petroleum industry in the United States.

152 center left The Houston Ship Channel leads from Galveston Bay into Buffalo Bayou and on to Houston. Ocean-going ships can gain access to the Port of Houston via the ship channel.

152 bottom right The Houston Astrodome was completed in 1965 with an innovative design involving a plastic dome 218 feet above the stadium floor. The Astrodome was the first stadium to use an artificial grass named "Astroturf." The Astrodome is home to the Astros baseball team and the Oilers football team, and seats as many as 66,000 people.

152 bottom left The city of Houston, Texas can be seen beyond the Astrodome, in the foreground. Between the skyscrapers and the stadium, urban dwellers can relax in Memorial Park with the city's Arboretum, or Hermann Park with the zoo and the Museum of Natural Science.

153 This magnificent bridge spans part of Galveston Bay, east of Houston.

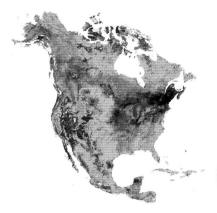

154-155 Indiana's magnificent sand dunes along Lake Michigan are preserved by both a state and a national park area. The south shore of Lake Michigan, which lies in the state of Indiana, has sandy beaches and rolling dunes which draw recreationists from neighboring cities, including Chicago and Detroit.

The Midwest

154 bottom This photo of the shore of Lake Michigan belies its enormous size. Third largest of the Great Lakes, it is the only one of the five totally within the borders of the United States. Measuring 306 miles long and up to 118 miles wide, Lake Michigan covers 22,300 square miles and is as deep as 922 feet in some areas. Lake Michigan is part of an enormous inland waterway system within the United States running from Minnesota to New York City, or past Quebec, Canada to the Atlantic Ocean.

155 The gleaming downtown of Detroit, Michigan is situated on the Detroit River, which along with the St. Clair River and Lake connect Lake Huron to Lake Erie. Detroit's position as the nation's preeminent automobile manufacturing hub was assured after Henry Ford perfected his assembly-line techniques in the early 20th century, which enabled him to turn out cheap autos quickly. Other major auto firms in the Detroit area include Chrysler and General Motors.

Another automobile reaches the end of a Detroit assembly line, while an Iowa farm is hit with a devastating tornado. A walk in a summer field of bright green grasses with a veteran of the Dust Bowl affords an incomparable vista over the lush flat lands of western Oklahoma. The gleaming 630 foot Gateway Arch marks the spot in St. Louis where western hunters, explorers and pioneer settlers prepared themselves for an epic journey. This is the land of Mike Fink the legendary keelboat man, and Davy Crockett, not to mention Mark Twain, Willa Cather, and Laura Ingalls Wilder's Little House

books. It is the land that formed the character of Abraham Lincoln, Dwight Eisenhower and Harry S Truman. It is a land of honest, mostly rural people, accustomed to plain dealing and plain talk. It is the land of Indian tribal peoples, many relocated from other parts of the United States, who preserve ancient customs and lifeways in the center of an ever-changing nation. The Midwest includes the skyscrapers of Chicago, the vastnesses of the Great Lakes, and the extensive horizons of a gently rolling landscape dominated by determined farmers.

The American heartland, the Midwest, is dominated by the Mississippi River, which slices through its center. Not long after Thomas Jefferson became President of the United States in 1801, he ordered his envoy to France to open negotiations with Napoleon's ministers for the purchase of the port of New Orleans. Unknown to Jefferson, Napoleon's ambitions in the Caribbean had failed, and he needed cash for impending hostilities with Britain.

Central Chicago was where Louis Sullivan first pioneered the use of steel in creating skyscrapers during the 1890s. Today these buildings are dwarfed by the towers of steel and glass which surround them.

156 top left The towers of downtown Chicago rise above a row of hotels fronting on Grant Park and the Chicago Yacht Club's boat basin on Lake Michigan. In the foreground, the Field Museum of Natural History at the far left houses plant and animal specimens, capped by one of the finest collections of fossil remains, including dinosaur skeletons, in the world. In the center foreground is the Shedd Aquarium, another of Chicago's stellar museum attractions.

156 center left The buildings of downtown Chicago fade into the distance in this view from the north side. The green band of Lincoln Park borders the lake at the upper left. The north side includes alternative theater, DePaul University, and Wrigley Field, home of the Chicago Cubs baseball team.

156 bottom left The south side of the Chicago River and the buildings of downtown are seen in this view. Trains coming out of "The Loop," Chicago's elevated railroad trestle for its mass-transit system, proceed to the west along the bridge shown in the lower foreground.

156 top right Hospitals and medical centers stand close to the river near Broadway in north Chicago. Near the upper end of Lincoln Park is Montrose Harbor, the encircling arm of greenery which protects the boat anchorage in the center of the photo.

156 bottom right The Sears Tower dominates downtown Chicago. Completed in 1974, the steel frame is clad in black aluminum and holds 16,000 bronze-tinted windows. Central Chicago was where Louis Sullivan first pioneered the use of steel in creating "skyscrapers" in the 1890s.

156-157 *Chicago stretches along Lake Michigan, looking westward. On the left, the 1,425 foot Sears Tower, which remains the tallest building in the United States, looms above "The Loop" and Grant Park. The sun reflects off the Chicago River to the left center, dividing downtown from the Near North Side. The festive attractions of Navy Pier can be seen jutting into the lake at the center, while the tall buildings along Michigan Avenue to the right culminate in the 1,107 foot John Hancock Center.*

157 bottom *Lincoln Park's Belmont Harbor, south of Montrose Harbor, forms another boat basin for the many who wish to sail the waters of Lake Michigan.*

The City of Chicago began on the shores of Lake Michigan in the 1770s, when a Haitian trader named Jean Baptiste Point du Sable set up a trading post there.

As a result, he offered the Americans not just New Orleans, but all of Louisiana for 15 million dollars! The Louisiana Purchase, probably the greatest real estate deal in history, doubled the size of the United States overnight, and seemed to seal the nation's destiny as a world power.

Early explorers loved the beauty of the newly-purchased area, but did not think its flat, treeless expanses could ever support American farmers. The prairies, those seemingly-endless plains of grassland seen by explorers like Lewis and Clark, once covered more than 800 million acres of what is now the Midwest. Today most of the original prairie has been turned by the farmer's plow, and has been converted to neat sections of agricultural land. But once there were vast areas covered by three types of prairie—the eastern tallgrass prairie, the mixed-grass prairie, and the western short grass prairie. These grasses actually were a complex ecosystem of plants. The tallgrass prairie, for instance, was composed of 150 species of perennial plants of the type which produce green stems, or "tillers," each

spring. After flowering in the summer, the tillers died, but the root of the plant continued to live and send up green shoots each spring. The short grass prairie contained plants which kept their shoots above ground longer, and were more dependant upon a longer growing season and more rainfall. The further west one traveled on the prairie, the dryer the climate was.

The prairie was once the realm of the American

buffalo along with the pronghorn antelope, the wolf, the coyote, the jackrabbit, and the black bear. Prairie dogs honeycombed the earth with their burrows. Rattlesnakes slithered through the grasses looking for prey, while birds like the grouse, pheasant and prairie chicken avoided the attacks of hawks and eagles. The balance of rainfall and temperature kept the area of the prairie grasslands constant for thousands of years, neither allowing forests to creep westward nor deserts to move further east. Wildfires killed invading trees and rejuvenated the soil.

158 Buildings line the Chicago River looking toward Lake Michigan, a location where the City of Chicago began in the 1770s, when a Haitian trader named Jean Baptiste Point du Sable set up a trading post there. The U.S. Army built Fort Dearborn at about the same spot in 1803. The settlement of Chicago did not begin to grow until the 1850s, with the advent of the railroads. The Great Chicago Fire of 1871 burned out 1/3 of the city, but left a blank slate for architects to build a modern city.

159 top left Diversey Harbor in Lincoln Park is one of three large boat refuges in the park. Residents of Chicago make good use of the lake for their recreation, including boating, swimming, walking and jogging.

159 bottom left Buildings along the lakeshore speak of Chicago's past and future. The city is the home of several institutions of higher learning, including Northwestern University and the University of Chicago. Chicago is also noted for cultural institutions like the Art Institute of Chicago, the Chicago Historical Society, the Du Sable Museum of African-American History and the Museum of Science and Industry.

159 top right The Near North Side of Chicago is dominated by the multi-use John Hancock Building. Along Michigan Avenue, which runs parallel to the lake on the west side of the building, is the heart of the commercial and shopping district of the city.

159 center right The John G. Shedd Aquarium exhibits more than 8,000 freshwater and ocean animals in over 200 naturalistic settings. In a 90,000 gallon coral reef exhibit colorful Caribbean fish delight visitors, especially at set feeding times.

159 bottom right The new Comiskey Park in South Chicago opened in 1991 and seats 40,000 spectators. It replaced an aging stadium across the street which was built in 1910. Comiskey Park is home to the Chicago White Sox. In addition to rivalries between Chicago and the sports teams of other cities, there is a rivalry within Chicago itself, between the White Sox on the south side and the Chicago Cubs on the north side, who play at Wrigley Field.

St. Louis is dominated by architect Eero Saarinen's stainless steel Gateway Arch.

160 left Downtown St. Louis continues to thrive and grow. In the foreground is the Thomas F. Eagleton Federal Building, to the left is the Southwestern Bell Building, third tallest in St. Louis. To the right is the Famous and Barr department store.

160-161 The Jefferson Barracks Bridge crosses the Mississippi River south of St. Louis, Missouri. Located near the confluence of the Mississippi and Missouri rivers in eastern Missouri, St. Louis was founded as a fur trading center in 1764.

160 bottom Looking north up the stream of the Mississippi River at St. Louis, one sees the city of St. Louis, Missouri on the

left and East St. Louis, Illinois on the right. Connecting the two cities is the Eads Bridge, the first steel truss suspension bridge in the world, completed in 1874, in the foreground. Immediately above Eads Bridge is the Dr. Martin Luther King, Jr. Bridge. The silver boat is the Admiral, an excursion boat built in 1940 now used as a casino.

161 top A bridge along the Mississippi evokes the history of the river. The river and its nearly 250 tributaries drain an area of 1,257,000 square miles in the heartland of the United States. Subject to periodic flooding, the river reached its highest crest to date in 1993, when many communities close to St. Louis were inundated

The predominant animal of the region was the bison. At least 40 million of these animals once roamed the Great Plains. American Indians hunted them in small numbers, seasonally, since originally they had no horses and had to walk to and from the hunting grounds. The advent of the horse changed life forever on the Great Plains. Horses escaped from the early Spanish explorers and became wild denizens of the plains. Indians captured, tamed and trained the horses, putting them to effective use in hunting the buffalo—both for transport to the site of the herds, as a swift hunting platform, and as beasts of burden to carry the meat home. As extensive European settlement on the east coast began to drive Indian tribes westward in a domino effect, entire tribes developed a nomadic lifestyle, no longer tied to fixed village sites but able to subsist on the buffalo herds they followed on horseback. This lifestyle was short-lived, however. In just over 100 years Euro-Americans invaded the plains, at first merely passing through what they described as a "desert" along the Oregon, California, Santa Fe and Mormon trails. Their routes divided the buffalo herds and encroached upon Indian hunting grounds. By 1869 steel rails had been laid across the prairie, and the buffalo slaughter casually begun by the Oregon emigrants was continued in earnest by professional hide hunters. Not far behind were the ranchers who took over the

161 bottom left The Dr. Martin Luther King, Jr. Bridge crosses the Mississippi River at Laclede's Landing, a revitalized section of St. Louis' historic levee district with original grid-pattern streets with brick and cobblestone paving and restored buildings which evoke the city's storied past.

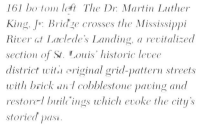

161 bottom right The pyramid-shaped cap of the City Courts Building, completed in 1930, rubs shoulders with Art Deco, Beaux-Arts, early- and post-modern architectural styles in downtown St. Louis. The St. Louis metropolitan area consists of 2.5 million people, while less than 400,000 live within the city limits.

162-163 St. Louis is dominated by architect Eero Saarinen's stainless steel Gateway Arch, at 630 feet the tallest structure in the city. The Arch was built between 1963 and 1965 to commemorate St. Louis' role in the westward expansion of the U. S. Below the Arch stands Busch Stadium, home to the baseball team the St. Louis Cardinals.

Forest Park was opened in 1876 and played host to the Louisiana Purchase Exposition in 1904, the largest world's fair ever held, which inspired the song and the movie Meet Me in St. Louis.

164 top left The Climatron in the Missouri Botanical Garden was designed by R. Buckminster Fuller and shelters a tropical rainforest environment.

164 top center The landscaped paths and colorful pavilions of the St. Louis Zoo hearken back to a proud heritage. Begun in the 1890s, the zoo is supported by a special tax adopted in 1916, which makes it free to the public.

164 top right The Saint Louis Art Museum served as the Palace of Fine Arts for the 1904 world's fair, and is one of its few surviving buildings.

164 bottom The Living World Pavilion of the St. Louis Zoo is located in 1,293 acre Forest Park, one of the world's largest urban parks. Forest Park was opened in 1876 and played host to the Louisiana Purchase Exposition in 1904, the largest world's fair ever held, which inspired the song and the movie Meet Me in St. Louis. *The Living World is an indoor exhibit area and meeting space for the extensive outdoor grounds of the zoo.*

165 This view of the Missouri Botanical Garden, in the western part of St. Louis, is dominated by the country mansion of the man who donated the land for the facility in 1859, Henry Shaw. It was one of the first botanical gardens in the United States. The restored grounds include Victorian-era formal gardens and a hedge maze.

grasslands for domestic cattle. By the 1880s irrigation methods and farming machinery made it possible to till the vast area of the plains, and farming homesteads took the place of the ancient prairie ecosystem. By 1900, there were less than 300 surviving bison; the species was saved from extinction only by the timely efforts of a few concerned individuals. Today, the bison population has returned on preserves and bison ranches, where at least 200,000 animals again graze on prairie grasses. Needless to say, the way of life of the Indian was changed forever.

The prairie region produced several of America's great figures, including Abraham Lincoln, William Jennings Bryan, the Lakota leaders Crazy Horse,

Sitting Bull and Red Cloud, the poet Carl Sandburg, and the architect Frank Lloyd Wright. These men, and others like them, carried the ideals, morals and culture of the heartland from America to the people of the world. Today, the Midwest struggles with many problems. Its people are leaving the rural areas for the cities. Family farms are being lost as a generation comes of age which seems to be uninterested in the life of the farmer. Midwestern cities are afflicted with the same problems as the large urban areas of the east and the west coasts. Chicago, Detroit, Cincinnati, Louisville, Kansas City and St. Louis are the region's largest cities. West of Kansas City and Omaha lies a region without large urban

concentrations, a patchwork quilt of farm fields and people who hold American values and patriotism high. The cities and towns of the region are characterized by their water towers and grain elevators. The water towers almost always sport the name of the town on their sides, and can be seen for miles across the flat landscape. The grain elevators, large storage silos for corn, wheat, milo and other crops, lend a character to each municipality, whether it be a "whistle-stop" or a city.

Chicago dominates the region with its cultural institutions, fascinating ethnic neighborhoods, recreational opportunities, and its spectacular architecture. In fact, it is a Mecca for lovers of architecture. Louis Sullivan, who pioneered the techniques of building tall structures with steel skeletons at the end of the 19th century, influenced many, including his protégée, Frank Lloyd Wright. The Carson-Pirie-Scott building in Chicago's downtown area (affectionately known as the "Loop" for its circuit of elevated train trestles) is one of the best surviving examples of Sullivan's work. In 1951, Mies van der Rohe's twin 26-story glass towers, the Lake Shore Drive Apartments, were completed, heavily influencing the worldwide direction of modern architecture.

The last four decades have brought Bertrand Goldberg's Marina City, as well as Bruce Graham's John Hancock Center and the Sears Tower.

The Hancock Center, completed in 1970, is 1,107 feet tall, and in its 100 stories mixes retail stores, parking, office space, condominium apartments and restaurants in a unique vertical experiment in city living.

The Sears Tower, strictly an office building, is 1,454 feet tall. It was the tallest building in the world when it was completed in 1974, and it remains the tallest building in the United States.

The wonders of the rural Midwest are more subtle, and take longer to recognize and appreciate. Although the land is generally flat, (there are no mountains in the region), there are substantial and beautiful hills which present lovely vistas, particularly when seen at sunrise or sunset.

Driving along a country road as straight as an arrow, between two fields of corn rising up on each side on a summer evening near dusk is one of the most calming experiences one can have.

The lovely green of the corn field, the glow of

orange from the setting sun, the wonderful surprises of vistas which suddenly open up on one side or the other, delight the mind and the senses. Views of farm houses, some old, some new, all neat, painted and cared for with pride, go swishing by as the sun sinks lower. Triangular ponds used as swimming holes by the kids, with their little docks and tire swings reflect the dying light in the sky.

The clusters of trees around farm houses and barns, marking their existence from far off across the plains, add a sense of order to the vastness.

And the rivers which border these farmlands; the Wabash, the Illinois, the Ohio, the Mississippi, the Arkansas, the Platte, and the mighty and seemingly endless Missouri, serve to define the area.

The people of the Midwest are honest, hardworking, conservative and gregarious. But after more than a century of Euro-American habitation, despite the incredible changes in the ecosystem and the new landscape which evolved with the demise of the prairie, it is the people who make the region a special place. The 21st century presents many challenges for these people as they strive to find a balance between themselves and the Midwestern landscape.

166 Sheds and grain storage bins line the side of a field in rural southern Illinois, across the Mississippi River from St. Louis. The humid continental climate provides a fairly long growing season of up to 180 days per year. An average of 48 inches of annual rainfall is combined with less than 10 inches of snow each year. Illinois ranks 5th in the U.S. in terms of annual farm income.

167 top This farmstead is built close to an earthen levee and a drainage channel of the Mississippi River. The levee, covered with trees and vegetation, protects the farm from flooding. Major crops in Illinois include soybeans, corn, wheat, hay and oats.

167 center Farming in Missouri does not differ in many ways from farming in Illinois. One difference is caused by the topography of Missouri, which is far more undulating than that of primarily flat southern Illinois. Missouri farmers must use contour plowing to prevent erosion. Missouri has more farms than Illinois, but they are on average 80 acres smaller than their Illinois counterparts. In the photo one can see a peaceful farm field sown with winter wheat, which glows bright green amidst the leaves of fall.

167 bottom This farm house is surrounded by a kitchen garden. When the first European settlers arrived, 45% of Illinois was forested. Today only 10% of the state is wooded. Illinois' 80,000 farms average about 354 acres in size.

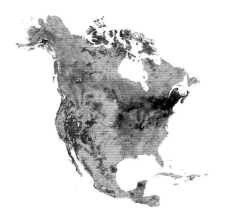

168-169 *The Rocky Mountains near Telluride, Colorado glow in the fading light of afternoon. Relative youngsters geologically speaking, the Rockies were created by uplift only 65 million years ago, during the late Cretaceous period. The Rocky Mountain chain runs for 2,000 miles from central New Mexico to British Columbia.*

The Rocky Mountain Region

168 bottom The rolling fields of a farm in eastern Wyoming, looking southwest from Steptoe Butte. Although livestock and ranching compose about 85% of the agricultural output of the state, farms in the river valleys along the eastern portion produce sugar beets, wheat, barley and hay.

169 Weird configurations of severely eroded, layered sedimentary rock compose Badlands National Park in southwestern South Dakota. The multicolored formations are constantly subject to change from the forces of the wind. The badlands have little plant or animal life, but there are populations of bighorn sheep, antelope and bison in some parts of the park. The area also abounds with fossils.

In 1909, a conservationist named Enos Mills led a campaign to preserve the area, and the U.S. Congress complied in 1915 by creating Rocky Mountain National Park.

One hundred fifty year old ruts mark the passage of covered wagons, while just a stone's throw away automobiles whiz along an interstate highway at 75 miles per hour. High up in an alpine meadow between two mountain peaks, fragile little blue flowers hug the ground, while tiny rodents called picas run for their burrows. Arriving at a point overlooking a peaceful valley, a hiker tries to imagine

a rowdy annual rendezvous of mountain men, the beaver trappers drinking themselves insensible and blowing an entire year's wages in the frolic. In Denver, one sees vestiges everywhere of the past amid the bustle of a modern city. The new (and controversial) airport mimics the mountains which can be seen in the distance. The traffic slows to a crawl in Yellowstone National Park, as tourists lean out their windows to photograph wildlife. For many urban dwellers, this may be the most intense natural experience of their lives.

170 top The high, snow-filled mountain valleys of Rocky Mountain National Park are seen by few visitors. They are the haunts of a few rugged animals.

170 center left No mining is allowed within the confines of Rocky Mountain National Park, although mining in other parts of the Rocky Mountain range has been taking place for nearly 200 years. Valuable minerals and other substances such as coal, copper, zinc, silver, gold, iron ore, natural gas, petroleum, lead and molybdenum have all been found in the Rocky Mountains.

170 center right Beautiful Alpine meadows and streams lead out of the mountain peaks at Rocky Mountain National Park.

170 bottom The lower elevations of Rocky Mountain National Park contain beautiful green forests and clear running streams. In 1859 Joel Estes and his son Milton settled in the area called Estes Park, but few pioneers ever made the area their home. In 1909 a conservationist named Enos Mills led a campaign to preserve the area, and the U.S. Congress complied in 1915 by creating Rocky Mountain National Park.

171 Snowy peaks rise above glistening lakes in Rocky Mountain National Park. Since a third of the park's land is above the tree line, visitors are treated to views of Arctic tundra and wildlife. The first non-Indians to see the mountains were fur trappers in the late 18th and early 19th centuries.

172-173 The Maroon Bells, two peaks higher than 14,000 feet, are located in the Colorado Rockies southwest of Aspen. This winter scene shows the peaks in all their beauty, but also hints at the danger of this inhospitable region above the treeline on a frozen winter day.

On the other end of the scale, experienced climbers arrive exhausted at the top of one of the lesser-known peaks in the region, a sweet payoff after months of planning and dreaming. Others don hip waders and cast for fish in a clear, fast-flowing mountain stream. These are the Rocky Mountains, the backbone of America.

After a seemingly endless drive across the Great Plains on an interstate highway, they seem to rise from the earth like a mirage—a line of blue, snow-covered peaks in the distance. The sun sets and a dramatic show of lightning begins in the still-distant mountains, silently stabbing the darkness with sudden flashes of light. The Rocky Mountains offer cool breezes, swift streams, dark green pine boughs and light green, shimmering aspen leaves. They are a wonderful vacation spot, but they are also home to a diverse set of people—ranchers, artists and prospectors as well as those who support life for native and tourist alike. Because of their natural and cultural history, "the Rockies" cover and define an entire region of the United States.

Where did these magnificent mountains come from? How were they created? The Rocky Mountains rose over a period of 60 million years as the Atlantic Ocean grew, pushing the North American tectonic plate over the Farallon plate in the Pacific Ocean.

174 The wondrous world of Yellowstone National Park can be glimpsed in this view along the Yellowstone River. In an area a world of geysers, hot springs, meadows, streams, lakes and wildlife has been preserved for the enjoyment of visitors.

175 top Yellowstone National Park's bison herd was one of the small remnants left alive in the early 20th century. The herd was augmented by other animals to create the 2,700 healthy animals visitors see today.

175 center right The Yellowstone River courses southward through the Grand Canyon of the Yellowstone to tumble over Upper Yellowstone Falls, partially obscured by a bend in the river to the left of the center of this photo. Lower Yellowstone Falls is just to the left of the photo.

175 center left Visitors follow designed tour roads within Yellowstone National Park, which take autos away from sensitive areas while allowing access to those on foot.

175 bottom right A ribbon of water forms a creek within Yellowstone National Park, eventually finding its way to rivers and to the oceans. Yellowstone sits on the Continental Divide, which means that water from its northern half flows toward the Missouri River and the Atlantic, while water from the southern half flows to the Pacific.

175 bottom left The National Park Service headquarters at Mammoth Hot Springs in Yellowstone National Park. The complex of buildings includes the former barracks used by U.S. Cavalrymen prior to 1916, when the National Park Service was created. The 1st U.S. cavalry used to patrol and maintain the park in its early years, and they were headquartered here, at what was once called Fort Yellowstone. A portion of the hot springs can be seen on the right.

A ribbon of water forms a creek within Yellowstone National Park, which sits on the Continental Divide

The name "Teton" probably originated with French-Canadian trappers, who referred to the mountains as the Trois Tetons, or Three Breasts.

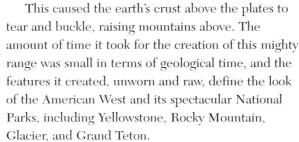

176 top Tallest mountain of its namesake range, Grand Teton stands 13,770 feet tall, a graceful and quintessential mountain peak. The name "Teton" probably originated with French-Canadian trappers, who referred to the mountains as the Trois Tetons, or Three Breasts.

176 center The Grand Teton range in all its glory, looking northward. The peaks from left to right are Nez Perce, Middle Teton, Grand Teton, Mount Owen and Teewinot Mountain. On the right, three lakes feed into the Snake River, starting with Jenny Lake in the foreground and continuing with Leigh Lake and the large Jackson Lake on the north.

This caused the earth's crust above the plates to tear and buckle, raising mountains above. The amount of time it took for the creation of this mighty range was small in terms of geological time, and the features it created, unworn and raw, define the look of the American West and its spectacular National Parks, including Yellowstone, Rocky Mountain, Glacier, and Grand Teton.

Rocky Mountain National Park is a premiere spot to see and study the mountain ecosystem. The park is located in Colorado, in the southern Rocky Mountains, which extend into New Mexico. Fully a third of the park is above the treeline, where tundra predominates. Growing amid and atop the rocks of these mountains are beautiful trees. The white-trunked aspens lend a magnificent aura of movement, their leaves rustling in the wind, catching the light. Lodgepole pines thrive on the mountainsides and in the valleys; Native Americans once prized their straight, tall, narrow trunks for use as tipi poles. The cones of these trees need the heat of forest fires to open and effectively release their seeds. Higher up the mountain slopes, above 9,000 feet, live the Douglas firs and Engelmann spruce, in a world of deep winter snows and damp summers. At the upper edges of this region trees assume stunted, twisted, grotesque shapes, reminding one of the trees in the film *The Wizard of Oz*. Above this level, the trees disappear and the climber finds himself in alpine tundra, where more than 1/4 of the low-lying plants can also be found in the Arctic.

The park teems with wildlife, including bighorn sheep, beaver, elk, moose, and cougar. In the autumn the mountains seem to glow as the aspen leaves turn yellow.

176 bottom Jackson Lake in Grand Teton National Park makes a spectacular mirror for the incredible peaks just to the west. Grand Teton became a National Park in 1929, but it was the efforts of John D. Rockefeller, Jr. that acquired the valley floor to add to the park. In recent years calls have come from conservationists to better manage an even wider zone around Yellowstone and Grand Teton to preserve the entire ecosystem from damage.

176-177 Hermitage Point juts into Jackson Lake in Grand Teton National Park, just south of Yellowstone. During the last ice age glaciers carved out basins, and then as they melted left mounds of debris known as terminal moraines. One such moraine captured the water of Jackson Lake, which was enlarged in the early 1900s by a man-made dam to provide irrigation in Idaho.

177 bottom left The craggy peaks of Grand Teton National Park seem to jump up suddenly from the valley of the Snake River below. Created only 9 million years ago, these are the youngest mountains in America.

177 bottom right A bay on Jackson Lake in Grand Teton National Park helps to support the area's thriving population of wildlife. Elk, moose, bear, pronghorn antelope, bison, eagles, swans and coyotes are among the many species that live here.

The golden leaves fall in October, signaling the onset of winter and an annual snowfall of 30 to 40 feet. The Rocky Mountain chain extends northward from Colorado into the central Rockies of Utah, Wyoming, Idaho and Montana. One of the premiere recreational areas of this region is Grand Teton National Park. Composed of incredibly picturesque peaks, the Tetons have a slightly different geological story to tell than does Rocky Mountain National Park. The Teton Range began rising about 10 million years ago along a 40 mile long fault. Plains east of the fault dropped, forming the valley of Jackson Hole. Broken sedimentary layers of ancient sandstone, shale, dolomite, and limestone still cap each end and the back of the Teton range. The area is so broken that a sandstone remnant now atop 6,000 foot Mount Moran once connected to another now estimated to be 25,000 feet below the valley floor.

178 The Lower Yellowstone Falls send water plunging 308 feet down into the Grand Canyon of the Yellowstone. The canyon's colors were created by hot underground water acting on the area's volcanic rock, causing a chemical reaction. The river got its name not from this canyon, however, but from the color of the rock near its confluence with the Missouri River, 671 miles to the east in western North Dakota.

179 top A river in Yellowstone National Park meanders through a valley. Wildfires in 1988 raged across 1.4 million acres in and around Yellowstone, but the damage has been quick to heal, especially since fire is a natural process in healthy forests.

179 center left The Grand Canyon of the Yellowstone plunges 1,000 feet from the plateau above to the river below. The canyon has been eroded during concentrated periods of time in the past, perhaps by floods caused by melting glaciers. Little erosion takes place today.

Wildfires in 1988 raged across 1.4 million acres in and around Yellowstone.

179 center right Sulphur Caldron and Mud Volcano border the Yellowstone River as it winds its way to Yellowstone Lake.

179 bottom left The Yellowstone River near its entry into Yellowstone Lake. The river will leave the far side of the lake to travel over 600 miles to join the Missouri. Eventually, this water will end up in the Gulf of Mexico below New Orleans.

179 bottom right Buffalo graze contentedly in Yellowstone National Park, the species of animal most often seen by visitors. In addition to other wildlife, the most popular recent addition to the park has been the grey wolf. Eradicated in the early 1900s, the wolves were reintroduced to the park in a controversial program which has neighboring ranchers up in arms and tourists for the most part delighted.

The wonders of Yellowstone are the result of three volcanic eruptions, the latest of which was 600,000 years ago.

Wind, water, ice and glaciers stripped away the surface, revealing rock now visible on the sides of the peaks, granite nearly as old as the Earth itself.

The glaciers, in fact, worked the most visible changes on the Tetons in relatively recent times sculpting lakes and other features throughout the area. The tallest peak is 13,770 foot Grand Teton. Altogether the Tetons are much younger than other mountains in the Rockies.

Abundant wildlife, including elk, moose, mule deer, black bear, bighorn sheep, buffalo, pronghorn antelope and coyote inhabit the region.

But like many other beautiful natural areas in the United States, the Grand Tetons are threatened by development. Nearby Jackson, Wyoming, has grown into a fashionable resort served by a modern airport, surrounded by million dollar vacation homes.

Unlike Grand Teton's spine of icy peaks, Yellowstone National Park is encompassed by an elliptical volcanic plateau ringed by mountains.

The wonders of Yellowstone are the result of three volcanic eruptions, the latest of which was 600,000 years ago. In fact, Yellowstone is a caldera, one of the largest in the world. Beneath the forests and meadows, geothermal heat creates over 200 hot springs and geysers.

Underground heat melts the winter snow, allowing the abundant wildlife of the park to sustain themselves on winter grasses. These animals include an estimated 93,000 elk and 2,700 bison.

180 top Geysers and hot springs inhabit this field at Yellowstone National Park. The same superheated water creates both phenomena, except that when the pressure drops suddenly the water flume turns into the steam of a geyser. This water can also create fumeroles, which lack enough moisture to flow and just vent steam; and mud pots, which form over fumeroles as acid gasses decompose rocks into mud and clay.

180 center left Mammoth Hot Springs at Yellowstone National Park are kept going by a hot spot deep in the earth's mantle. Magma is sent toward the surface in the Yellowstone caldera, producing 30 times more underground heat than normal for this region. Between 1923 and 1985 the caldera rose three feet, before falling eight inches on the northeastern end. This warping, combined with earthquakes, may be signs of renewed volcanic activity in the future.

180 center right Possibly the most famous spot in Yellowstone National Park, Old Faithful Geyser is the focal point of recreational development. The semicircular walkway and fence looks out on the geyser field with Old Faithful at the center. The large building to the right is the Old Faithful Lodge, while to the left is the roof of Old Faithful Inn, the world's largest hotel made of logs, with a lobby more than 90 feet high.

180 bottom Another view of hot springs in Yellowstone National Park.

181 This photo of the Grand Prismatic Hot Spring shows the spectacular colors created by colorful photosynthetic bacteria. Surface water seeps down into porous rock where it is

heated under pressure and rises back to the surface as geysers or hot springs. Hot springs occur when water emerges that is not superheated or under pressure. The size of the spring can be judged by the walkways curving near its right side, where visitors can be seen walking.

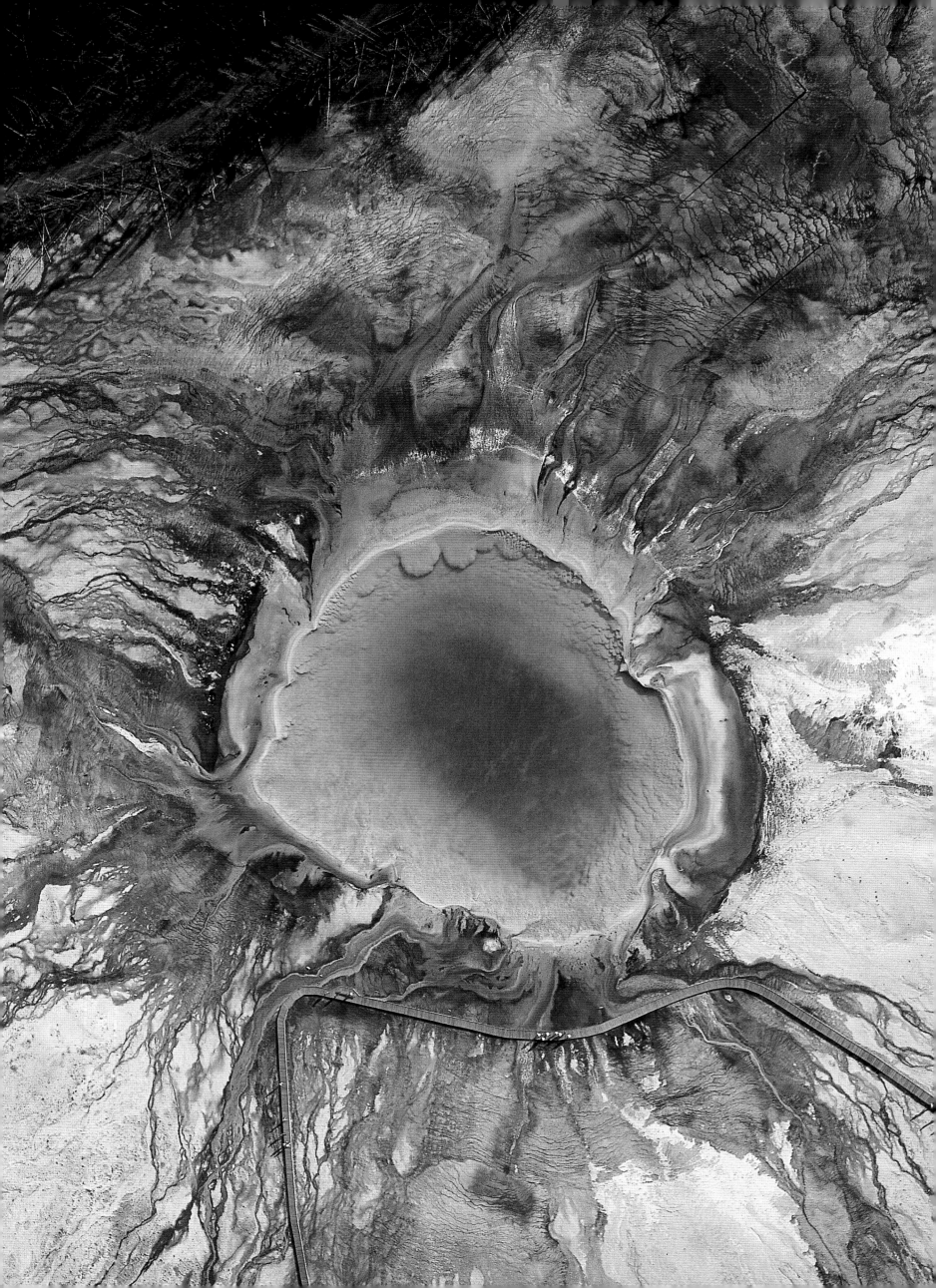

182 top *Clouds obscure part of the view of Custer State Park in the Black Hills of South Dakota. A favorite vacation retreat that showcases history and nature, the park has its own bison herd.*

182-183 Scotts Bluff, Nebraska rises 800 feet above the surrounding valley of the North Platte River. The bluff was a landmark on the Oregon Trail, an often tedious march across a flat and featureless landscape for the first portion of the 2,000 miles from Independence, Missouri to the Willamette Valley of Oregon. Between 1842 and 1869 an estimated 300,000 people traveled the Oregon Trail. A National Park Service visitor center complex is in the center of the photograph.

182 bottom The wilder aspects of the American West, and the way that the pristine West once looked, left, can be contrasted in this photo with the changes wrought by the hand of man in irrigated farm fields on the right. The topography of the area to the right was always flat, but originally covered with prairie grasses; while the area to the left is too rocky, wild and undulating to ever be fit for agriculture.

The wilder aspects of the American West, and the way that the pristine West once looked, left, can be contrasted in these photos.

Jackson Hole, Yellowstone and the Tetons cannot help but evoke images of the past. Fur trappers from the United States began to work and live in the Rocky Mountain region soon after the explorations of Meriwether Lewis and William Clark in 1804-1806. Their successful reports of plentiful beaver in the mountains led entrepreneurial Americans to organize and dispatch groups of trappers or "mountain men" to these regions, whether or not they were then within the boundaries of the United States. It was mountain man John Colter, a veteran of the Lewis and Clark Expedition, who became the first non-Indian to see the Grand Tetons and the Yellowstone region.

By the early 1840s, the beaver were nearly

extinct, but mountain men like Colter, Jim Bridger, Kit Carson and Jim Beckwourth put their stamp on the region.

Later, minerals replaced furs as mining towns were built throughout the Rockies. Many of these quaint towns survive today, particularly in Colorado—places like Telluride, Ouray, Leadville and Silverton. Their colorful Victorian homes, covered with wooden "gingerbread" ornamentation, look more like movie sets than authentic Western towns, with the unbelievable grandeur of the mountains rising behind their roofs.

Today, these towns draw tourists from all over the world to enjoy the summer scenery or winter skiing. Steamboat Springs, Aspen, and Vail, Colorado have become legendary as ski resorts. One of the region's biggest industries is tourism, and 20 million people a year visit Colorado alone. In addition, although the region is far more sparsely settled than most other areas of the country, more and more people are finding it a desirable year-round place to live.

This, of course, is placing stress on the ecosystem and causing long-term residents to wince.

183 left Farm fields along the flat plain of the Platte River near Fort Laramie, Wyoming.

183 top right Irrigating the dry western lands of the United States is necessary for efficient farming. Center pivot irrigation is often employed in the West. Long lines of sprinklers move around a circular field from a central point, like the hand of a clock.

This method of irrigation can be seen in this photo of fields near Scotts Bluff, Nebraska.

183 center right Chimney Rock, near the Platte River in Nebraska, delighted weary travelers on the Oregon Trail. Most could not resist carving their names on the shaft, which since their time has been reduced in height due to crumbling and erosion.

183 bottom right Farmers plow their fields around rock outcroppings near Scotts Bluff, Nebraska. Different forms of irrigation and plowing are used depending upon the type of crop, the topography of the land, and the amount of water needed.

The four heroes on Mount Rushmore in the Black Hills of South Dakota were carved by sculptor Gutzon Borglum and a team of workers between 1927 and 1943.

Luckily, the region has not yet been affected to a destructive degree. Moving north of Yellowstone one comes to the northern Rockies, which are located in Idaho, Montana and western Washington. This section of mountains also has its exemplary park— Glacier, in northwestern Montana. The park has more than 50 glaciers and 200 glacier-fed lakes; the maximum elevation is the top of Mount Cleveland, at 10,448 feet. The park's glaciers are only 4,000 years old, and move very slowly—only about 30 feet per

year. Glacier extends into the Waterton Lakes National Park in Canada, and comprises one of the most beautiful regions in the world. In 1932 the two parks were combined as the world's first international peace park. Under a unique arrangement, each country administers its own park lands but cooperates in the areas of visitor services, scientific research and wildlife management. This spirit of cooperation epitomizes the attitude of the people of the Rocky Mountain region—a can-do spirit and an abundance of friendly howdy-doos characterize its residents.

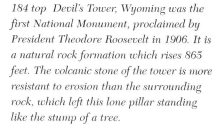

184 top Devil's Tower, Wyoming was the first National Monument, proclaimed by President Theodore Roosevelt in 1906. It is a natural rock formation which rises 865 feet. The volcanic stone of the tower is more resistant to erosion than the surrounding rock, which left this lone pillar standing like the stump of a tree.

184 center Near the faces on Mount Rushmore, the Crazy Horse monument honors the brilliant Lakota leader who died in 1877 at the hands of a U.S. soldier while being held in captivity. Asked in 1948 by Lakota leaders to carve a memorial to an Indian as a counterpoint to the faces on Mount Rushmore, Boston-born sculptor Korczak Ziolkowski accepted the project.

184 bottom Beautiful hills and meadows in Custer State Park support a wide variety of wildlife. The park's herd of 1,400 bison roam freely through the area. The park is also home to wild turkey, deer, elk, antelope, mountain goats and bighorn sheep.

184-185 The four faces carved on Mount Rushmore in the Black Hills of South Dakota represent Presidents George Washington, Thomas Jefferson, Theodore Roosevelt and Abraham Lincoln. The faces were carved by Gutzon Borglum between 1927 and 1943.

185 bottom Pinnacles of rock reach for the sky in Custer State Park, South Dakota, a 73,000 acre area in the Black Hills. The park is a perfect place for hiking, rock

climbing, horseback riding, fishing and mountain biking. The park takes its name from Gen. George Armstrong Custer, who found gold in the region in 1874, starting a stampede of miners who quickly supplanted the Lakota people.

186-187 Badlands National Park in South Dakota is located to the east of the Black Hills. The park covers nearly 244,000 acres, which in addition to rock formations includes the largest protected mixed grass prairie in the United States. Sixty four thousand acres of the park have been designated wilderness areas, where the black-footed ferret, the most endangered land mammal in North America, has been reintroduced.

Glacier National Park was combined in 1932 with Waterton Lakes National Park in Alberta, Canada as the first International Peace Park.

188 top The exposed sedimentary rock of Glacier National Park is unique in that it is unaltered since the Proterozoic Age, 1,600 to 800 million years ago. The rock still contains fossils, and other phenomena of long ago.

188 center The views are extensive and unparalleled in Glacier National Park, with high mountain lakes such as Lake MacDonald, shown in this photo, and gorgeous mountains ringing nearly every location. Lake MacDonald actually straddles the Continental Divide.

188 bottom Established in 1910, Glacier National Park covers an area of 1,600 square miles. Designated a World Heritage Site, Glacier is home to many species of animals, including wolves, grizzly bears and cougars, the only place in the lower 48 states where all three predators continue to live, never having been eradicated during the 19th and early 20th centuries. The park was combined in 1932 with Waterton Lakes National Park in Alberta, Canada as the first International Peace Park.

188-189 A summer thunderstorm rolls in over Mount Reynolds in Glacier National Park. The park contains 50 glaciers, 200 glacier fed lakes, and tall peaks culminating in 10,448 foot Mount Cleveland.

189 bottom left A dusting of winter settles on Glacier National Park's Lake MacDonald, mirroring the usually snow covered peaks in the distance. The topographical features of the region were sculpted by the massive glaciers of the last Ice Age.

189 bottom right The Lewis Overthrust Fault in Glacier National Park provides scientists with comparative information about worldwide geologic processes. The Lewis Overthrust was created 170 million years ago by a collision of the Earth's tectonic plates which thrust rocks of ancient age over the top of newer rocks, a rarity in geology.

Ice near the surface of a glacier is often hard and brittle, but the pressure of the ice above enables the ice near the bottom to move downhill, due to gravity's pull.

190 top The glaciers in Glacier National Park were all formed within the last few thousand years, and all are shrinking because more snow melts each summer than is replenished each winter. As the climate changed over the last two million years, glaciers have come and gone.

190 bottom Glaciers sculpt the land due to rocks and debris which fall into them and become part of their composition. This debris causes a glacier to act like a giant piece of sandpaper, sculpting the land before it as it moves.

190-191 Grinnell Glacier is an example of the over 50 glaciers in the National Park. A glacier is formed by snow in areas where climactic conditions keep it from melting in the summer months. An accumulation of snow begins to weigh on the layers below, compacting them into ice. Ice near the surface of a glacier is often hard and brittle, but the pressure of the ice above enables the ice near the bottom to move downhill, due to gravity's pull. It is a pack of snow and ice which is able to move in this fashion which is called a glacier.

191 top The huge sheets of ice of ancient times exist no more, but the smaller glaciers in Glacier National Park have much to teach us about this fascinating phenomenon of nature.

192-193 *The beautiful mountains of the Flathead Valley's Mission Range rise on the Flathead Indian Reservation near Ronan, Montana. The reservation also includes the National Bison Range. The Flathead Reservation is home to the Confederated Salish and Kootenai tribes, and is the third largest in Montana.*

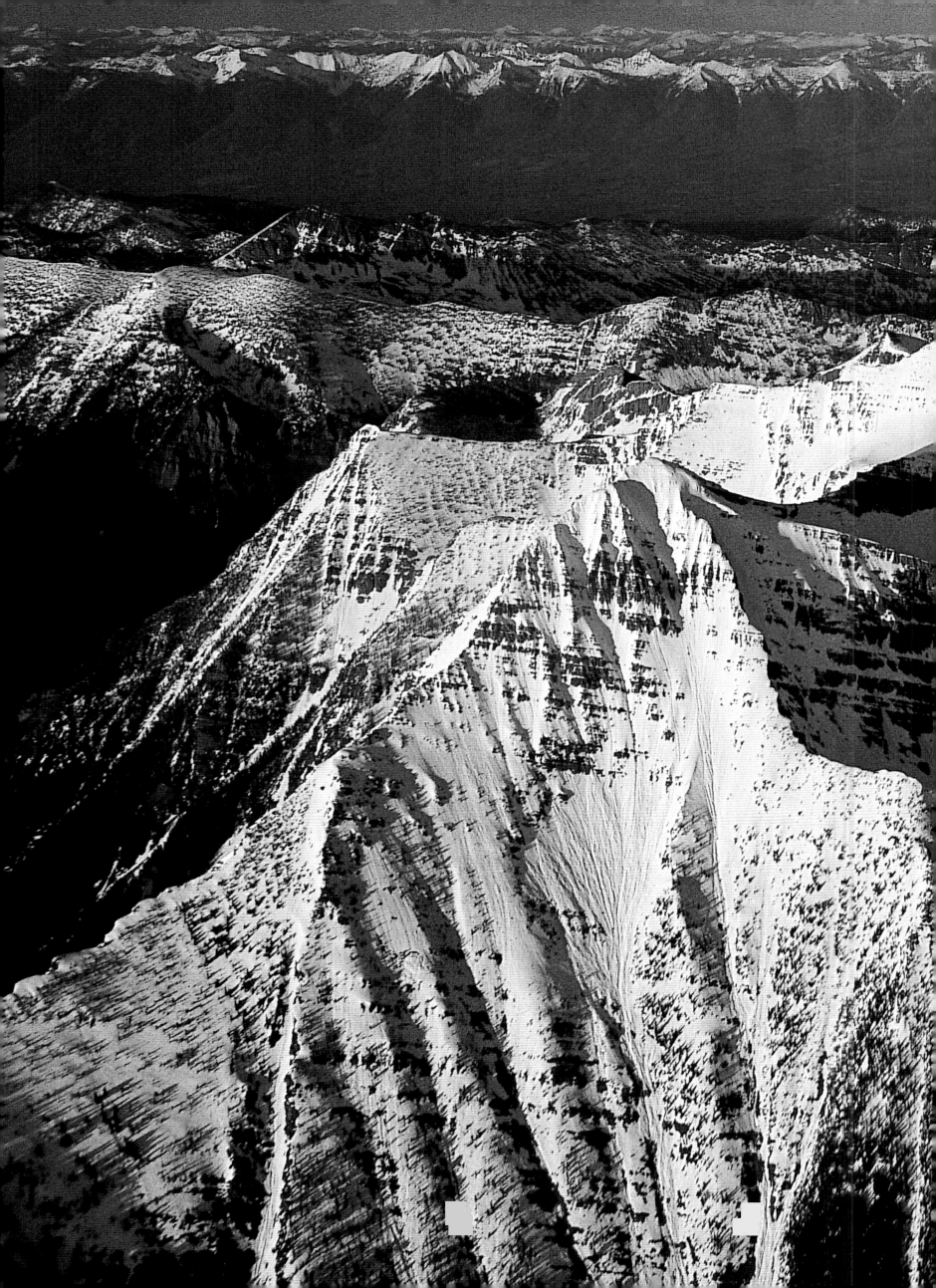

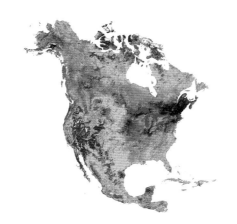

194-195 The second largest reservoir in North America, Lake Powell has 1,960 miles of shoreline. The Glen Canyon Dam backed up the Colorado River behind it into this lake, which put a large body of water in the midst of the desert. The lake was named for explorer John Wesley Powell, who led the first team of men to successfully navigate the length of the Colorado River canyons. Ironically, the reservoir has changed the landscape and beautiful Glen Canyon itself from what Powell saw in 1869.

The Desert Southwest

194 bottom An entrance to Las Vegas' MGM Grand Hotel uses the film studio's symbol, Leo the Lion. The facility is the world's largest resort hotel, with 5,005 rooms. The State of Nevada legalized gambling in 1931, and Las Vegas began to boom after World War II when big investors, some linked to organized crime, began to construct hotels and casinos. The city drew international visitors to this former watering stop in the middle of the Mojave Desert, due to big-name entertainers and glitzy floor shows.

195 A desert resort community, Palm Springs, California has been a playground for celebrities and the wealthy from Los Angeles' movie colony since the 1930s. Famous residents have included Bob Hope, Frank Sinatra and former President Gerald Ford, who enjoyed the fine weather and the local golf courses.

196 top left As the Colorado River nears the Grand Canyon, it cuts deeper into the Kaibab Plateau. As the rock walls broke down over the eons, the canyon widened. It has been estimated that it took three to six million years for the canyon to evolve to its present appearance.

196 top right The result of nature's handiwork can be seen all along the length of the Grand Canyon. What water did not accomplish, wind, ice, ancient volcanism and rockslides finished. The Grand Canyon is an amalgam of nearly every type of force that can be exerted upon rock by nature.

196-197 Visitors are awestruck by their first glimpse of Arizona's Grand Canyon of the Colorado. Their first question inevitably is "how could this have been created?" Scientists have been trying to answer that puzzle for many years. The Grand Canyon is probably the world's most spectacular example of erosion—a chasm which follows the river for 277 miles and is up to 18 miles wide in some places. Below Yavapai Point the canyon bottom is 2,400 feet above sea level and 4,500 feet below the rim.

The Grand Canyon is probably the world's most spectacular example of erosion—a chasm which follows the river for 277 miles and is up to 18 miles wide in some places.

A raven lets out its shrill call as it soars above the walls of the canyon, driving off eagles and hawks that dare to challenge it. Below, a mountain sheep rests on an impossibly steep rock outcropping. Millions of twinkling lights set aside the glitter of Las Vegas from the lonely miles of desert around it. At the top of a steep street in Jerome, Arizona, original buildings left over from the wild mining days of the Old West speak volumes about the recent history of the region. A hot, overcast August day suddenly erupts into a driving rainstorm, bringing much-needed water to the desert ecosystem. Boats pull into a small side canyon of Lake Powell which leads to Rainbow Bridge, the tallest natural arch in the world, a sacred site to the Navajo people. As a sudden October snowstorm blankets northern Arizona, the Grand Canyon is transformed into a fairyland, its rocky mounts and outcrops looking like frosted layer cakes. A wooden ladder is placed up against the side of an ancient Indian dwelling a hundred feet above the valley floor. Wind whistles through the juniper trees on the rim of a canyon, the varicolored rocks below bearing witness to millions of years of erosion and life.

Heat, sand, cactus, animal pests. Most people think of the desert in these terms. When traveling through the desert, they long for tall trees, lakes or oceans, and fields carpeted with grass or grain.

197 bottom It is very difficult for a camera to capture the awesome wonder of the Grand Canyon. In this view, Marble Canyon winds its way through the Painted Desert, delivering the river to the deeper and more spectacular wonders of the Grand Canyon below. Although it may look barren to the first-time visitor, the Grand Canyon supports about 70 species of mammals, 250 species of birds, 25 species of reptiles and 5 species of amphibians. Plant life is also varied, and includes wild flowers.

196 bottom The Grand Canyon is composed of a series of layers of different types of rock. Starting at the very bottom of the Canyon is the Vishnu Schist, some of the world's oldest-known rock. Next comes the Tapeats Sandstone, followed by Bright Angel Shale, Mauv Limestone, Redwall Limestone, the Supai Group, Hermit Shale, Coconino sandstone, the Toroweap Formation, and, at the top, Kaibab Limestone. Since most of this rock was formed as sediment beneath oceans, it is thought that the area of the Grand Canyon was once buried under a vast inland sea.

197 top Millions of years of the movement of continents, tectonic plates, and the advance and retreat of the oceans created the rock layers seen in the Grand Canyon. But the canyon itself was created after the oceans receded and the Rocky Mountains rose about 70 million years ago. The action of rainwater falling on the mountains caused streams to unite into a river bed. This formed the ancient Colorado River, which began to carve its way through a flat plain. At the same time, the Colorado Plateau beneath it was actually rising due to pressures deep in the earth. This "uplift" acted like one person holding a board another is sawing, allowing the river to cut through the rock of the plateau very efficiently.

The first European to see the Grand Canyon was Don Lopez de Cardenas, commander of a splinter group sent out from Coronado's expedition in 1540.

But there are others for whom the desert is the most beautiful of places, a region of abundant diversity in flora, fauna and scenery.

These people see the differences in the many types of exposed rock, the beauty in the gorgeous colors of the plants and flowers, the serenity in the ribbons of water in the rivers and seasonal creeks which course through the desert country. The United States has not just one desert but three.

The Mojave Desert is the westernmost, smallest and driest, with less than 2 inches of rainfall each year. The next desert, the Sonoran, extends from southern Arizona into Mexico. The third is the Chihuahuan, most of which lies in Mexico but a small portion of which extends into Texas and New Mexico. These deserts evolved about 40 million years ago, when the beginnings of a high pressure weather system still in existence coupled with coastal mountains to prevent rainfall from reaching them throughout most of each year.

Despite the prejudices of those who dislike the desert, the region is lush with plant life, with over 250 species of wildflowers found in the Mojave Desert

alone. The Sonoran Desert harbors 600 species of plants, and the Chihuahuan has over 100 species of cactus, including the ubiquitous giant agave.

The region is strewn with occasional mountains, which serve as cool green havens for bears, bighorn sheep and bobcats. The surprising variety of this country can be seen in a drive from Phoenix to the Grand Canyon. With the gentle rise in elevation, the mesquite trees, saguaro and cholla cactus give way to forests of short pinon and juniper trees, which in turn give way to ponderosa pine on the Canyon's rim.

The Grand Canyon, a mile deep, from rim to rim ranging from 600 feet to 18 miles wide, and altogether 277 miles long, defines the desert country for most visitors. The water running through the canyon, combined with wind, gravity, and the energy of expansion and contraction caused by fluctuating temperatures, has created the Grand Canyon over millions of years of time. The canyon's north and south rims are a five hour drive away from one another.

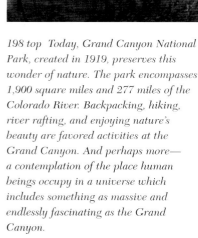

198 top Today, Grand Canyon National Park, created in 1919, preserves this wonder of nature. The park encompasses 1,900 square miles and 277 miles of the Colorado River. Backpacking, hiking, river rafting, and enjoying nature's beauty are favored activities at the Grand Canyon. And perhaps more— a contemplation of the place human beings occupy in a universe which includes something as massive and endlessly fascinating as the Grand Canyon.

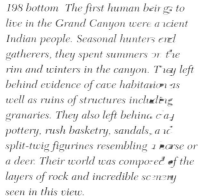

198 bottom The first human beings to live in the Grand Canyon were ancient Indian people. Seasonal hunters and gatherers, they spent summers on the rim and winters in the canyon. They left behind evidence of cave habitation as well as ruins of structures including granaries. They also left behind clay pottery, rush basketry, sandals, and split-twig figurines resembling a horse or a deer. Their world was composed of the layers of rock and incredible scenery seen in this view.

198-199 Storm clouds roll in during a beautiful sunset over the Grand Canyon. Although the view from the rim or from the air is spectacular, nothing compares with walking down into the canyon to try to grasp its vastness and complexity. A hike takes one down through the layers of ancient rock, just as it proceeds down through six of the seven climactic belts recognized around the world. Vegetation varies from that of the Mexican desert on the canyon floor to that of Alpine regions on the North rim.

199 bottom The first European to see the Grand Canyon was Don Lopez de Cardenas, commander of a splinter group sent out from Coronado's expedition in 1540. The canyon was not fully explored until John Wesley Powell and his men ran the rapids in 1869. He returned in 1872 with a larger team to illustrate and photograph the wonders of the canyon. Prospectors were just beginning to cast covetous eyes on the canyon in 1908, when Theodore Roosevelt declared it a National Monument, thus making it off limits to commercial exploitation.

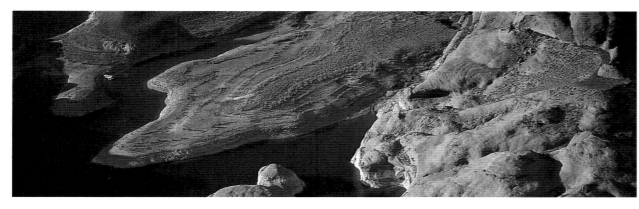

201 center left The desert is home to many animals. Coyotes and foxes, ringtails, deer, rats, mice all conserve energy by holing up during the day. Lizards like the chuckwalla are out in the daytime, as are snakes.

201 bottom left Towering rock formations and soaring red cliffs compose the desert lands surrounding Lake Powell. The rugged area landscape is impressive and memorable, perhaps more so than the man-made lake in its midst. Away from the lake one can find quiet and solitude.

201 top right One of the chief criticisms of the creation of Lake Powell is that even if the canyon was drained, irreparable damage has been done to the resource. One of the often-cited problems is the so-called white "bathtub ring," clearly evident in this photo, caused by the bleaching effect of the water on the red sandstone. Depending on the level of the river, the white band protrudes from the water 6 to 10 feet, while providing evidence of what is happening below the surface.

201 bottom right For all of its vaunted attributes, including the production of hydroelectric power, water storage and flood control, Lake Powell and the Glen Canyon Dam have constituted one of the most controversial projects ever undertaken by the U.S. Government. Many environmentalists criticize not only the innundation of Glen Canyon, but also the altered environment of an artificial lake ecosystem above the dam and the elimination of the annual spring floods below.

200 Lake Powell, formed by the waters of the Colorado River behind the Glen Canyon Dam, winds for 186 miles. The Glen Canyon Dam was built between 1956 and 1964 of five million cubic yards of concrete. Its power plant generates 1.3 million kilowatts.

201 top left Sometimes the sweep of desert rock obscures the thriving plant life that makes its home near Lake Powell. Lichens, cactus and bayonet-tipped yucca grow widely. Wildflowers bloom in the spring and even after a particularly heavy summer rainy season.

The quick route between them is the trail that crosses the Colorado River on a small suspension bridge wide enough to carry a person and a mule—but it is at least 10 arduous miles down and then 15 more back up to go from the south to the north by this route.

The North Rim averages 300 feet higher than the South, and is composed of spruce fir forest. But what most visitors marvel at are the huge twisted shapes of the mesas and mountains within the canyon itself, the breathtaking panorama of something so unimaginably huge that we tiny humans will never obtain a real lock on the enormity of it all.

For in the end, the Grand Canyon is humbling, and perhaps more than any other place on earth illustrates the insignificance of human beings in the midst of God's nature.

Through it all runs the mighty Colorado River. Even with damming, this powerful river can easily carry boulders weighing more than a ton.

And the river points up that enduring paradox that the uninitiated are never ready for—water in the midst of the desert. Of course, with the needs and actions of man there is more—and less—water there now than traditionally.

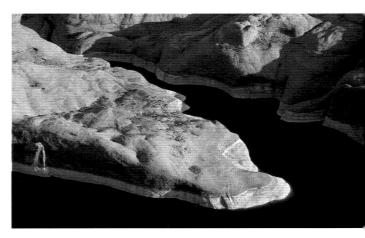

The Glen Canyon Dam was built between 1956 and 1964 of five million cubic yards of concrete. Its power plant generates 1.3 million kilowatts of electricity.

202 top and 202-203 The Lake Powell area was once inhabited by ancient Indian tribes who hunted herds of now-extinct large-horned bison and mammoths. Later, as the climate grew warmer and the terrain more desert-like, Indian people built pueblos, villages of rock-walled homes on the desert floor or in the natural caves in the cliffs. The peak of the "Ancestral Puebloan" culture was between 1050 A.D. and 1250. The Ancestral Pueblo people left the region for unknown reasons in the late 1200s, and other Indian groups such as the Paiute, Ute and Navajo moved in. These tribal groups continue to live in the Colorado Plateau region today.

203 top Lake Powell has become a fisherman's paradise, since it has been stocked with largemouth bass, rainbow trout, walleye pike, striped bass, catfish, crappie and northern pike. Record fish catches in the lake included a 48 pound striped bass, a 24 pound catfish, a 32 pound carp and a 17 pound brown trout.

203 center Boats crowd the docks of Wahweap Marina on Lake Powell. Boating is one of the most popular forms of recreation on the lake, and many different types of boats are available for rent, including speedboats and houseboats. Many families or groups rent a houseboat for a week, motoring about the lake and investigating its side canyons.

Lake Powell, formed by the waters of the Colorado River behind the Glen Canyon Dam, winds for 186 miles.

On a drive northwest toward Las Vegas, you get used to the desert scenery, when suddenly the unfamiliar color of blue is juxtaposed with the pinks, reds and browns of the rock. And then as you drive down a twisting road, you see the unbelievable work of man, the dam, holding back a lake of water. The 726 foot tall Hoover Dam (1935), near Las Vegas, created 110 mile long Lake Mead. In the midst of an unforgiving desert, where summer temperatures average 100 degrees Fahrenheit each day, people now swim, water-ski, boat and fish in a huge recreational area. To the northeast, 710 foot Glen Canyon Dam backs up 180-mile Lake Powell. Both dams provide recreation and hydroelectric power, and both were controversial with environmentalists, especially the Glen Canyon Dam, completed in 1964. Many felt the dam ruined an incredible resource, the Glen Canyon itself, now inundated with water, and authors such as Edward Abbey wrote about removing it with dynamite.

Then there is the story of too little water, the story of the disappearing Colorado. Water rights divided up the river among farmers and municipalities along its length, but today it is a rare season when any water at all reaches Mexico along the Colorado River bed. It is simply all used up within the United States.

North of the deserts lies the basin and plateau region, that is, the Great Basin and the Colorado Plateau. It is a land of over 300,000 square miles, where water is scarce and wind carves rock into unbelievably beautiful forms. The plateau provides visitors with wonderful sights like the sculpted forms of Monument Valley and Arches National Park. In the midst of the plateau lies Zion National Park, entered along Route 1 through Pine Creek Canyon and a mile-long tunnel which suddenly opens up on

203 bottom Like the towers of castles or a strange fantasy world from a science-fiction film, Lake Powell's blue waters surround the red sandstone mesas of the southwestern desert. Filmmakers have been drawn to Lake Powell since the completion of the dam for this reason, and such films as The Greatest Story Ever Told *and* Planet of the Apes *have been shot there.*

the incomparable Zion valley. The original Mormon inhabitants reported that the stunning view looked like Zion itself, the promised land. Many visitors are inclined to agree. Beautiful rock outcrops mesh with the waters leading to the Virgin River. Water seems to drip from everywhere, percolating out of the rock itself and downward to the washes which lead to the river. The spectacular "narrows" is a slot canyon which flanks the Virgin River with sheer walls on each side of its course through the park.

The desert country is too full of delights to recount them all. Apparently, many folks agree, since the states of Nevada and Arizona are the second and third-fastest growing areas of the United States (the first is Alaska). Arizona alone experienced a population increase of 34% between

1980 and 1990.

Although the region is famous for its traditional mining and continues to provide a full half of the nation's annual copper yield, the image of the grizzled prospector with his burro is a historical fantasy. Today the southwestern United States depends far more upon the entertainment and tourist industries, commercial firms and government agencies for its income.

The desert continues to be a subtle land of mystery. Despite the population influx, which has primarily been to urban areas like Phoenix, Tucson and Las Vegas, there are still plenty of wild places in this country. American Indians of many cultures, including Hopi, Zuni, Navajo, Taos, Acoma and Apache people of several bands continue to call the region home. This was the land of the "Anasazi"—

the "ancient ones" in the Navajo language—who built fantastic structures into caverns and on the flatlands between 900 and 1200 A.D. These people were talented architects, traders and jewelers whose descendants, the Hopi and other pueblo tribes, carry on the old traditions. Some of the Anasazi (a term disliked by many modern Pueblo tribes) lived in structures like those at Mesa Verde in Colorado, Montezuma Castle in Arizona and Bandelier in New Mexico. They also built enormous villages like those illustrated by the ruins of Pueblo Bonito in Chaco Canyon, New Mexico, which once housed 1,000 people in four-story tall structures built without mortar on three square acres of land. That a good share of the ancient village is still standing is a testament to the builders.

204 top left Lake Mead is a man-made reservoir created by the 726 foot tall Hoover Dam, which was completed in 1935 after five years of back-breaking work. Like Lake Powell to the northeast of the Grand Canyon, Lake Mead to the west presents a starting contrast to the Mojave Desert which surrounds it. An extreme desert environment, the area supports only plants and animals that have adapted to living under grueling conditions.

Lake Mead is a man-made reservoir created by the 726 foot tall Hoover Dam, which was completed in 1935 after five years of back-breaking work.

204 center left Before the advent of Hoover Dam, few people ever came to the stretch of desert and river which became Lake Mead. American Indian people were later joined by a few adventurous fur trappers and explorers, but it was not until modern times that the lake has drawn thousands of visitors deep into the desert. They come with recreation in mind, but many also leave with a greater appreciation for the challenging but beautiful desert environment.

204 bottom right One hundred ten mile long Lake Mead begins at the western end of the Grand Canyon and ends at Hoover Dam. Boulder Basin is less than 20 miles from Las Vegas, providing an immediate recreation playground for the city.

204-205 Despite the barren appearance of the desert surrounding Lake Mead, the area actually supports a wide variety of wildlife. During daylight hours, desert bighorn sheep often make their way down to the lake for a drink, while aquatic plants and animals revel in the warm water. A profusion of birds, including ducks, cormorants, geese, egrets, herons and pelicans find good fishing on and under the waters of the lake.

205 bottom Callville Bay on Lake Mead provides a ranger station, camping and picnicking facilities, as well as a boat anchorage. The bay is located across Boulder Basin from the Hoover Dam, about seven miles to the south.

206-207 An evening scene along the Las Vegas strip provides an overview of this modern, unusual city located in the middle of the Mojave Desert. A building boom which began in the 1980s has transformed Las Vegas into a hotel-resort complex, complete with attractions to satisfy the family. Each hotel, in the fashion of Walt Disney World, tries to attract patrons of many different age groups. Some of the large hotels visible here include the Bellagio, Treasure Island, Stardust, and Circus Circus.

206 bottom Away from the casinos Las Vegas is a city which caters to a large number of people who want to be married without the usual fuss and bother. Wedding chapels do a thriving business in this city. It is no wonder that a city which somehow evolved in the middle of a desert with little water, food or amenities and which today includes all the modern conveniences, should be remembered as a place where one sees Elvis Presley impersonators and hundreds of wedding chapels.

207 top The glittering lights of Las Vegas recede into the distance behind the Palace Station hotel. The Palace Station, a 5,000 square foot building, was opened in 1976, and served as a model for the "new look" in Las Vegas hotel-casinos.

207 bottom Las Vegas hotels clustered along "the Strip" include the green MGM Grand, the Mandalay Bay, the colored castle towers of Excalibur, the mock-skyscrapers of New York, New York, and the more traditional Flamingo Hilton on the right. Entertainment in the hotels ranges from gambling to concerts. The MGM Grand Adventures provides an amusement park with rides, shops, restaurants and theme streets.

208-209 An example of Las Vegas' "new look," the Wet 'n' Wild Aquatic Park provides every imaginable use of the rare desert commodity, including a pool shaped to look like a roulette wheel. The natural character of the land can be seen at the top left.

The desert has many stories to tell, and Indian people tell many of them through the antics of coyote, the trickster. It is no wonder that Indian tales involve animals, for the fascinating creatures of the region never cease to amaze. For instance, each summer evening at dusk, denizens of the underground world of caves invade the world above: Mexican freetailed bats. Weighing only half an ounce, with a wingspan of 12 inches, millions of the night-feeding bats fly to heights of 10,000 feet and cover thousands of square miles of territory. In just one night a large colony of bats, like those at Bracken Cave or Carlsbad Caverns, can consume up to 250 tons of insects, including mosquitoes and crop pests.

The night is a special time in the desert for both bats and humans. People marvel at the millions of stars they can see at night, and perhaps for the first time understand how the Milky Way got its name. The sky can be seen with such clarity in the midst of the desert because there is no moisture in the air, and in most areas no reflected lights from large cities to obscure the view.

The clear, pleasant nights of the desert are punctuated by the calls of many nocturnal animals. In the distance a coyote calls to us, reminding us of the ancient past and the exciting future of the desert world.

A building boom which began in the 1980s has transformed Las Vegas and the older casinos into a hotel-resort complex, complete with attractions to satisfy the entire family.

210 top A model of the Sphinx crouches in front of the glass pyramid of the Hotel Luxor, an architectural stand-out among the many new theme hotels on the strip. The hotel is actually fronted by a lagoon called Karnak Lake with reeds, palm trees, rock formations and statues of pharaohs. The 2,526 interior guest rooms cling to the sides of the pyramid and are decorated with furniture accented with hieroglyphs. A reproduction of King Tut's Tomb is available as a diversion. Female cocktail servers in the huge casino are decked out with Cleopatra wigs.

210-211 Imitations of some of New York City's most famous buildings and landmarks compose the facade of New York New York, with 2,033 guest rooms and an 84,000 square foot casino. Around the perimeter runs a Corey Island roller coaster, while the restaurants inside imitate all sorts of typical New York ethnic foods. The posh Monte Carlo, to the right, caters to a different clientele with rooms decorated with turn-of-the-20th century décor including Italian marble, and a 102,197 square foot casino.

211 top left Las Vegas' Hotel Excalibur is built to resemble an old English castle. Merlin the Magician battles a dragon every night in a free laser light show beneath the castle's drawbridge. In addition, a medieval shopping village, complete with jugglers, magicians and minstrels is located inside, as is a "dungeon" fun zone for children. The hotel's main show is King Arthur's Tournament, a live jousting tourney which takes place in a 900-seat theater where food is eaten with the fingers.

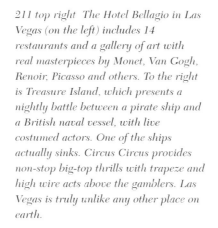

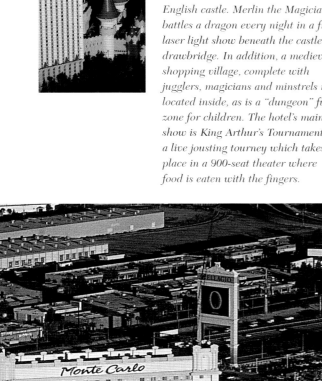

211 top right The Hotel Bellagio in Las Vegas (on the left) includes 14 restaurants and a gallery of art with real masterpieces by Monet, Van Gogh, Renoir, Picasso and others. To the right is Treasure Island, which presents a nightly battle between a pirate ship and a British naval vessel, with live costumed actors. One of the ships actually sinks. Circus Circus provides non-stop big-top thrills with trapeze and high wire acts above the gamblers. Las Vegas is truly unlike any other place on earth.

211 center The buildings of Las Vegas and the distant mountains form a backdrop for the Stratosphere Tower, an observation deck which provides spectacular views of Las Vegas and the surrounding countryside. Within 40 miles of Las Vegas, beautiful mountain ranges and the Toiyabe National Forest supply gorgeous scenery and an environment which looks more like preconceptions of Colorado's Rockies than Nevada's deserts.

211 bottom The success story of Las Vegas continues, despite widespread legalization of gambling in various forms in many regions of the United States. Las Vegas has kept its appeal because it continues to draw big-name entertainers from around the world, and keeps its home-town favorites like Wayne Newton and the magicians Siegfried and Roy in the city. It also has diversified its appeal to families with children with theme hotels and experiences.

Within 40 miles of Las Vegas, beautiful mountain ranges supply gorgeous scenery and an environment that looks more like Colorado's Rockies than Nevada's deserts.

Death Valley lies in a "rainshadow" of the mountains to its West, meaning that the tall ranges absorb the rain-laden clouds before they ever reach the valley.

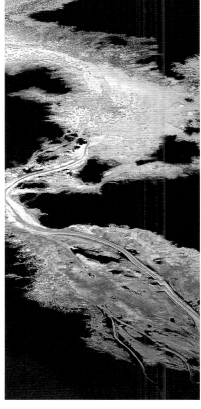

212 center right Death Valley is the lowest elevation in the Western Hemisphere, 282 feet below sea level at Badwater Basin. Summer temperatures average 100 degrees Fahrenheit, and may exceed 120 degrees on many days. Winter temperatures average about 60 degrees. Death Valley contains one of the world's largest salt pans, which includes many types of salts. Groundwater is close to the surface but too salty to drink.

212 bottom Death Valley's Zabriskie Point is part of a complex geological puzzle within the park. The rock layers in the region tell nearly the whole story of earth's history, but that story is out of sequence. Only in recent geological time have the mountains risen, and they have pushed and pulled the layers which exist in the rock. Dry stream beds like this one carry water quickly from the mountains to the valley, causing intense erosion.

213 Alkali salts shimmer in the sun like water in this view of "Devil's Golf Course," Death Valley National Monument located about 140 miles north of Las Vegas. In fact, this is one of the driest places on earth. Death Valley lies in a "rainshadow" of the mountains to its West, meaning that the tall ranges absorb the rain-laden clouds before they ever reach the valley. Death Valley receives an average of but 1.5 inches of rain each year.

212 top left Death Valley looks arid, formidable and boring. Actually it is a fascinating place with unique natural areas, historic sites, and recreation. It received its name from a group of 30 pioneers who in 1849 thought they were taking a shortcut to California. Only 18 survived the trek due to heat and inadequate food and water, thus the motivation for the name. Death Valley ranges from 4 to 16 miles wide and is 140 miles long.

212 top right About 2,000 years ago, Death Valley contained a lake about 30 feet deep. But tall mountain ranges to the west and east of the valley, nearing 11,000 feet in height, cut off the water supply and the lake dried up. The difference between the elevation of the tops of these ranges and the floor of the valley is over two vertical miles.

212 center left American Indians called the area "Tomesha," or "ground afire" because of its extreme summer temperatures. Death Valley offers more than just cracked earth and alkali salt flats, however. Spring and autumn temperatures are quite pleasant, and travelers can see wildflowers, sand dunes, abandoned mines, snow-covered peaks, date palms, oases, and wildlife.

Death Valley is a land of animals that have adapted to the heat and lack of water in the desert.

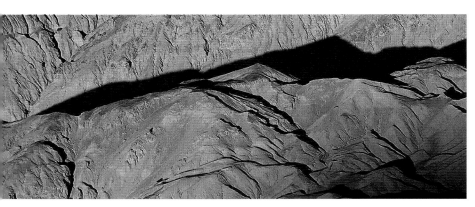

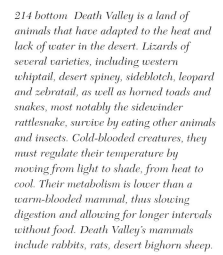

214 top and center Death Valley was proclaimed a National Monument in 1933, and in 1995, with the passage of the Desert Protection Act, it grew by 1,200,000 acres and was designated a National Park. Today the park is composed of 3,336,000 acres, of which 3 million are designated as wilderness. Evidence of human habitation exists in Death Valley in addition to natural beauty. One of the most unique spots in the park is Scotty's Castle, built in the 1920s as a vacation getaway by Midwesterner Albert M. Johnson. Johnson befriended a crusty old prospector named Walter E. Scott, affectionately called "Death Valley Scotty." Scott spent so much time at Johnson's ranch that the two began to tell visitors that Scotty was the owner and Johnson the guest. The name "Scotty's castle" stuck, and the home is today open for tours.

214 bottom Death Valley is a land of animals that have adapted to the heat and lack of water in the desert. Lizards of several varieties, including western whiptail, desert spiney, sideblotch, leopard and zebratail, as well as horned toads and snakes, most notably the sidewinder rattlesnake, survive by eating other animals and insects. Cold-blooded creatures, they must regulate their temperature by moving from light to shade, from heat to cool. Their metabolism is lower than a warm-blooded mammal, thus slowing digestion and allowing for longer intervals without food. Death Valley's mammals include rabbits, rats, desert bighorn sheep.

214-215 A sunset at Artist's Palette in Death Valley reveals the subtle beauties of the desert. Yet plants and animals must adapt to survive in such a harsh environment. Desert plants have small leaves or none at all, because tiny openings on leaves allow water to escape. Cacti have spines instead of leaves, which allow no water loss and protect the plant from animals. The pads and stems of cacti act like mini-reservoirs, with inner tissues consisting of 90% water after an infrequent rainstorm. Plants such as the creosote bush dump unneeded leaves, stems and branches in a drought, and can survive up to four years without water.

215 top An evening view of Artist's Palette gives a more temperate appearance to an area where the relentless, baking sun of summer drives all animal life underground. The highest temperature ever recorded in the United States, 134 degrees Fahrenheit, occurred in Death Valley in 1913. Deposits of gold, silver, copper and borax were found and mined in these hills before the area became a National Park.

Capitol Reef protects a 60 mile long sandstone ridge cut by deep canyons. Petroglyphs and cliff dwellings of Ancient Pueblo people are also found within the park.

216 top The wild terrain near Bryce Canyon, Utah invites adventurous backpackers who wish to experience the pristine air quality, beautiful fir-spruce forests, and gorgeous stargazing opportunities of the area. Ancient puebloan people once inhabited this region, leaving their marks behind in petroglyphs pounded into the rock.

216 bottom The Waterpocket Fold is located in Utah, north of Glen Canyon, in Capitol Reef National Park. Capitol Reef protects a 60 mile long sandstone ridge cut by deep canyons. Petroglyphs and cliff dwellings of ancient puebloan people are also found within the park.

216-217 About 200 million years ago, in the late Triassic Period, the region of Petrified Forest in Arizona was a vast floodplain crossed by streams. Giant creatures and small early dinosaurs inhabited this plain. As the water table rose and the trees died, they were covered by silt, mud and volcanic ash. As they decayed their tissues were replaced by silica deposits, which hardened and created the petrified wood visitors can see today.

217 top The desert country of southern Utah near Bryce Canyon reveals mountains, dry riverbeds and snowy hills. The only certain thing about traveling in the desert is that the visitor will be surprised by the variety, beauty and extraordinary scientific and cultural resources preserved there. Evidence in the rock of the earth's origins and the lives of ancient Indian people has drawn scientists to the American West since the earliest days of the nation.

Monument Valley is a scenic area encompassing about 2,000 square miles in northeastern Arizona and southeastern Utah. Tall red sandstone rock formations rise as high as 1,000 feet from the surrounding plain.

218 top left, bottom, and 218-219 Monument Valley is a scenic area encompassing about 2,000 square miles in northeastern Arizona and southeastern Utah. Tall red sandstone rock formations rise as high as 1,000 feet from the surrounding plain. Many people think the area is a National Park, but it is not. It is owned and maintained by the Cultural Resource Department of the Navajo Nation, and falls within the boundaries of the Navajo Indian Reservation. The Navajo are a very tradition-minded people. Omens and signs, gleaned especially from the natural world around them, dictate what it is possible for an individual to do and what actions might throw the cosmos out of balance.

219 top right Roads and a hogan are dwarfed by soaring pinnacles in Monument Valley. The Navajo reservation covers 15 million acres, and is the second largest in the United States. The Navajo people number some 219,000, and have become prosperous due to oil and minerals which have been found on their lands. The Navajo Nation earns money from leases on oil and gas reserves, mineral resources like coal, and forest lands.

219 bottom left and bottom right Monument Valley's "mitten" buttes form a picturesque foreground for the subtle hues of the desert beyond and the blue sky. Visitors can see the valley from a visitor center and drive a 17 mile tour road into the heart of this natural wonder. All lands off the tour road can be seen only with an Indian guide, which helps control access to sacred sites and private lands.

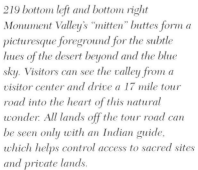

The dramatic scenery of Monument Valley evokes a West that never was. In reality, Monument Valley is a land of traditional Navajo tribal people.

220 top Monument Valley embodies the quintessential view of the American West. It is wild, raw and otherworldly, and the image has been stamped into our minds by Hollywood movies, television programs and commercial advertisements, which use Monument Valley on a regular basis. By the late 20th century, the features of Monument Valley have become icons that stand for the Old West. Well-known films made in Monument Valley include Stagecoach (1939), My Darling Clementine (1946), Fort Apache (1948), She Wore a Yellow Ribbon (1949), The Searchers (1956), and Italian director Sergio Leone's Once Upon a Time in the West (1969).

220 center and bottom The great director of western movies, John Ford, returned to Monument Valley year after year during the golden era of Hollywood. The films he produced, especially those with John Wayne, created the legend of the American West. Many Navajo people portrayed Indian bands in these films, obligingly attacking cavalry troops, stagecoaches or railroad trains for the famous director.

220-221 and 221 top The dramatic scenery of Monument Valley evokes a West that never was. In reality, Monument Valley is a land of traditional Navajo tribal people. It was never the scene of a mining camp, a pitched battle with Indians, or an American fort. It was not an overland trail route, and pioneers in covered wagons did not pass through, nor did any railroad line. Yet for millions of people around the world, Monument Valley means The West.

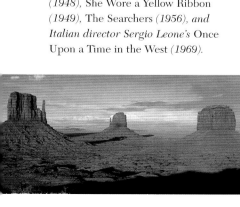

222 In 1923, Bryce Canyon was set aside as a National Monument, and five years later was designated a National Park. It consists of 37,277 acres of scenic, colorful, and unique rock formations called "hoodoos," like the ones in this photo. The rock itself is Claron limestone, sandstone and mudstone, carved from the eastern edge of the Paunsaugunt Plateau in southern Utah.

223 top A spectacular view from the hoodoos of Bryce Canyon toward the plateau's pine forests presents a rainbow of natural colors. Bryce Canyon was named for a Mormon settler named Ebenezer Bryce, who came to the area in 1875 to harvest timber. The canyon behind his home was named "Bryce's Canyon," a name which eventually was applied to the entire locale and later the National Park.

Bryce Canyon was named for a Mormon settler named Ebenezer Bryce, who came to area in 1875 to harvest timber.

223 center Snow-covered hoodoos stand out against the rim of the plateau of Bryce Canyon, which is covered with Ponderosa pines and fir-spruce forests. The hoodoos were created ten million years ago by uplift and fault, when one set of stone blocks was thrust upward and another became the Paunsaugunt Plateau. Ancient rivers sculpted the tops of the upper blocks, and with time tall thin ridges called "fins" emerged. Sculpted by wind and ice, the fins eroded into

the amazing hoodoos. For the native Paiute people, the hoodoos of Bryce Canyon were "legend people" who were turned to stone by coyote, the trickster. Coyote is more than an animal and more than a supernatural being for the people of the desert. He is the mischievous, somewhat evil central character in a series of tales that define life the way it is on earth. Without coyote life might be better, but it certainly would not be as interesting.

223 bottom Bryce Canyon is not really a canyon, but 14 amphitheaters of eroded limestone. This view shows a ridge line at the base of one of the amphitheaters.

224-225 Bryce Canyon on a clear, warm summer day is a perfect locale for a hike to contemplate nature's wonders. The park has many hiking trails which are often silent, as many visitors come to take a quick look and then pass on to better-known wonders at Zion or the Grand Canyon.

The famous Route 66, one of America's earliest highways, was designated in 1926. It ran from Chicago to Los Angeles and passed prominently down Central Avenue in Albuquerque.

226 left Aging commercial airliners are put out to pasture in the desert, where they can be used for spare parts or reconditioned if necessary at some future date.

226-227 All manner and color of hot-air balloons are inflated at the annual Kodak Albuquerque International Balloon Fiesta, held for nine days each year during the first week in October in Albuquerque, New Mexico. The fiesta began in 1972 with 13 balloons, a number which has blossomed to 850 balloons and 1200 pilots since. Special events include a gas balloon race, mass ascensions, and night ascents called "Magic Glows."

226 bottom Balloons soar over Albuquerque during the annual International Balloon Fiesta. Spanish pioneers established a settlement in the area in the 1690s, and in 1706 it was named for a Spanish Viceroy with the power to bestow the official title of villa, or village, upon it. Albuquerque remained a small place until after the Civil War and the advent of the railroad. The famous Route 66, one of America's earliest highways, was designated in 1926. It ran from Chicago to Los Angeles and passed prominently down Albuquerque's Central Avenue.

227 top right The center city of Phoenix, Arizona, another burgeoning desert city in the "Sunbelt." Settled by entrepreneurs who widened an ancient Indian canal in 1865, the town was named for the mythical bird which consumed itself in fire then arose from its own ashes. In 1889 the successful and growing community became the territorial capital, and in 1912 when Arizona became a state, retained its status. With a population topping 1 million in the city and 1.5 million more in its suburbs, Phoenix is quickly becoming the premiere city of the desert and is the ninth largest in the nation.

227 center right Tucson, Arizona is a rapidly-growing desert community of over 440,000 people located south of Phoenix. The town has been a favorite of retirees for many years, with a dry, warm and healthful climate. The region has become known as a convention center, with resorts and many golf courses. Tucson is also home to the fabulous Arizona-Sonora Desert Museum, which interprets desert ecology through a botanical garden and live animals.

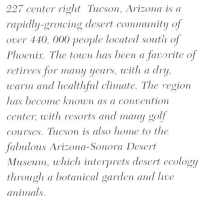

227 bottom left In 1911 Theodore Roosevelt Dam was completed, backing up the Salt River into a reservoir which continues to supply Phoenix and the surrounding area with water. Irrigation allows farming even in the midst of the desert. Crops grown near Phoenix include cotton, alfalfa, durum wheat, vegetables and citrus and other fruits.

228 top The Bartlett Reservoir, north of Scotsdale and Phoenix, Arizona, is created by a dam on the Verde River. Similar reservoirs on the Salt and Fria rivers supply much-needed water for these growing cities.

228-229 Saguaro National Park is located near Tucson, Arizona, and was established in 1933 to preserve the awesome giant cacti of the desert, along with other forms of plants. In the photo, the vast number of these tall monarchs can be observed. In addition, the preservation of this section of Sonoran Desert provides undisturbed habitat for thousands of desert creatures.

Saguaro cacti grow very slowly, but can reach a height of 50 feet and may weigh as much as 10 tons. They can live to be at least 200 years old.

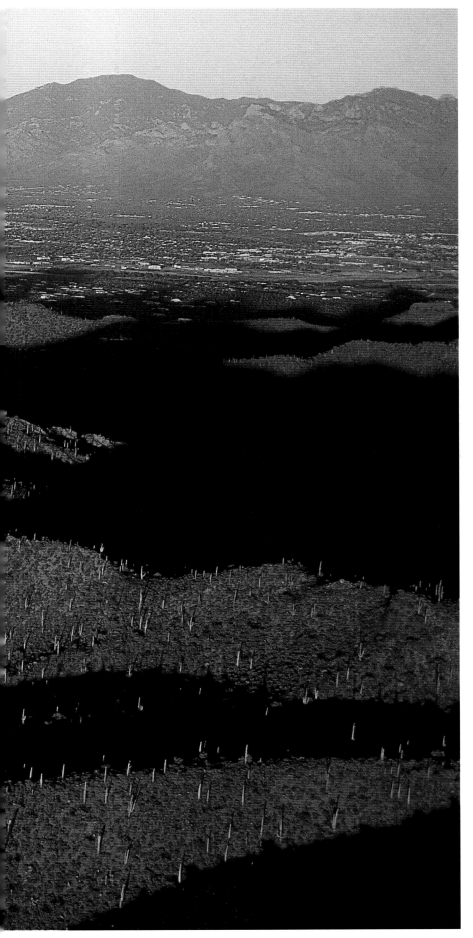

229 top Saguaro National Park preserves desert ecosystems ranging from lowland desert to high mountain. The saguaros grow very slowly, but can reach a height of 50 feet and may weigh as much as 10 tons. They can live to be at least 200 years old.

229 center Shiprock, New Mexico, is located about 20 miles southeast of the "Four Corners," where the four states of Utah, New Mexico, Colorado and Arizona meet.

229 bottom Tucson is seen beyond the hills within Saguaro National Park. The park is divided into two sections, the smaller on the west side of Tucson and the larger on the east. The low elevation of the Sonoran Desert contributes to a wide variety of plant species, including many varieties of cactus: prickly pear, cholla, staghorn, organ pipe and barrel.

230-231 Organ Pipe Cactus National Park, like Saguaro, preserves a portion of the Sonoran Desert which includes three unique desert habitats. The organ pipe cactus is a variety rarely found in the United States. The park comprises an area of 517 square miles and preserves an essential segment of the American desert ecosystem.

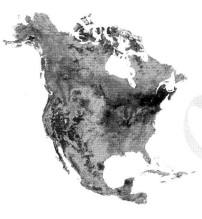

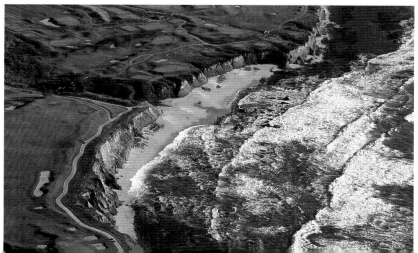

232-233 One of the richest underwater marine habitats in California lies off the Point Lobos State Reserve along the California Coast. In this photo Headland Cove and Sea Lion Point reflect the golden light of a California sunset, while waves crash onto shore. In the ocean waters, amid sea kelp forests which grow to a height of 70 feet, animals such as seal, sea otters and even whales sometimes swim by, while lingcod, cabezone and rockfish are among the permanent residents.

The Pacific Coast

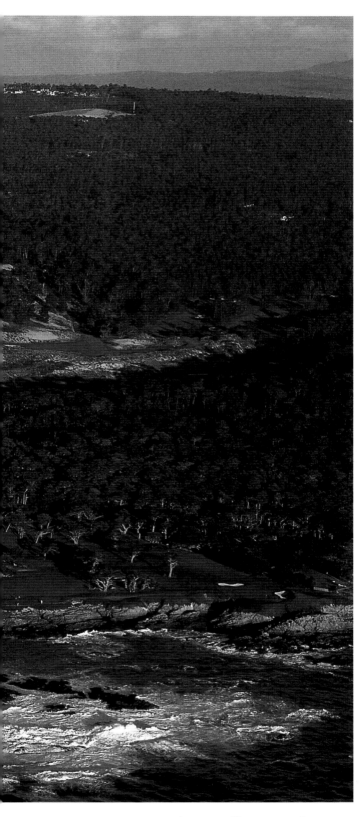

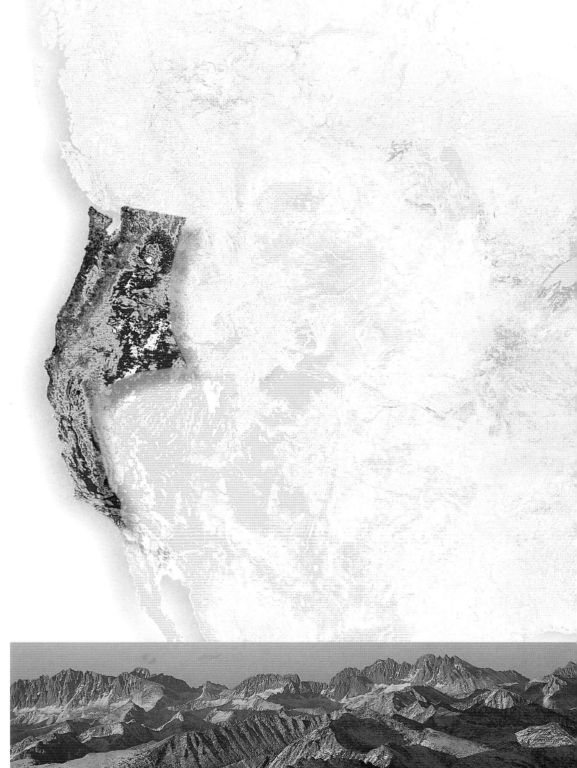

232 bottom Golf Courses on the Monterey Peninsula, north of Carmel, California, are some of the most beautiful in the world. A 17 mile road winds along the Pebble Beach coastline, high above the Pacific Ocean.

233 The Sierra Mountains in California's Sequoia Kings-Canyon National Park are but one attraction of this second-oldest National Park in the nation. The park was established in 1890 to protect the Sequoia trees in Giant Forest which include the General Sherman Tree, the world's largest living thing. Today, the park also includes the south fork of the Kings River, 456,552 acres of backcountry wilderness, Mineral King Valley and Mount Whitney, the highest point in the lower 48 states.

Olympic National Park includes glacier-capped mountains, lakes, a temperate rain forest and an unspoiled coast which includes tide pools teeming with marine life.

The glow of a misty sunset turns the pine boughs a lovely salmon color, while the waves of the Pacific pound the sandy shore below. A cable car is slowly drawn up the side of one of San Francisco's fabled hills, affording fabulous views to all its riders. Inside the chapel of a restored Spanish mission, tourists mix with the local faithful. All marvel at the interior of the structure, decorated 200 years ago by Native American artisans. Through pounding rain and sleet, a fishing boat approaches the entrance to Puget Sound and safe harbor. Off the California coast, sea lions play in the surf near Anacapa Island, while cormorants dive for fish in the deep offshore waters. Near the devastated cone of Mt. St. Helens, visitors come to understand the awesome power of the volcanic explosion which ripped the top off this mountain. Tourists walk in the

234 bottom left The Cascade Mountain Range near Seattle dates to about 2 million years ago, and was caused by the folding and buckling of the earth due to the pressure of tectonic plates.

234 bottom right and 235 Olympic National Park is located on the Olympic Peninsula, across Puget Sound to the west of Seattle, Washington. The park includes glacier-capped mountains like this, along with lakes, valleys, meadows, a rain forest, and an unspoiled coast which includes tide pools teeming with marine life.

236-237 Mount Rainier, a currently-dormant 14,410 foot volcano in the State of Washington, is yet another site protected and managed by the National Park Service. Mount St. Helens, located only 30 miles to the southwest of Mount Rainier, erupted in 1980, proving that these volcanoes may be silent for long periods without being silent forever. The West Coast of the U.S. is younger geologically and located along a fault line, making it far more subject to dramatic volcanic or seismic disturbances than most other parts of the country.

234 top Olympic National Park includes 7,695 foot Mount Olympus and the Olympic Mountains which were created through the clashing of tectonic plates 35 million years ago.

234 center right More than three million people visit Olympic National Park each year. The park was established in 1938.

234 center left As visitors enter the fog-shrouded valleys of Olympic National Park, they may contemplate the park's history. Northwest coast Indian people lived here, including the Skokomish, Quinault, Quileute, Hoh, Makah, Klallam and Chehalis tribes.

The City of Seattle, Washington is nestled in an area of perpetual greenery, surrounded by the blue waters of Puget Sound, bays, lakes, rivers and canals.

238 top Seattle's waterfront was once crowded with prospectors headed to Alaska for the great gold rush of 1898. Today, the city has transformed the waterfront into an international conference center, the home of the Seattle Aquarium, and tour cruises on Puget Sound and up the Canadian Coast.

238 center Seattle's abundance of water makes bridges necessary over the southern tip of Puget Sound and the waters to the east. Ferries still help to carry people and vehicles across the wide expanses of water in the area.

238 bottom Seattle's most famous landmark is the 605 foot tall Space Needle, which includes a revolving restaurant at the top. Built in 1962 for the Century 21 Fair, it was once the tallest building west of the Mississippi River. The structure has already survived 90 mile-per-hour winds and an earthquake measuring 7.3 on the Richter Scale.

courtyard of the Chinese Theater in Los Angeles, trying to fit their shoes into the footprints in the cement left by Marilyn Monroe, Bob Hope, the Marx Brothers and Harrison Ford. From the balcony of the central courtyard of San Diego's Hotel Del Coronado, a full moon rises above the ocean waves on the most romantic of nights for a honeymooning couple.

The Pacific Coast region is comprised of many such scenes, all tied together by the incredible physical beauty of each diverse element. A world of crashing ocean waves, volcanic mountains, deserts, rainforests, and lush man-made agricultural regions, the western United States cannot be pigeon-holed. The character of the coast and all its intricate variations is due to geology—specifically the Farallon tectonic plate, a piece of the earth's crust which continually moves eastward and under the North American plate, creating a deep trench offshore and the coastal ranges of Washington, Oregon and California.

The northern coast is wet—very wet. Much of this coastline receives as much as 10 feet of rain per year. When it is not raining, it is usually foggy, a result of warm land air meeting cool offshore water.

238-239 The City of Seattle, Washington is nestled in an area of perpetual greenery, surrounded by the blue waters of Puget Sound, bays, lakes, rivers and canals. In the distance, Mount Rainier looks down upon the town, nicknamed by residents "the Emerald City." Several international corporations, including Boeing Aerospace, Microsoft Computers, Nordstrom, and Starbucks are based in Seattle.

239 top Seattle, Washington is seen here with gorgeous Mount Rainier in the background. Seattle is a rapidly growing city with over 2.7 million inhabitants. Water tends to divide the city into small, intimate neighborhoods where the scale of a city dissolves into the feel of a small town.

Summer rainfall is often low, yet the condensed moisture of fog keeps the evergreen flora fresh. The moderate temperatures and year-round rainfall create a temperate rainforest which extends from California's Big Sur country on the south to Alaska's Kodiak Island on the north. In this lush region, some evergreens reach six to eight feet in diameter and live from 600 to 800 years. Topping even these statistics, the Redwood forests of northern California sustain trees twenty feet in diameter which live 3,000 years.

One of the best-known and most incredible stories of the northwest involved the salmon. Millions of these fish were spawned in specific natural hatcheries on specific rivers, then swam downstream and out to the ocean to live their adult lives until the urge to spawn made them complete their life cycle. They

found the same path to the same stream where they were hatched and continued their species by spawning and dying there. The cycle continues today, although not to the extent that it once did. The old salmon runs have been depleted, as stocks have dwindled dramatically due to over logging, over development, and the taming of wild rivers by damming.

Behind the shoreline of Washington and Oregon can be seen the lofty, glacier-covered peaks of volcanoes—the Cascades. Mt. Rainier in the state of Washington, 14,410 feet tall, was once more than 16,000 feet tall—but that was 75,000 years ago, before it blew its top for the last time. Magnificent conifer forests surround the slopes of these mountains, which support twenty species of evergreens. This area is the heart of America's timber industry, excellent for growing trees and for replenishing cut stock. Some Douglas firs can grow trunks a yard in diameter in less than 40 years. Unfortunately, the region's virgin forests continue to be cut, despite the widespread area of the trees and the ability of the cut forests to regenerate, primarily due to the wonderful climate. The forests abound with animals, birds and plants, including cougars, bears, elk, deer, otter, eagles and insects— plenty of insects.

San Francisco, founded in 1776 , did not grow until the glut of fortune-seekers during the 1849 gold rush. Today the city of 724,000 is at the center of a metropolitan area of over 6 million.

240 Some of the famous landmarks of San Francisco can be seen in this photo, looking to the southeast. In the foreground is the marina for the Aquatic Park of San Francisco Maritime, which includes the 1886 square-rigged Balclutha and an 1890 paddle-wheel ferryboat, the Eureka. To the left of the pier is the Fisherman's Wharf area. The major street leading toward the Trans America Pyramid Building in the financial district is Columbus Avenue, which runs through North Beach and near Chinatown. To the far left is Telegraph Hill, topped by Coit Tower, and the Oakland-Bay Bridge.

241 top right Telegraph Hill and Coit Tower dominate this view of San Francisco, with Alcatraz Island in the center of the bay. On the far side of the bay is Alameda, and to the left Oakland and Berkeley. To the left of Coit Tower is North Beach, to the right the Embarcadero. In the center foreground is the Jackson Square Historical District.

241 top left A section of Lombard Street in San Francisco, where it descends from Russian Hill, has been labeled "the Crookedest Street in the World." The one-way street—going down—is a favorite of tourists. Beautiful restored Victorian homes line the street, which is maintained with hedges and flowers throughout the year.

241 center left This long-range view of San Francisco from the west highlights the Pacific Coast side of the city. The grid pattern of streets in Outer Richmond, left, and Inner and Outer Sunset, right, contrast with the severe hills of the downtown area. The park at the center left is the Presidio, with the Golden Gate Bridge spanning off to the left. Lincoln Park at the lower left marks the south entrance to the "Golden Gate."

241 center right Colorful row houses dominate sections of San Francisco, which takes pride in its heritage of structures which pre-date the fire of 1906. The city, founded in 1776 , did not grow until the glut of fortune-seekers during the 1849 gold rush. Today the city of 724,000 is at the center of a metropolitan area of over 6 million.

241 bottom left Alcatraz Island was fortified during the American Civil War,

then used as a military prison beginning in 1907. Between 1933 and 1963, a federal security prison was maintained on the island, nicknamed "The Rock." Today it is a historic site.

242-243 Downtown San Francisco and the heart of the Financial District are seen in the middle of this photo, with the Oakland-Bay Bridge in the background. A portion of San Francisco's famous Chinatown can be seen in the lower left corner.

Further south lie the Sierra Nevada Mountains, crowned by three incredible National Parks—Yosemite, Sequoia and King's Canyon. The parks include the 2,425 foot tall Yosemite Falls, third highest waterfall in the world, King's Canyon, at 8,240 feet even deeper than the Grand Canyon of the Colorado, and the Giant Sequoia trees. The Sequoias grow in a narrow band which stretches along 260 miles of the Sierras and is limited by elevation—the trees can only grow between 4,500 and 7,500 feet. Today there are about 13,000 of these trees, growing in 75 groves throughout the mountains. The tallest stands 275 feet tall and is 36 feet wide at the base; it is named for the Civil War general William Tecumseh Sherman, who was not only still living when it was named, but was yet to be born when the tree had already been thriving for over 1,000 years.

Yosemite National Park is an unbelievable world of sheer rock cliffs and running, plunging water. It embraces a vast tract of scenic wildlands, a portion of which was first set aside by Abraham Lincoln in 1864. Due to the agitation of environmentalist John Muir, Yosemite became a national park in 1890 in order to preserve a portion of the Sierra Nevada Mountains. Yosemite features alpine wilderness, three groves of Giant Sequoias, and the incomparable Yosemite Valley.

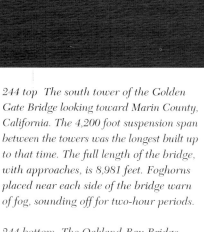

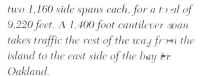

244 top The south tower of the Golden Gate Bridge looking toward Marin County, California. The 4,200 foot suspension span between the towers was the longest built up to that time. The full length of the bridge, with approaches, is 8,981 feet. Foghorns placed near each side of the bridge warn of fog, sounding off for two-hour periods.

244 bottom The Oakland-Bay Bridge carries vehicular traffic across the bay from San Francisco to Oakland. Opened in November 1936, the bridge utilizes four towers and two suspension bridges joined by a center anchorage to carry it to Yerba Buena Island in the center of the bay. The center span of each suspension bridge measures 2,310 feet in length, with

two 1,160 side spans each, for a total of 9,220 feet. A 1,400 foot cantilever span takes traffic the rest of the way from the island to the east side of the bay at Oakland.

244-245 The Golden Gate Bridge crosses the bay entrance to Golden Gate National Recreation Area, in the upper left. The explorer John C. Fremont named the Golden Gate in 1846 after a strait he had seen in Istanbul, Turkey. The bridge was opened in 1937. Consulting architect Irving F. Morrow selected the color to accentuate the area's natural beauty. Called "Golden Gate Bridge International Orange," the distinctive shade is as much a part of San Francisco as the bridge itself.

The explorer John C. Fremont named San Francisco's Golden Gate in 1846 after a strait he had seen in Istanbul, Turkey.

245 center left The City of San Francisco, seen from the tower of the Golden Gate Bridge, looks deceptively concentrated and flat. It is actually a very large city spread over incredibly steep hills. The ingenious cable cars, introduced in 1873, solved the problems of getting up such inclines by running steam-powered cables under the streets like the pulley lines used to dry laundry. A gripper device on the car itself could hitch a ride on the continuously-moving cable merely by gripping it and letting go when it wanted to change direction or come to a stop. The same system is still in use on several San Francisco car lines today.

245 bottom left Sailboats on the San Francisco Bay are a common sight year-round. The people of the San Francisco area love recreation and have many opportunities and locales close at hand. In addition to the bay and the ocean, several recreational parks and natural areas exist just across the Golden Gate Bridge in Marin County, including Point Reyes National Seashore and Muir Woods National Monument.

245 top right The Golden Gate Bridge's stylish Art Deco design was formulated by consulting architect Irving F. Morrow.

245 bottom right The Oakland-Bay Bridge has two levels, each supporting one way traffic across the bay.

245

Vineyards north of San Francisco in Sonoma and Napa Counties produce some of America's finest wines.

Geologically, the Yosemite story began 500 million years ago with the thick layers of sediment beneath an ancient sea. The sediment was folded, twisted, and eventually thrust above sea level. At the same time, molten rock bubbled up from below the Earth's crust and cooled slowly beneath the sediment to form granite. Millions of years of erosion wore the sedimentary layers away, leaving a solid spine of granite, the Sierra Nevada, to be weathered by glaciers and water. Today, the Yosemite Valley is a seven mile long, one mile wide grassy meadow flanked by sheer granite walls, including the 7,500

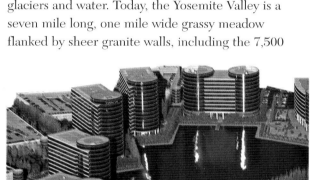

foot El Capitan and the 8,800 foot tall Half Dome, both immortalized by the photographs of Ansel Adams.

Traveling from the mountains to the coast, the visitor gets some idea of the vastness of California, its cultural and natural diversity. Each of the California coastal cities has a style—and a charm—all its own. San Francisco, Monterey, San Luis Obispo, Santa Barbara, Los Angeles, and San Diego vary in size and appeal. Like the east coast of the United States, the west coast has become a popular place to live for large numbers of people. Unlike the east coast, however, a drive down California's Route 1 along the Pacific Ocean reveals little waterfront development and affords spectacular views without leaving the roadway.

One of the most fascinating stops along this route is Monterey. Founded as a mission site in 1770, Monterey served as the capital of Spanish/Mexican California from 1775 to 1846. The town is prized for its original adobe architecture, cypress trees and sand dunes. Cannery Row, formerly a pungent sardine processing area made famous by novelist John Steinbeck, is now a shopping mall and home to the world-famous Monterey Bay Aquarium. The bay itself is one of the deepest marine areas immediately near a shoreline anywhere in the world, thus affording a relatively easy and sustained study of deep water ocean life. The town is inhabited by artists, writers, actors and other creative people who make its lifestyle unique.

California was once the home of numerous American Indian tribes, groups of people who could live off the abundance of the land. When the Spanish

246 top left A close-up view of Fisherman's Wharf in Monterey, California. The Spanish first settled Monterey in 1770. Once a whaling and fishing center, the town includes several historic buildings.

246 bottom left Vineyards north of San Francisco in Sonoma and Napa Counties produce some of America's finest wines. The region caters to tourists through tours and samples of wines at nearly every winery, plus hotel accommodations coupled with fine restaurants.

246 right The headquarters of the Oracle Corporation, the world's second largest software company, is located in Redwood Shores, Santa Clara County, California. The company is situated in the area known as "Silicon Valley." The valley's nickname comes from the semiconductor, with its silicon chip "brain," and was coined by electronics writer Don Hoeffler in 1972.

246-247 The Monterey Marina and Fisherman's Wharf in the city of Monterey, California. The wharf includes fishmonger's stands and whale watching boats. Nearby is the Monterey Aquarium, with a million-gallon indoor ocean, a three story kelp forest, and about 100 galleries on marine wildlife.

247 bottom left The burgeoning computer industry of Santa Clara County's "Silicon Valley" has supplanted the former cash crops of fruit. The spirit of invention in technology was fostered at Stanford University in the early 1900s with the financial assistance given to Lee DeForest, inventor of the vacuum and audion tubes.

247 bottom right The Silicon Valley's roots go back to the 1950s, when major companies like GE, Sylvania, Westinghouse, IBM and Ford Philco established facilities in Palo Alto, Mountain View and San Jose. In 1958, under the direction of Robert Noyce, the first integrated circuit was produced at Fairchild Semiconductor. Ten years later, Noyce formed a company called Intel, and manufactured the first integrated semiconductor chips. Since that time, each year has brought increases to random access chip memory, spurring the computer revolution and the further growth of Silicon Valley's industry.

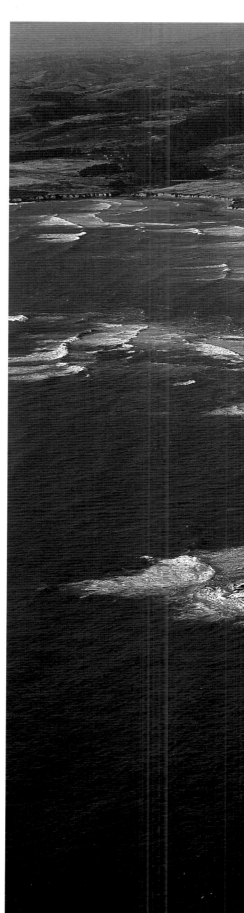

arrived to set up missions in 1769, they were baffled by the Indians' self sufficiency, and did not have the ability to use the region's resources as the Indians did. The Spanish were determined to convert the Indians to Christianity and to use them as "substitute citizens" in a land they could not entice Spaniards to settle. European diseases killed many of the Indians, and Christianity factionalized the tribes. In 1846, after years of trade with the relatively isolated Spanish/Mexican missions, the United States was able to easily conquer the sparsely-settled region and take it away from Mexico. Today, the legacy of the region's early history is chronicled in the chain of 21 missions which were established in California, from San Diego to Sonoma, between 1769 and 1821. Most of the missions are exquisitely preserved, with museums and displays which tell the early history of the state. A journey along the Mission Trail passes through some of the most picturesque regions of the state, educating the traveler about the cultural and natural history of the region.

Since 1846 times in California have changed. The gold rush of 1849 lured hundreds of thousands of Americans to the region, which became a state in 1850.

248 top A private home on Cypress Point, near the Cypress Point Golf Course on the Monterey Peninsula north of Carmel. The renowned golf course is one of 19 on the Monterey Peninsula.

248 center The Seventeen Mile Drive along the Pacific Coast between Monterey and Carmel is one of the most beautiful roads anywhere. Skirting the edges of several well-known golf courses, the drive is bordered on the west by the private homes of local residents.

248 bottom South of Carmel is a beautiful stretch of Route 1, the Pacific Coast Highway, which has become popularly known as the "Big Sur Country." There are few towns along the highway, only scenic views and twisting, winding roads that follow the contours of the coast and canyons which carry rivers and creeks from the interior to the ocean. This beautiful lighthouse complex is placed on a typical point of land along the route.

248-249 *Point Lobos State Reserve south of Carmel on the California coast has been called the "greatest meeting of land and sea on earth." The area is rich in natural beauty and abundance of animal and marine life. Sea lions, harbor seals, elephant seals, sea otters, and whales and dolphins are seen in the waters near the reserve. The area is a designated California Sea Otter Game Refuge.*

249 top *Private residences are seen on Cypress Point, backed by the Del Monte Forest, on the Monterey Peninsula north of Carmel. This is part of the route skirted by the Seventeen Mile Drive.*

The telegraph, shipping lines and railroads linked the state to the rest of the nation prior to the settlement of the Great Plains and the Rocky Mountains. Just before World War I, filmmakers from New York traveled to the small city of Los Angeles in search of strong sunlight and good year-round weather for their movie-making. Los Angeles soon became a boom town, and the former orange groves of Century City, Hollywood and Anaheim became film studios and entertainment centers. Migrations in the 1930s and 1940s to the factories established for the war effort swelled California's population, and the tide of emigration from other regions and nations has yet to recede.

The West Coast of the United States is substantially different from the East, not only geologically and in terms of its history but in the cultural differences of its citizens. The lifestyles are vastly different, even though they all occur within areas of the same country. It is these differences, of course, which make the United States such a fascinating place to visit or in which to reside. The nation's strength and charm lies in its diversity.

250 Some private homes, like these, have been built along the coast in the Big Sur Country, but for the most part the area is delightfully undeveloped, unlike major portions of the U.S. Atlantic Coast. The drive along the coast is spectacular, with a seemingly endless abundance of new vistas with every turn. One of the few towns along the route is Big Sur, from which the name for the region is derived.

251 top and bottom Waves crash onto the shore below the Pacific Coast Highway in the Big Sur region. Point after point of rocky land can be seen as one looks up and down the coast, each adding further dimension and beauty to the scene.

251 center The Pacific Coast Highway in the Big Sur region, close to Morro Bay, has many turn-outs for cars to pull over and admire the scenery.

252-253 Yosemite National Park, in the Sierra Nevada Mountain range in eastern California, includes the glacially-carved Yosemite Valley.

The West Coast of the United States is substantially different from the East, not only geologically and in terms of its history, but in the cultural differences of its citizens.

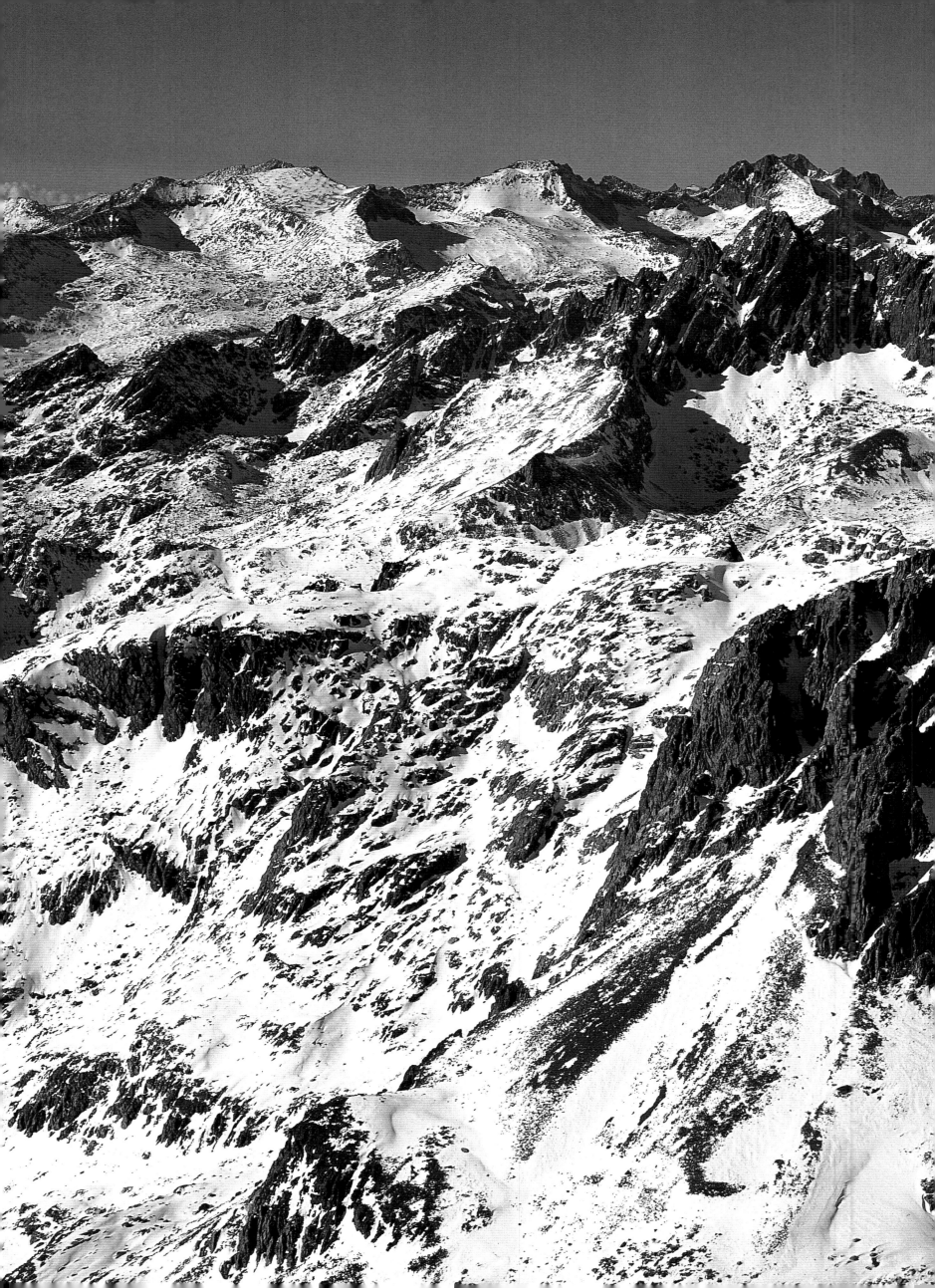

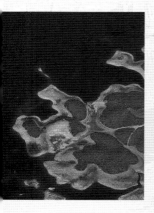

Sequoia Kings-Canyon National Park includes Mount Whitney on its eastern border. At 14,494 feet, Mount Whitney is the tallest peak in California.

254 top left Cherry Lake is a reservoir created by damming the Cherry River in Stanislaus National Forest, just to the west of Yosemite National Park. It is one of many reservoirs created to provide fresh water for San Francisco only 209 miles away.

254-255 This panoramic shot of Sequoia-Kings Canyon National Park includes hot springs and a glacial lake, at the center. The rugged Sierras present a challenge to hikers even in the summer months. Consequently, the winters in this backcountry wilderness truly belong to the creatures of the forest.

254 bottom Looking down the valleys of Sequoia Kings-Canyon National Park, one feels the insignificance of human beings and the incredible nature of the earth and the mighty forces that shaped it.

255 top right Mono Lake, a California State Park located to the east of Yosemite, is surrounded by mountains of the Sierra chain. The water is salty and alkaline. Towers of calcium carbonate along the shoreline of the lake are called tufas. The lake is an active site for wildlife and many bird species.

255 center right Sequoia Kings-Canyon National Park receives about 1.5 million visitors each year, who want to see the gorgeous scenery, climb mountains, or "get away from it all" into the backcountry. The park includes Mount Whitney on its eastern border, at 14,494 feet the tallest peak in California.

255 bottom left Hot springs on the valley floor at the base of the Sierras in Sequoia-Kings Canyon National Park cause snowmelt which runs into a glacial lake. The winter months in the park are explored by the hardy few, who are rewarded by their solitary encounters with pristine wilderness.

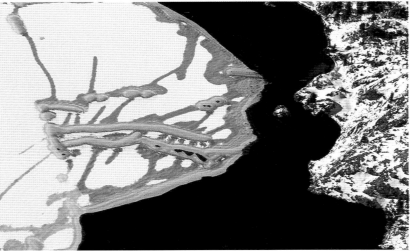

The highest canyon wall in the United States rises from the south fork of the Kings River a sheer 8,350 feet, over 1 1/2 miles.

256 In addition to mountain fastnesses, Sequoia Kings-Canyon National Park, which encompasses an area of 628.9 square miles, has many other attractions. They include the General Sherman tree, the world's largest living thing, which stands 275 feet tall and has a diameter of 36.5 feet. Kern River Canyon and Crystal Cave, a marble cavern, are also of note. The highest canyon wall in the United States rises from the south fork of the Kings River a sheer 8,350 feet, over one and a half miles.

257 Sun and water vapor create the illusion of a fire on the mountains of Sequoia Kings-Canyon National Park. Park managers conduct prescribed burns in the park in the proper seasons to clear deadfall and prevent devastating forest fires.

258-259 Moonrise over 13,114 foot tall Mount Lyell, located on the east side of Yosemite National Park near the border with Inyo National Forest. The mountain is located in one of many nearly inaccessible areas of the park, away from all roads and trails. The Pacific Crest Trail passes within about two miles of the peak.

Yosemite National Park harbors an amazing ecosystem with some 1,300 types of flowering plants, 31 species of trees, 220 species of birds and 60 mammal species.

260-261 Yosemite National Park's Halfdome, one of the most photographed landmarks in the world, is a gigantic boulder of granite located in the Yosemite Valley. The park harbors an amazing ecosystem with some 1,300 types of flowering plants, 31 species of trees, 220 species of birds and 60 mammal species, including deer and black bear.

260 bottom Few visitors see the seemingly endless mountain peaks within Yosemite National Park. Most tourists spend their time in the Yosemite Valley, a very small portion of this gigantic park.

261 top left Yosemite National Park's El Capitan and its sheer walls provide an almost irresistible challenge to rock climbers. And it is a rock—a solid boulder of granite rising 3,604 feet from the floor of the Yosemite Valley. Formed by the Merced River, the valley is seven miles long and a mile wide, with every foot providing a new and fascinating experience.

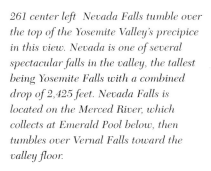

261 center left Nevada Falls tumble over the top of the Yosemite Valley's precipice in this view. Nevada is one of several spectacular falls in the valley, the tallest being Yosemite Falls with a combined drop of 2,425 feet. Nevada Falls is located on the Merced River, which collects at Emerald Pool below, then tumbles over Vernal Falls toward the valley floor.

261 bottom left Backcountry trails and wilderness campsites allow access to views like these in Yosemite National Park, but only with the sweat and determination of hikers who revel in the outdoors and the hardship of such treks. The park includes 750 miles of trails. Cross-country skiing and snowshoeing have become popular as winter backcountry use increases.

261 right The Merced River spills over Vernal Falls, seen at the lower right, and flows down the Yosemite Valley. The dramatic impact of this park and the effect it has had on countless numbers of visitors in encouraging an appreciation for wilderness is staggering. Whether a visitor learns simple nature facts or takes an extended backcountry hike at primitive campsites, Yosemite helps to provide instruction to all, including urban-dwellers and savvy backcountry experts.

The Channel Islands comprise an island chain lying off the west coast of California in the Pacific Ocean.

262 top Santa Cruz Island is about 24 miles long and comprises 96 square miles. The highest of the Channel Islands' mountains is found on Santa Cruz, standing 2,470 feet. Several areas on the island provide important habitat for nesting sea birds, plants and animals. More than 600 plant species and 140 land bird species live here. The cliffs along the shoreline, offshore rocks and tidepools all provide breeding habitat.

262 center The topography of Santa Cruz Island is rough. To the uninitiated it looks barren, yet it supports some 85 species of plants, nine unique to Santa Cruz. Biologists enjoy studying the ecosystem of the islands, where many plant and animal species have adapted to the special conditions and differ from similar species on the mainland.

262 bottom Santa Cruz Island is a place of great scenic beauty, with two rugged mountain ranges, deep canyons, a wide central valley, year-round water supply in springs and streams, sea cliffs extending for 77 miles, huge sea caverns, tidepools and beaches.

262-263 The Channel Islands comprise an island chain lying off the west coast of California in the Pacific Ocean. Five of the eight islands are parts of Channel Islands National Park. Anacapa Island lies 11 miles off the coast from Oxnard. It is composed of three islands, seen in this view, about five miles in length comprising 699 acres. National Park Service buildings and a light house can be seen on the closest island. In the distance to the north is Santa Cruz Island, at 60,645 acres the largest in the group.

263 top Chumash Indians were the original inhabitants of Santa Cruz Island, dwelling there for more than 6,000 years. As many as 2,000 probably inhabited the island in 1542 when the explorer Juan Rodriguez Cabrillo made the first European contact with the region. Ranching was carried on at Santa Cruz from 1839 to the early 1980s. Today, the Nature Conservancy owns 90% of the island, while the eastern 10% is part of Channel Islands National Park.

Santa Monica is located near Beverly Hills and features a revitalized downtown and shopping district. Its beach is a favorite place for Los Angelenos.

264 Part of the beach at Santa Monica and the Santa Monica Pier can be seen in this photo. Santa Monica is a city located just north and west of Los Angeles along the Pacific Coast.

265 top left Malibu, California, and the Malibu Colony, is a private community favored by show business celebrities. Beachfront houses give the residents of Malibu a connection with the Pacific. Malibu is located to the west of Santa Monica.

265 top right Located 92 miles northwest of Los Angeles, Santa Barbara is a sunny city with little of the rush and hassle of L.A. In this view the beachfront area of the resort town can be seen, with Route 101 making a sweeping arc to the right and out of the photo at the right center. The Spanish presidio is located in the green area at the upper right, with the mission church beyond a few more blocks to the north.

265 center right Santa Monica and the full length of the pier can be seen in this photo. A community of about 90,000 people, Santa Monica is located near Beverly Hills and features a revitalized downtown and shopping district.

265 center left Santa Monica Beach on a crowded summer weekend. Just 5 miles from Beverly Hills, Culver City, The University of California at Los Angeles (UCLA) and 10 miles from Los Angeles International Airport, Santa Monica is a central location in the western Los Angeles area.

265 bottom Marina Del Rey is the next community down the coast from Santa Monica, with Venice Beach in between. The extensive marina attends to the needs of many of the sea-loving residents of Los Angeles. Marina Del Rey is one of the few protected harbors along the coast.

266 top The Hollywood Bowl is set in a natural amphitheater in the Hollywood Hills. Seating just under 18,000 people, it opened in 1922 as the scene of concerts under the stars by the Los Angeles Philharmonic Orchestra. The orchestra continues to play there today, and the Bowl is the scene of jazz, pop and mariachi concerts as well.

266-267 This view of downtown Los Angeles shows the newer skyscrapers near Pershing Square on the left and the City Hall building, at the lower right center. Behind the City Hall complex at the middle right is the L.A. Music Center. At the lower left is the "Little Tokyo" neighborhood. In the distance on the horizon are the Santa Monica Mountains.

266 bottom Hotels and high-rises line a major thoroughfare running through West Hollywood, California.

267 top right One of many homes in the Beverly Hills-Hollywood Hills area of Los Angeles, this nicely-landscaped property includes a tennis court and palm trees.

The community of Beverly Hills was laid out in 1906 and incorporated in 1914. The very name of the town has become a synonym for large mansions and extravagant lifestyles.

267 center right Universal Studios in Hollywood opened part of their backlot for tours after the demand for location filming grew in the 1970s, 80s and 90s. The old studios, where weather, lighting, sets and costumes could be controlled and crowds were nonexistent are today used for television production and some interiors for feature films. Some of the studio lots, so important in the "Golden Age of Hollywood" have become tourist attractions similar to Disneyland and Disney World.

267 bottom right In the heart of one of the best-known celebrity addresses in the world, the Beverly Hills Hotel, built in 1912 and renovated in 1995, is available for guests. The community of Beverly Hills was laid out in 1906 and incorporated in 1914. The very name of the town has become a synonym for large mansions and extravagant lifestyles.

267 bottom left Many entertainment personalities have homes in the Hollywood Hills above Los Angeles. In this view, the winding canyons and steep roads of the area can be seen clearly.

268 top right A beautiful view of the Pacific oceanfront near Malibu, with the Santa Monica Mountains in the background. The National Park Service maintains a National Recreation Area in the mountains, preserving the ecosystem of this portion of the built-up Los Angeles area.

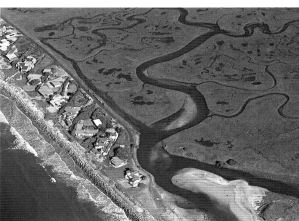

268 center left Homes and apartments along the oceanfront at Long Point, Rancho Palos Verdes, are located just south of Los Angeles. Palos Verdes is nestled between Redondo Beach and San Pedro, and is located on a natural peninsula of land which helps to enclose San Pedro Bay to the east.

268 bottom left Marshy land behind a land spit near the Los Angeles oceanfront backs a row of expensive homes.

268-269 Point Dume west of Los Angeles is close to a state beach which features headlands, cliffs, secluded coves and tidepools. Westward Beach is a sandy stretch of shore popular for surfing, swimming and scuba diving.

269 top. The oceanfront near Malibu along the Pacific Coast Highway was subject to mudslides in the late 1990s, when heavy rains broke a long spell of drought in southern California. Evidence of a mudslide can be seen at left center.

269 bottom The Point Vincente Lighthouse is located adjacent to Rancho Palos Verdes and not far from the Cabrillo Marine Museum. The lighthouse was completed in 1926, and has been automated since 1973. The light, augmented by a Fresnel lens built in Paris, France in 1886, can be seen for 20 miles out to sea. The still-operating lighthouse points up the continued need for such installations along the coasts, even in an era of radar and sophisticated communications.

Point Dume west of Los Angeles features headlands, cliffs, secluded coves and tide pools.

San Diego became the second largest city in California when it grew by nearly 200,000 people during the 1980s. Today it is home to over 1,110,000 people.

270 The graceful sweep of the San Diego-Coronado Bay Bridge at San Diego takes vehicles between the City of San Diego and Coronado, on a peninsula which protects the San Diego Bay. Coronado is the home of the U.S. Navy's Naval Air Station on North Island. There are also public beaches on the peninsula, including Coronado and Silver Strand State Beach.

271 top left Many modern buildings grace San Diego, one of the fastest growing cities in the U.S. The pleasant weather of the region, one of only five places on earth with a true Mediterranean climate, draws new residents, retirees and casual visitors alike. San Diego became the second largest city in California when it grew by nearly 200,000 people during the decade of the 1980s. The photo shows the Convention Center.

271 top right A building boom took place in downtown San Diego during the 1980s, but military spending reductions in the 1990s slowed the pace. Here, modern structures stand alongside the turn-of-the-century U.S. Grant Hotel, bottom left. San Diego boasts attractions as Sea World, Old Town San Diego, the Gaslamp Quarter and proximity to Mexico.

271 bottom right The U.S. Naval Station at San Diego is seen with several ships docked for repairs, including one in a floating drydock. The U.S. Navy has been a presence in San Diego since the time of the Mexican War in the 1840s, and the port has remained a proud home station for the U.S. Pacific Fleet. The military provides a major source of income for San Diego and the immediate area.

271 center left Downtown San Diego is seen in this view not far from the city's waterfront on the bay. At the far left center is the Santa Fe Railroad Station. Horton Plaza Shopping Mall is at the right center. The indentation of green at the top center is Balboa Park.

271 bottom left Horton Plaza, a shopping mall in the heart of downtown San Diego, is a marvelously appealing conglomeration of architectural styles. Unlike most malls, most of the central court area is open to the sky, providing a light, airy feel.

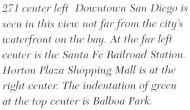

San Diego is a popular location for yacht racing. The Pacific coast off La Jolla draws many visitors who watch sea birds and the ocean waves.

272 top San Diego is a popular location for yacht racing, as in this photo of the Kenwood Cup race in 1996. San Diego is also the site of recent America's Cup races. Recreational opportunities also include surfing, swimming and deep-sea fishing.

272 center The romantic cliffs near La Jolla along the Pacific Coast are located just north of San Diego. The San Diego region offers many institutions of higher learning, including San Diego State University (1897). The University of California, San Diego is located in La Jolla, and affiliated with the Scripps Institution of Oceanography (1903). The Jonas Salk Institute for Biological Studies, with buildings designed by Louis Kahn in 1959, is also located in La Jolla.

272 bottom The Pacific coast off La Jolla draws many visitors who watch sea birds and the ocean waves. La Jolla means "the Jewel" in Spanish, and the community offers beaches, cultural activities and restaurants.

272-273 The massive sweep of the San Diego-Coronado Bay Bridge terminates near the fabulous Hotel Del Coronado. Built on the Pacific Ocean in 1888, the hotel has housed many famous guests over the years. It was one of the first hotels in the world to be wired for electricity, a process personally supervised by Thomas A. Edison. The famous hotel was a major location for the 1959 film Some Like It Hot with Marilyn Monroe, Jack Lemmon and Tony Curtis.

273 bottom left The U.S. Coast Guard's Point Loma lighthouse stands below Cabrillo National Monument on the Pacific side of San Diego Bay. An older lighthouse high above on the bluffs was closed in 1891 and is now a historic site. Tidepools near Point Loma are a major attraction of Cabrillo National Monument, where all manner of sea creatures can be observed at low tide, a fitting way to wind up a visit to the Pacific Coast.

273 bottom right The community of La Jolla, located just north of San Diego, joins a southern European resort atmosphere with southern California tastes. The affluent community is a pleasant place to go shopping and antiquing.

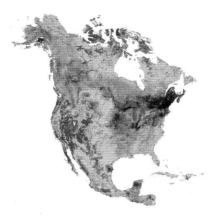

A "FINAL FRONTIER" OF PRISTINE BEAUTY:

274-275 The Harding Icefield in the Kenai Mountains of Alaska covers 300 square miles and encompasses 34 major glaciers. Only isolated mountain peaks interrupt its nearly flat, snow-clad surface, which rises a mile above the surrounding coastline.

Alaska

274 bottom The rugged Alaska Range, near Mount McKinley, continually challenges mountain climbers. The mountains stretch for 600 miles from the Aleutian Range in south central Alaska to the Yukon boundary in southern Alaska. The range separates the interior tundra prairie from the Pacific coastal region. In the center of the range is Mount McKinley, the highest point in North America.

275 A beautiful summer scene of the Alaska Range, near Denali National Park. The region comprises a habitat for caribou, wolves, Dall sheep, moose and grizzly bears, as well as diminutive tundra plants and fir trees.

Sixty percent of all land managed by the National Park Service is in Alaska—54 million acres—most as a result of the Alaska National Interest Land Conservation Act of 1980.

276-277 A misty autumn day in the Kenai Mountains, south of Anchorage, Alaska. Fjords punctuate this beautiful region—long, narrow fingers of ocean water which penetrate the interior below the plateau. Kenai Fjords National Park is a 650,000 acre area on the Pacific Coast, which includes the offshore Alaska Maritime National Wildlife Refuge.

A moose wades through the shallow water near the shoreline of Wonder Lake, while the magnificent white mountains of Denali rise precipitously in the background. The colors of the aurora borealis light up the evening sky, silhouetting the evergreen trees outside Nome. Huge Kodiak brown bears, 10 feet tall and weighing 1,700 pounds each, fish in a waterfall along the waters of the Yukon River. A colorful totem pole rises above a Tlingit Indian village, each of its symbols representing a family. A fishing boat's crew hauls in a net full of salmon on a dark spring day. The green onion-shaped dome of a Russian Orthodox church rises above the city of Sitka, pointing to the rich cultural past of this vast land.

A land of mystery and excitement, a "final frontier," Alaska continues to beckon to those who wish to exploit her resources, those who prefer solitude, and to those who truly love the natural world. The Aleuts called it Alysehka—the Great Land. Fully one-fifth the size of the entire lower 48 states, Alaska contains a vast, nearly unexplored wilderness, containing hundreds of species of animals and birds. The fourteen tallest mountains in the United States are in Alaska, as are three million lakes and 51,000 square miles of glaciers. Alaska's Yukon River is one of the longest on the continent, and flows from east to west, emptying into the Bering Sea. Although Alaska is the largest state, it has the smallest population of any at about 600,000. Less than 10% of the state is even inhabited by human beings, although it is the fastest-growing of all. Sixty percent of all land managed by the National Park Service is in Alaska—54 million acres—most as a result of the Alaska National Interest Land Conservation Act signed by President Jimmy Carter in 1980.

The entire southern coastal area of Alaska belongs to the Pacific Mountain system. The area is geologically unstable, with volcanic and seismic activity quite common. The state has two "tails," island chains that extend from the southwestern corner (the Aleutians) and the coastal islands to the southeast (the Alexander Archipelago) which run along the Pacific Coast of British Columbia and the Yukon Territory in Canada.

276 bottom The Yukon River flows past the Southern Brooks Range in this view. The mighty, 1,979 mile-long river drains an area of 329,730 square miles. The region is inhabited by a few thousand Inuit people, who continue to make a living by hunting and trapping.

277 top A coastal area of Glacier Bay National Park and Preserve is seen in this view. The park is a land of intense beauty which includes glaciers, floating icebergs, over 100 miles of coastline and 15,320 foot Mount Fairweather. Bears, river otters and mink, mountain goats and hoary marmots live in areas where glaciers have retreated, while in the offshore waters whales, Dall porpoises, and harbor porpoises thrive.

277 center Streams wander across the face of the land near Fairbanks, a city founded in 1903 as a trading post for the distant gold fields. Today, Fairbanks has a population of over 31,000 people.

277 bottom The Chulitna River flows out of Denali National Park, winding its way toward the Yukon and the Bering Sea to the west. The rivers in this region are young and laden with pulverized rock, called rock flour. They meander across broad, flat valleys and carve new channels in a matter of days.

Denali National Park and Preserve covers six million acres. The park was originally established as Mount McKinley National Park in 1917.

At the northern limit of the Alexander Islands and their junction with the main body of the state is the St. Elias Range, with some of the highest mountains on the continent, mostly snow-covered, as well as the Malaspina Glacier, the largest in the state. Moving northwest, the Wrangell Mountains include the 14,006 foot Mt. Wrangell, the largest active volcano in Alaska. Further to the northwest is Mount McKinley, the continent's tallest peak and part of the arc-shaped Alaska Range. In the northern part of the state is the Brooks Range, composed of mountain tundra and alpine vegetation. The Brooks Range extends northward to the North Slope, composed of treeless arctic tundra, which gradually descends in elevation to the Beaufort Sea.

The arctic region contains huge mountain ranges and flatlands stretching as far as the eye can see.

There are prolonged periods of total darkness in this area during the winter months, and the sun does not set during the summer. Rainfall may not be great, but permanent swamps are created because water cannot drain through the permafrost below the surface. Plants must be able to withstand prolonged low temperatures, then flourish and reproduce during the brief summer season. Regional plants are frost-resistant and low-growing, so that they can be sheltered from the wind by the winter snows. A small number of mammal and bird species have adapted to survival in the arctic region, using layers of fat and fur to insulate themselves from the cold. Very large species of mammals have been successful here, such as the moose, the Alaskan brown bear, caribou, and the polar bear. The waters that surround Alaska contain whales, fur seals, walrus and sea otters.

279 bottom White Pass, north of Juneau, Skagway and Haines, was the 3,290 foot entrance to the gold country during the Alaska gold rush in 1898. Seen here from the Alaska side, the pass itself is in the Canadian Province of British Columbia, with the Yukon Territory on the far side.

White Pass, north of Juneau, Skagway and Haines, was the 3,290 foot entrance to the gold country during the Alaska gold rush of 1898.

278 left In this view, the Trans-Alaska Pipeline snakes its way across the state's landscape. In 1968 vast petroleum deposits were discovered on Alaska's North Slope at Prudhoe Bay, and the nearly 800 mile long pipeline was completed in 1977 to carry crude oil to Valdez on the southern shore of the state.

278-279 Denali National Park and Preserve covers six million acres, an area larger than the state of Massachusetts. The park encompasses a complete sub-arctic ecosystem. The park was originally established as Mount McKinley National Park in 1917. The title was changed to reflect the original name given to the mountain by the indigenous people in 1980. The park became an International Biosphere Reserve in 1976.

279 top The Arrigetch Peaks are located in the Gates of the Arctic National Park. The park's south side begins with foothills which sweep up to the jagged peaks of the Brooks Range, shown here. Beyond the mountains to the north lies arctic tundra which stretches to the Arctic Ocean. Six national wild rivers traverse the park, which has no formal trails.

279 center Tundra on the north slope of the Brooks Range is seen here in the Arctic National Wildlife Refuge, in the northeast corner of Alaska. The refuge is home to diverse arctic wildlife, including 36 species of fish, 36 of land mammals, 9 marine mammals, and more than 160 migratory and resident bird species. Free-roaming herds of musk-oxen, caribou, Dall sheep and wolves make the refuge their home, as well as wolverines, polar bears, and grizzly bears.

Known to the indigenous people as Denali, "the tall one," it was named Mount McKinley in 1896 to honor President-elect William McKinley.

280 top and center The Alaska Range of perpetually snow-covered peaks in central Alaska, in addition to Mount McKinley, also includes Mount Hunter, Mount Hayes and Mount Foraker, all of which exceed 13,000 feet. The range is crossed at Isabel Pass by the Trans-Alaska Pipeline which carries oil from the North Slope to Valdez in the south.

280 bottom The aptly-named Broken Tooth Mountain in Denali National Park glows in the foreground of this view.

Parklands have been created to preserve the animals and their environment.

One of the most fascinating of Alaska's animals is the moose, the largest subspecies of which lives in the state. Moose can eat 40 to 60 pounds of forage each day. They prefer willow shoots, which they digest with the aid of their four-chambered stomachs. They feed most often in ponds, ducking to the bottom for sodium-rich plants. An adult bull moose may weigh 1,600 pounds, stand seven feet tall and raise 70-pound antlers that spread seven feet.

Many of Alaska's wildlife species are on the endangered list. Although oil accounts for 85 percent of the state's revenues, it poses a potential threat to the region's flora and fauna. The Trans-Alaska pipeline and oil spills like the Exxon Valdez disaster of 1989 suggest future scenarios involving the natural world which would be incomprehensible and unacceptable.

280-281 The southern summit of Mount McKinley rises to 20,320 feet, the tallest mountain in North America. The upper two thirds of the peak are covered with permanent snow fields that feed several glaciers. The mountain stands 17,000 feet above the treeline. It was first sighted by the English navigator George Vancouver in 1794. Known to the indigenous people as Denali, "the tall one," it was named Mount McKinley in 1896 to honor President-elect William McKinley. Of the 20 highest mountains in the United States, 17 are in Alaska.

281 bottom Denali National Park encompasses 19,088 square miles, one of the largest parks in Alaska. The park has few roads. Visitors can only gain access to the interior via shuttle or tour bus to cut down on pollution and protect fragile resources. The primary visitor season is from May through September. Valleys below the Alaska Range are seen in the view on the left of Denali National Park. The only visitor accommodations within the park are at the Denali Park Hotel and seven campgrounds. Nearby Healy, Alaska also offers services.

282-283 The face of Mt. McKinley is seen in this close-up view. Many tried to scale its peaks unsuccessfully, beginning in 1903. The north peak was scaled in 1910, and the taller south peak on June 13, 1913 by the Anglo-American clergyman and explorer Hudson Stuck and three companions, including Harry Karstens.

284-285 *Grewingk Glacier flows out of the Kenai Mountains in southern Alaska. Glaciers move under the influence of gravity by the combined action of sliding over the rock on which they lie, and by deformation, the gradual displacement between and within ice crystals. Maximum speeds occur near the surface and along the centerline of the glacier.*

284 bottom *The lessons of Glacier Bay National Park can be interesting, even staggering, to ponder. Ten percent of the globe is under ice today, and polar ice caps and glaciers store more water than lakes, rivers, groundwater and the atmosphere combined. If all this ice melted, half the world's cities would be under water.*

Although there are modern cities in Alaska, the rough terrain and small population make the remainder of the state one of sparsely-settled, isolated towns.

Government agencies are doing their best to cope with the many problems confronting species preservation, despite opposition from many Alaskans who support development and economic opportunities for their area.

The population of Alaska is primarily white, although native peoples compose about 15%. There are several native groups in Alaska—the Inuit (Eskimo) are the largest single group, followed by Aleuts in the Aleutian islands, and three principal Native American groups who live in the southern and southeastern portion of the state—the Tlingit, Haida and Athabaska. Contrary to public perception, most Inuit people do not live in historic ways, and own oil fields, hotels and lands adjacent to parks. They do, however, continue to practice traditional beliefs, festivals and hunting methods.

The Inuit probably migrated across the Bering Strait at a far later time than anthropologists claim for American Indians, and retain many common traditions and characteristics of people throughout the arctic region, from Canada to Greenland and Siberia. The Inuit invented the kayak, the dogsled, and the temporary shelter of snow called an igloo (igloos were indigenous to the Canadian Inuit, not Alaska natives).

The Aleuts are a subgroup of the Inuit who moved to the Aleutian islands. Their hunting skills were exploited by the Russians in the 18th and 19th centuries, and their population decreased dramatically

due to poor treatment and disease. Today, about 2,000 Aleuts live in wood frame houses and engage in fishing, hunting and raising sheep.

Although there are modern cities in Alaska, like Juneau, Fairbanks and Anchorage, the rough terrain, lack of infrastructure and small population make the remainder of the state one of sparsely-settled, isolated towns. These areas may lack amenities, but their residents are richly compensated by the glorious surroundings. One of the most beautiful drives in Alaska, for instance, is down the Seward Highway. Near the highway is the fairly typical little town of Hope, across the Cook Inlet from Anchorage. Hope was the first gold mining town in the state, and today supports about 200 people. Alaska is composed of many such towns.

Due to geography, many Alaska towns can be reached only by air or water. From October to May, roads into Denali National Park are not plowed, leaving access open only to skiers or dogsledders. Glacier Bay National Park and Preserve has no roads leading to it, and is isolated by mountains and glaciers.

285 top left Glaciers of Glacier Bay National Park can be seen flowing toward the bay in parallel, sweeping arcs in this aerial view.

285 bottom left Glacier Bay National Park is a favorite haunt of tourists, who often arrive by cruise ship in the summer months. A limit of 139 cruise ships per year is maintained by the National Park Service in order to protect endangered humpback whale populations offshore.

285 top right Glaciers flow down to the bay at Glacier Bay National Park in Alaska. The park contains 16 tidewater glaciers, 12 of which are actively "calving" icebergs into the bay. These shores were covered with ice 200 years ago, when explorer George Vancouver first saw them in 1794.

285 bottom right The flowing stream of a glacier at Glacier Bay National Park moves slowly toward the bay in the background. The extraordinarily fast movement of these glaciers intrigues scientists, who study and document the changes in these vast ice fields.

The Sun never sets during Alaska's summer season, due to the Earth's tilt at that time of the year. The Sun never rises between the end of November and the middle of January.

286 top The North Slope of Alaska has become known as a national petroleum reserve, and the famous Alaska Pipeline carries the crude oil down to Valdez on the south shore. Trees do not grow north of the 66 degree 34 minute latitude mark, but many species of smaller plants thrive and turn the tundra green in the summer. The sun never sets during the summer season, due to the earth's tilt at that time of the year. The region has a mix of people, including many native Inupiaq living in eight villages.

The only way in is by air or water. Why live there or visit the park? At Glacier Bay people can witness the retreat of glaciers, one of the few places in the world where this can be done. Huge blocks of ice break off from the glaciers and crash into the Pacific, causing waves of more than 30 feet. This process is called "calving." Although Alaskan towns and parks are often a long way from anywhere, their residents can enjoy the natural splendor of their surroundings.

One of the best-known annual events in Alaska is the Iditarod Trail sled dog race. Running from Anchorage to Nome, the race covers from 1,135 to 1,165 miles of the central highlands and basin regions. The great enemies of the racers are the rugged terrain, fatigue, and bad weather. In many ways the participants in this race epitomize the state of Alaska and the character of its people—tough, uncompromising, using traditional means to run a race toward the future.

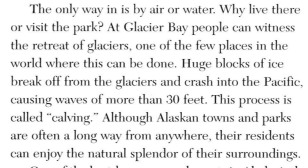

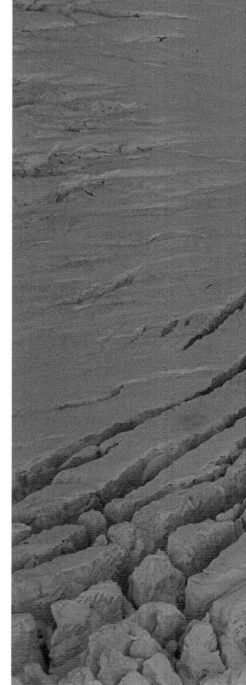

286 bottom right Prince William Sound, on the south shore of Alaska, is the location of communities like Valdez and Cordova. The sound is surrounded by rugged mountains and fjords, and has one of the most diverse ecosystems along the Pacific coast, with salmon, sea otters, sharks, halibut, seals and whales

286 bottom left The North Slope in its wintry whiteness is home to walrus, caribou, seals and polar bears. Winter lasts from autumn until June, with little precipitation. The small amounts of snow that fall stay, however, and accumulate to drift about for several months. The sun never rises between the end of November and the middle of January. There is only one road, the Dalton Highway, which was recently opened, but it is unpaved and there are no amenities. Most travel is by airplane in this, the world's largest municipality—89,000 square miles.

286-287 A floatplane flies over a crevassed glacier in the Coast Range of Tongass National Forest in southeastern Alaska. Tongass is the largest National Forest in the United States, encompassing nearly 17 million acres, larger than the state of West Virginia. The region is composed of glaciers, mountains, waterways and thousands of islands.

287 bottom left An inlet near Haines, Alaska, near the Tongass National Forest and on the road of the gold rush pioneers of 1898. The town is located on America's longest fjord, the Lynn Canal seen here. Just over the mountains in the distance is Glacier Bay National Park.

287 bottom right The town of Skagway, Alaska, just north of Haines, was created literally overnight during the Klondike gold rush of 1898. The Klondike Gold Rush National Historical Park is located in the downtown area as well as the nearby town of Dyea, the Chilkoot Trail and the White Pass Trail. A three hour train trip departs twice daily during the summer for the summit of White Pass.

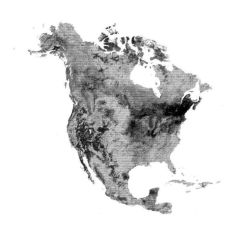

PARADISE ON EARTH:

288-289 One of the most famous places in the world, Waikiki Beach on the island of Oahu is lined with hotels. In the distance Diamond Head rises above the Pacific. The beach and its surrounding area offer every kind of recreational activity involving water, as well as hula dances, tennis, hikes on Diamond Head, concerts and museums.

Hawaii

288 bottom and 289 top The island of Kauai boasts incredible natural beauty. Nicknamed "the Garden Island," it is a tropical paradise with a mild climate, wide sand beaches, and breathtaking waterfalls in the mountains. Geologically it is the oldest and northernmost of the Hawaiian Islands. Hanalei Bay, Waimea Canyon, the Na Pali Coast and the Kokee Forests are all highlights of Kauai.

289 bottom Maui is a resort area known throughout the world. The prime resort locations are at Kapalua, Kaanapali, Kihei, Wailea and Makena along the western and southern shores of the island. Maui features golf courses and 42 miles of beaches, including the black sand beach at Waianapanapa State Park.

Each of the Hawaiian Islands offers something special and unique to the visitor.

A young couple hold hands as they walk down the black sands of a gorgeous beach, as the sun sets behind them. Birds soar over dramatic mountains covered with greenery, while fields of sugar cane stretch out before them. Outrigger canoes and surfboards vie for space along Oahu's busy Waikiki Beach, while stately hotel towers loom in the background.

The red fiery river of a stream of lava flows from an active volcano, its sizzling contents dumped into the ocean, protesting as two ancient elements, fire and water, meet.

Each of the Hawaiian islands offers something special and unique to the visitor. The eight major islands and 124 islets, reefs and shoals, with a surface area of 6,459 square miles, extend in an arc 1,490 miles long in the central Pacific. Temperature varies with elevation, but remains close to 75 degrees Fahrenheit year-round. High rainfall on the east sides of the islands is caused by the condensation of the moist ocean trade winds, while the west sides are drier because they are shielded by mountains. Mount Waialeale on the island of Kauai is the wettest spot in the United States, with an average annual rainfall of 460 inches—over 40 feet!

The Hawaiian Islands have the most ethnically diverse population of any state in the United States, with a large proportion of their estimated 1.2 million inhabitants of Japanese, native Hawaiian, Filipino, Chinese, Korean and Samoan ancestry. The native language is still spoken on the islands of Hawaii and Niihau. The Hawaiian language utilizes a 12-letter

290 top left Tourists relax on a Maui beach. In addition to water activities, Maui has many breathtaking hiking trails, including those at the Hawaii Nature Center in Iao Valley and at the dormant volcano of Haleakala National Park. Maui also has a large number of historic sites which help to tell the story of the island's heritage.

290 bottom left Makapu'u Head forms the southeast corner of the island of Oahu on the Kaiwi Channel, which separates Oahu and Molokai islands. Just to the left of the photo is Koko Head, with Diamond Head and Honolulu about 6 miles further along the coast. The small island at the upper center is Manana Island.

290 top right Lush vegetation surrounds Kaheohe Bay on the east, or windward, side of Oahu. Because it is on the windward side, rains stop up against the mountains and dump their moisture on the area, thus creating a green paradise around the bay. In addition to recreational activities on its beaches, the bay is also home to a U.S. Marine Corps Air Station.

290 bottom right Two-lane roads around the coast of Oahu can comprise a 100 mile scenic circuit of the island. Starting in Honolulu and traveling east the visitor passes Makapu'u Head, continuing on through Kailua and Kaneohe along Kaneohe Bay on the north side. Winding past Kahuku Point on the north and Kaena Point on the west, a major highway continues back through Pearl City to Honolulu.

291 A rainbow arcs over the wild Na Pali Coast, on Kauai. The Hawaiian island chain, the Na Pali Coast on Kauai, has been the scene of many T.V. shows and movies, including Magnum P.I., The Thorn Birds, the opening sequence of Raiders of the Lost Ark, and both Jurassic Park films. Its cliffs loom 4,000 feet above the Pacific Ocean and are covered with lush vegetation.

*The first
Polynesian
settlers of
Hawaii
probably
migrated
from the
Marquesas
Islands
over 1,600
years ago.
They sailed
across 2,400
miles of
open sea
without
landfall in
huge double-
hulled
canoes.*

alphabet, and each of its words ends in a vowel. The Hawaiian people have worked hard to preserve the cultural heritage of their islands, through museums, study centers, and historic sites.

Geologically, millions of years ago layer after layer of lava flows formed the islands of Hawaii, resulting in a barren landscape of volcanic rock, upon which new life began. Hundreds of species of plants and animals somehow crossed the enormous Pacific Ocean on wind, water, or with birds in flight.

Seventy million years of evolution resulted in an edenic paradise untouched by the hand of man.

But all of this was disrupted with the advent of the first settlers, the Polynesians. Later arrivals, including Europeans and Americans, altered the landscape and imported plants and animals which wreaked havoc with the Hawaiian ecosystem so long in the making.

Today, the National Park Service, the state of Hawaii, and conservation groups work to save the native species, which are in danger of extinction from introduced plants and animals.

The first Polynesian settlers of Hawaii probably migrated from the Marquesas Islands over 1,600 years ago. They sailed across 2,400 miles of open sea without landfall in huge double-hulled canoes, bringing pigs, dogs, chickens, sweet potatoes, bananas, sugar cane and cocoanuts. About 800 years later another group of Polynesians from the Society Islands arrived and claimed descent from greater gods, taking over the rule of Hawaii. After several centuries of contact between the Hawaiian Islands

and Polynesia, a 400 year period of isolation began, during which a unique Hawaiian culture emerged.

A strict caste system developed, along with unique religious and social practices. All of this was changed forever when the English explorer Captain James Cook made landfall on the islands in 1778. In the 1790s Europeans and Americans began to arrive. The Americans sent Christian missionaries and company men who set up plantation businesses, primarily in sugar cane and pineapples. These newcomers disrupted the traditional ways of the islands, outlawed ancient beliefs and customs, and unwittingly introduced devastating epidemics which killed off many Hawaiians.

292 left A portion of the National Memorial Cemetery of the Pacific above Honolulu honors America's war dead, particularly those who lost their lives in the Japanese attack on Pearl Harbor on December 7, 1941.

292-293 Condos and hotels line the shore of Nawili Wili Bay, on the island of Kauai, located on the east side of the island near Kalpaki Beach, Ninini Beach, and the Ninini Lighthouse. The Lihu'e Airport is not far away. The entire 33 x 25 mile island of Kauai was created by a shield volcano which became extinct 6 million years ago.

292 bottom U.S. naval vessels are anchored in Pearl Harbor, still an important and active Navy port. A base was established in the harbor in 1887. The coral reef at the entrance to the harbor was dredged in 1911, allowing the largest naval vessels access to the harbor's 60 foot deep main channel.

293 bottom *The U.S.S. Arizona Memorial in Pearl Harbor is a beautiful white structure which rests above the sunken battleship, one of 18 sunk or badly damaged during the Japanese attack in 1941. The sunken form of the Arizona can be seen below the water, running perpendicularly to the memorial. A regular schedule of tour boats brings visitors to the memorial each day, the site is visited by 1.5 million people annually.*

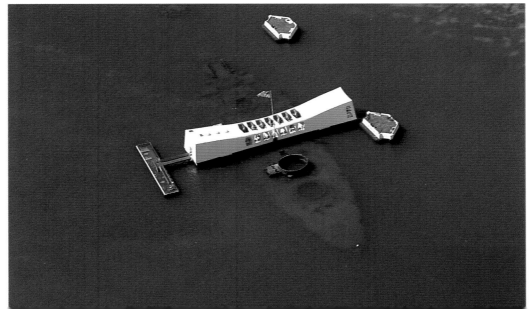

294-295 The beautiful northern coastline of Kauai, the Na Pali Coast, has drawn tourists and filmmakers for many years. Just behind the cliffs on the interior of the island is Waimea Canyon, 10 miles long, 2 miles wide, and 3,600 feet deep. The canyon can only be entered from the south side of the island at Waimea. The gorgeous colors and waterfalls make the canyon a hiking and camping treat.

294 bottom Agricultural fields on Kauai are primarily used to grow sugar cane, the island's cash crop. Kauai is generally more quiet and less tourist-oriented than Oahu or Maui, with many plantations on its shores.

Hawaii, and especially the beautiful northern coastline of Kauai, the Na Pali Coast, has drawn tourists and filmmakers for many years.

Many Japanese and Chinese laborers were brought to the islands to compensate for the loss of a large portion of the Hawaiian workforce. Although the native Hawaiians tried to regain control of their islands in the 1880s and 1890s, the grip of big American business was too strong.

The last Hawaiian monarch, Queen Liliuokalani, was deposed in 1893, and a government chaired by American businessman Sanford B. Dole was set up to rule the islands. In 1898, the United States annexed the islands, which became a territory and an important naval base.

Although most Americans were unfamiliar with the Hawaiian Islands or their strategic importance, a crash-course in Hawaiian history was necessary after December 7, 1941, when a surprise attack on naval and army bases by Japanese forces suddenly brought the United States into World War II.

Hawaii tried to achieve statehood for many years, but suspicions about the large Japanese population as well as suspected Communist forces within the labor union movement delayed statehood until 1959, when Hawaii finally became the 50th state.

The largest and easternmost of the eight islands, Hawaii, is noted for its active and inactive volcanoes, including Kilauea, Mauna Loa, and Mauna Kea. Mauna Loa is the most massive mountain on earth, occupying an area of 10,000 cubic miles. Its base is on

295 bottom left All roads lead to the beautiful beaches on Kauai, where thundering Pacific waters provide a doorway to a unique underwater world filled with whales, porpoises and tropical fish.

295 bottom right A peninsula juts out from the coast of Kauai in the Kilauea area on the northeast side of the island, not far from the popular Princeville resorts and airport. The island has one of the largest populations of permanent European residents in Hawaii. Its main sources of income are agriculture, tourism and the military.

The largest and easternmost of the eight islands, Hawaii, is noted for its active and inactive volcanoes.

the floor of the Pacific Ocean, and only its top can be seen, rising 13,796 feet above the waves. Measured from its base on the bottom of the ocean to the top, it rises at least 30,000 feet, more than 1,000 feet taller than Mount Everest. Kilauea and Mauna Loa, the island's active volcanoes, are less explosive and gaseous than their continental cousins—they usually produce fountains of fire and rivers of molten lava. Kilauea's latest eruption cycle began in 1983, and is now the longest in duration of any in modern Hawaiian history.

Moving westward from the large island of Hawaii, the next island, Maui, is renowned for its pineapple and sugar plantations as well as cattle raising. The world's largest dormant volcano, 10,023 foot tall Haleakala, dominates the scenery of the east side of the island. Haleakala's crater is 20 miles wide and over 3,000 feet deep. A narrow isthmus connects the east side to the more eroded west side and Puu Kukui, its highest point. Maui is very fertile, particularly the east side of the island, with rare plants such as the silversward fern growing there. Tourism is important to the island's economy, but it is crucial to balance the potentially destructive effects of visitation with the fragile ecosystem and its needs.

Molokai, the next island in the chain, has a plateau in the west and rugged mountains in the east. Projecting from the northern coast is Kalaupapa Peninsula, once the site of a colony for the victims of leprosy (Hansen's disease) begun by a Belgian priest named Father Damien in 1873. Today the historic site is administered by the National Park Service. Coffee and cattle are raised on Molokai, and of course it is a popular tourist spot.

296 Coast of Molokai is seen in this view, the fifth largest and least developed of the main Hawaiian Islands. Although most famous as a historical settlement for sufferers of Hansen's Disease, the island is also renowned for its great beauty. The eastern side is composed of dense wilderness, with mountains and deep green valleys. The western side is a rolling fertile plain used for agriculture.

297 top Kilauea Lighthouse is located on the north shore of Kauai, with Secret Beach on the far side of the point in the background. The Kilauea area is very popular with tourists.

297 center Manana Island is a small, uninhabited island off the east coast of Oahu. It is a good example of the many small islands which occupy the same archipelago with the better-known six larger Hawaiian Islands.

297 bottom A point of land on Kauai trails off into the ocean. Kauai is constantly shrinking due to heavy erosion by both water and wind. Ownership of about 90% of the island is in the hands of a few private individuals who are involved in the sugar cane business.

Next comes Oahu, the third largest of the Hawaiian islands and by far the most populated. Roughly 40 miles long by 26 miles wide, the island is composed of two heavily eroded shield volcanoes which form the Koolau and Wainanae mountain ranges. Between the two ranges lies a central plateau, on which sugar cane and pineapple are raised. The extinct volcanoes of Diamond Head and the Punchbowl are both tuff cones—volcanic features caused by ash explosions. Honolulu, the state's largest city and its capital, lies on a coral plain at the southeastern end of the island. Contrary to popular belief, nearly 90% of Hawaii's population is centered in urban areas, making it the most urban-oriented of all the 50 states. Oahu is the most cosmopolitan of the Hawaiian Islands, and the one most often visited by tourists. Waikiki Beach, with its hotels and its

298 top left A spectacular view of the Kilohana Crater on Kauai, covered with vegetation and leaking forth a waterfall. The trees in the lower foreground give some idea of the massive scale of the cliff.

298 top right The Kauai rainforest on Kawaikini Peak, the wettest place on earth with 450 inches of rain per year. The water runs down from the mountains to the Alakai Swamps, then empties into the Wailua River, the only navigable river in the archipelago.

298 bottom left Coastal Kauai rises above the waters of the Pacific in this view. The island was first visited by Europeans with the arrival of British Capt. James Cook in 1778. Missionaries and entrepreneurs followed, and Kauai, like the other islands, went through decades of turbulence in the 19th century. Today, its economy is thriving due to tourist dollars.

298 bottom right A sandy and inviting beach on Kauai gives some idea of the attraction the island has for tourists. The size of the beach can be determined by looking at the auto tracks running over the dunes.

299 The rugged Na Pali Coast of Kauai is a stunning, even unbelievable sight. The view often looks more like a movie set than something that is real. Perhaps that is why so many movies have used it as a backdrop.

300-301 The big island of Hawaii lies shrouded in clouds in this view. Hawaii is the opposite of Kauai; it is the youngest of the islands, it is the furthest south, it is growing every day rather than shrinking. This is due to the fact that Hawaii is located directly above one of the primary underwater hot spots of the Pacific Ocean. Lava bubbling forth from Kilauea volcano flows into the ocean, killing trees, fields and everything else in its path while forming new land when it hits the cooling waters.

magnificent surf, is famous throughout the world as a honeymoon or vacation destination. Pearl Harbor, focus of the 1941 Japanese attack, continues to be a United States Navy base. A beautiful white memorial built atop the sunken battleship Arizona in the harbor commemorates the men who lost their lives in the attack, and is one of the state's most visited sites.

The island of Kauai is composed of a single eroded volcanic shield, with steep cliffs and a number of inland canyons. Waimea Canyon, the deepest and most impressive, is ten miles long and half a mile deep. Kauai's Na Pali Coast, on the northwest side of the island, is so rugged that a road could not be built across it. Kawaikini Peak, the highest point on the island, rises to 5,243 feet.

Lanai is composed of a single shield volcano with a fertile plateau, on which is located the world's largest pineapple plantation. The island is privately owned, and all available space is used to grow pineapples. Ancient Polynesian petroglyphs and abandoned traditional and missionary villages are of historical interest.

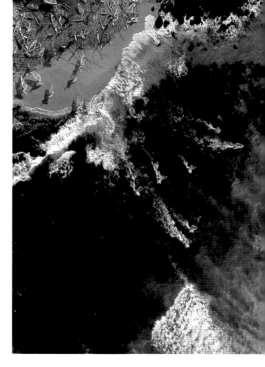

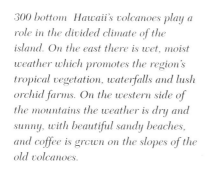

300 bottom Hawaii's volcanoes play a role in the divided climate of the island. On the east there is wet, moist weather which promotes the region's tropical vegetation, waterfalls and lush orchid farms. On the western side of the mountains the weather is dry and sunny, with beautiful sandy beaches, and coffee is grown on the slopes of the old volcanoes.

301 bottom left Land's end on Kauai looks out on the lovely Pacific Ocean, which the daring ancestors of the natives crossed in wooden boats without compasses to reach this island paradise.

301 top right Black volcanic rock created by ancient lava flows is seen in this photo of Oahu. This type of rock is plentiful on all the islands, as they were all created from volcanic activity.

301 center right Surfing is a sport created by native Hawaiians, and although it is practiced all over the world, Hawaii's waves are still the best. The north shore of Oahu has become a favorite region of young surfers, who have their own slang and hand signals. The south shore of the island on Waikiki Beach has not lost its popularity, but has more amateurs and tourists trying their hand at the sport.

301 bottom right Windsurfing has become a popular sport in the islands, joining snorkeling, scuba diving, boogey boarding and other forms of marine recreation. On land, hiking, visiting cultural demonstrations, or looking for adventure by driving around the island are popular pastimes.

Lava bubbling forth from Kilauea volcano flows into the ocean, destroying trees, fields and everything else in its path. The lava forms new land when it hits the cooling waters.

Further west lies Niihau. One of the smallest of the islands with a population of only 230 people, it is privately owned and composed almost exclusively of native Hawaiians. Its chief industry is cattle raising and the cultivation of rushes, from which mats are woven.

Lastly, the island of Kaahoolawe is barren and unpopulated. Once used by the U.S. Navy as a target site, it will be opened to the public after 2003, when all the unexploded ordnance is removed.

Hawaii, one of the smallest states in the union, is also one of the most complex in terms of its diverse population and natural and cultural history.

The history of the islands mirrors the history of the United States as a whole, with incredible natural beauty balanced against threats to its ecosystem, with a fierce cultural pride being multiplied and synthesized amid an expanding polyglot citizenry, with nostalgia for traditional lifeways pitted against commercial exploitation, and with the narrowly-averted destruction of native peoples measured against the rapid homogenization of world—and especially U.S.—culture.

Hawaii symbolizes in microcosm the great and mystic mosaic of the United States.

302 top The sides of Mauna Loa Volcano are seen here in 1984, flowing with lava. Mauna Loa, at 13,677 feet the largest active volcano in the world, erupts about once in every four years. Lava from Mauna Loa covers about 50% of the island of Hawaii. Both Mauna Loa and Kilauea are broad shield volcanoes, the only type that exist in Hawaii; their volume consists of lava eruptions alone. The other type of volcano, the composite, is created from alternate eruptions of lava and ash.

302 bottom Lava is seen in the Pu'u O'o vent on the side of Kilauea in Hawaii Volcanoes National Park. On some days only steam issues from the vent, while on others red lava flows can be clearly seen, especially at night.

302-303 In a land of fire and smoke, the eruption and lava flow of Kilauea Volcano on Hawaii in 1989 was still impressive. Kilauea has been erupting since January 3, 1983, the longest eruption event ever recorded on the island. It shows no signs of abatement. In 1989 Kilauea destroyed the National Park Service visitor center and employee housing. By 1995 it had added 500 acres of land to the island, and the flow continues at about 525,000 cubic yards per day.

303 center left The 10,023 foot summit of the extinct Haleakala volcano on the island of Maui is a favorite tourist attraction.

303 bottom left An aerial view of Pu'u O'o, a vent located on the flank of Kilauea about seven miles from the Kilauea Caldera. Lava from Kilauea flows through a natural volcanic tube for seven miles to emerge at Pu'u O'o and run down the face of the shoreline to fall into the ocean.

303 bottom right Extinct smaller volcanoes on the Island of Hawaii have become part of the landscape. The tallest mountain in Hawaii, 13,700 foot Mauna Kea, is a dormant volcano which dominates the scenery of the island. A popular form of recreation is to ski on its summit; in one day, a person could ski and swim in the warm waters of the Pacific to observe marine wildlife, all within a small radius. The variety of the terrain of Hawaii mirrors the diversity of the people and culture of the United States, a true mosaic of the best the world has to offer.

304 The classic curve of St. Louis' Busch Stadium is capped by arch-shaped openings, meant to accent the catenary curve of the 630-foot Gateway Arch nearby. It was in Busch Stadium that Mark McGwire made baseball history by hitting 62 season home runs and beating a 38-year-old record in 1998.

303

PHOTO CREDITS